Mystery Of The Future Past

*The Rebuilding of the Jewish Temple
and Coming Kingdom of Antichrist*

Mystery Of The Future Past

The Rebuilding of the Jewish Temple
and Coming Kingdom of Antichrist

by
Mark A Weller

DayStar Publishing

PO Box 464 • Miamitown, Ohio 45041

Many THANKS to Meaghan Troup for creating the INCREDIBLE cover art of this book.

Books by this Author

Lobster Boy *(Considered in the Light of Romans 14)*

Abundant Life *(Letting the Cup Run Over)*

Wee Texas Willie *(A Children's Book)*

Things That Accompany Salvation

Broken Bodies, Broken Hearts

Mystery OF The Future Past

The Gospel Nutshell

Precious Places

Ripped*!*

DEDICATION

Like all people, I have made a multitude of decisions in the course of my life, and I've lived long enough now to regret many of them. But there is one decision I have never regretted, not even for a single moment. That was my decision to accept the Lord Jesus Christ as my personal Saviour. This book is therefore dedicated to the Everlasting Father who is also the Eternal Son, before whose name every knee will bow, and who has declared *"I have magnified my word above all my name"*.

Table of Contents

	Page #

	Page#

END

A SCARLET THREAD
What Can You Expect from This Book?
Look and See!

BEHOLD, the Beauty of a Simple Scarlet Thread

This book contains both loose and unique considerations upon the subject of the *"Kingdom of Heaven"*. It is presented through a collection of recurring biblical *"patterns"* which stand individually complete in their own right; but when viewed collectively, they present a collage, or mosaic, of God's plan from eternity past to eternity future. In some places, it may initially seem as if the numerous events being discussed are totally unrelated. But as we continue our examination the reader will discover there is a thread of truth that runs through them from beginning to end. God's word is much like a magnificent tapestry with a weave containing many long threads in the warp and perhaps an even greater number of crossing threads in its shorter woof. The sacred threads of scripture reveal not only secrets from the past, but they also shine a light on future prophetic events. All of this is often done in the most unexpected and surprising ways! I think the best way to demonstrate this phenomenon is to simply pull a *"scarlet thread"* from scripture which creates a picture for the reader to consider. The following example will help to aim your expectation and adjust your focus so you will better understand what lies ahead.

Using the Authorized Version (KJV) text in a Bible program, the following search parameters were entered: *"**scarlet & thread**"*. The results of that search are listed below, and it has produced 4 occurrences found in what turns out to be 3 passages. Let's consider them in order, one at a time.

1) A woman named Tamar is found in the process of giving an unusual birth.

[Genesis 38:27-30]   And it came to pass in the time of her travail, that, behold, twins were in her womb. And it came to pass, when she travailed, that the one put out his hand: and the midwife took and bound upon his hand a **scarlet thread**, saying, This came out first. And it came to pass, as he drew back his hand, that, behold, his brother came out: and she said, <u>How hast thou broken forth?</u> this breach be upon thee: <u>therefore his name was called Pharez.</u> And **afterward came out his brother, that had the scarlet thread upon his hand: and his name was called Zarah.**

In the passage, Tamar is giving birth to twins. One boy enters the birth canal, and his hand even comes out of the womb. The midwife quickly ties a *"scarlet thread"* on the boy's hand naturally assuming he would be the firstborn of the two. The hand belonged to Zarah whose name means *"rising"*, and the scarlet thread was used to identify the boy as the oldest so they could tell the twins apart, but something remarkable happened. The first boy's hand went back in and somehow the other twin entered the world first. He was named Pharez which means *"breaker"*, matching the midwife's remark about his unusual birth.

2) A woman named Rahab makes an agreement with Israel's spies.

[Joshua 2:18] Behold, when we come into the land, thou shalt bind this line of **scarlet thread** in the window which thou didst let us down by: and thou shalt bring thy father, and thy mother, and thy brethren, and all thy father's household, home unto thee.

Israel's leader, Joshua, had sent two men to scout out Jericho before they waged war against its inhabitants. The presence of the spies was discovered by the leaders of the city, but Rahab (a citizen of Jericho) hid them and saved their lives. The context of the passage reveals that Rahab was a sinner; she was a harlot. Even so, she understood that Israel's God was the true God, so she helped the men, and as a result they made an agreement with her. Her life and the lives of her family members would be saved, provided they stayed securely in her house with a *"scarlet thread"* hanging out the window so her home could be readily identified.

3) **King Solomon boasts about the beautiful attributes of the lady he loves.**

[Song of Solomon 4:3] Thy lips are like a **thread of scarlet**, and thy speech is comely: thy temples are like a piece of a pomegranate within thy locks.

Many are the attractive qualities of Solomon's lover. But in this verse the son of David calls attention to her graceful speech and thin red lips which are like a *"thread of scarlet"*.

Is there nothing more to see?

At first glance these three passages appear to be totally unrelated with the exception of the seemingly unintended coincidence that each contains a scarlet thread. But is there a deeper connection? As is so often the case with the word of God, there is more!

The twin boys picture the two natures of our Lord Jesus Christ, both divine and human. Zarah, the *"rising"* son, was first and he wore the scarlet thread to prove it. He represents the deity of

Christ, who will, one day, as: *"...the Sun of righteousness **arise** with healing in his wings..."* [Malachi 4:2]. On the other hand, Pharez, who is in the earthly lineage of Jesus, typifies the Lord's humanity. Jesus the Messiah, the Son of man, identified as Emanuel which means *"God with us"* [Isaiah 7:14/Matthew 1:23] also *'broke forth'* into this world in a most remarkable manner. In this way, like Zarah, the eternal deity of Christ was obviously first; but like Pharez, the humanity of our Lord and Saviour was first to enter the world. But just as surely as Zarah followed Pharez, the scriptures reveal that when the man Christ Jesus returns to earth He will come in the glory of His deity as *"King of kings and Lord of lords"* [Revelation 19:16].

Rahab was a prostitute. The kind of person civic leaders and religious people tend to look down upon. But she was spiritual enough to recognize the judgment of God was headed to Jericho and she didn't want to be on the side fighting against Him. To be saved, all she had to do was trust in the scarlet thread typified by Pharez and Zarah. And if any of her family wanted to escape the coming judgment with her, they had to put their faith in the same scarlet thread that she trusted. In like manner, the apostle Paul pointed a Philippian jailer to our scarlet thread, Jesus the Messiah, saying: *"Believe on the Lord Jesus Christ, and thou shalt be saved, and thy house."* [Acts 16:31]

Solomon, the King whose name means *"peace"*, boasted of the gracious words proceeding from his true love. We are told they came from lips that were like a scarlet thread. So it is with the redeemed bride of Christ. She is a sinner who tells all that will listen how she trusts her Beloved King of Peace who shed His scarlet blood to save her life. The scriptures express it this way: *"Husbands, love your wives, even as Christ also loved the church, and gave himself for it... This is a great mystery: but I speak concerning Christ and the church."* [Ephesians 5:25/32]

What have we found in these scarlet threads?

It must be understood that the passages containing these scarlet threads were written by three different men. Moses wrote the book of Genesis about 1500 B.C. during his wilderness wanderings. Joshua put ink to scroll around 1450 B.C., in the land of Canaan, presumably as it was being acquired by Israel through conquest. And Solomon wrote the "Song of Songs" about his true love over four hundred years later in the solidly established nation of Israel. Accordingly, it is not possible that these men conspired in their writings to reveal the following pattern.

1) A divine, yet mortal, **Saviour** who is like a scarlet thread.

2) A **Sinner** who has trusted the scarlet thread to escape God's righteous judgment.

3) And the scarlet thread of the Redeemer upon the lips of the people God has redeemed by His sacrifice, the **Saints,** who speak with swollen hearts of their love and appreciation for their Saviour, the Lord Jesus Christ.

Like these three scarlet threads, what lies ahead is often elegant in its simplicity yet profound in its revelation. Take a moment to adjust your eyes. There is much to be seen!

Blessings...

The Scarlet Thread

A Scarlet Thread on a wooden cross,
Where earthly gain was counted loss.
The Scarlet Thread, He took my place,
And offered me Amazing Grace.

A Scarlet Thread on a twin boy's hand.
He's the Rising Sun, do you understand?
One Son of God - One Son of man.
These two reflect God's master plan.

Once sin's allure had lost its thrill,
I hung a Scarlet Thread from the windowsill.
When judgment came, this soul was spared.
My heart did see the Creator cared.

These lips now speak of the Scarlet Thread.
They boast of One no longer dead.
He gave His life to die for me.
The Scarlet Thread has set me free.

My Scarlet Thread, His wooden cross.
All earthly gain, I now count loss.
The Scarlet Thread now takes my place,
And I stand in His Amazing Grace.

By Mark A Weller

PART 1

LOCATION, LOCATION, LOCATION

WHY ISRAEL? WHY JERUSALEM? WHY MOUNT ZION?

WHY THE THRESHINGFLOOR OF ORNAN THE JEBUSITE?

Where does one begin when he sets out to tell a story that spans both before and after all of recorded time? This is my dilemma. Yet the story is so compelling, so intriguing, so interwoven through the history of the universe that I can't resist the lure to tell it. I simply must take up the challenge. In doing so, I will pull on a single thread that begins with the first verse in the book of Genesis, passes through the Jewish Temple Mount, and then runs out into eternity beyond the last verse in the book of Revelation. It will leave the reader with a very different, but fresh perspective regarding the *"kingdom of heaven"*. To accomplish this objective, I have decided to approach the subject by arranging many of the repeating patterns found in the Bible so as to form a chain like that of dominoes. The biblical dominoes will not always run in a straight line, but at times will twist and curve through a variety of subjects. They will even head off in an entirely different direction on occasion. But once aligned and the reader sees how the dominoes fall, a most fascinating picture will emerge of what has happened in the age's past, and what is likely to arrive in the not too distant future.

I will begin by asking the few simple questions; those which compose the title of this chapter. Why Israel? Why Jerusalem? Why Mount Zion? Why the threshingfloor of Ornan the Jebusite? We live in a big world do we not? What's so significant about that visually unattractive arid region of the world that biblical history and prophecy is so consistently focused there? Why did God choose it in the first place, and why does He continue to choose it? What's the big deal?

> [Zechariah 1:17] …the **LORD** shall yet comfort Zion, and shall yet choose Jerusalem.

Scripture emphatically proclaims that God knows *"the end from the beginning"* [Isaiah 46:10]. Somewhere in eternity past, before the Earth was formed, God chose Earth, and he chose Jerusalem as the place to make His stand. Why? What's the attraction? It's certainly not the most beautiful place a person could visit on this planet. Truthfully, in many ways, the land of Israel is much like the scripture's prophetic description of the Lord Jesus Christ in Isaiah 53, *"there is no beauty that we should desire"* it. Although, I admit this is changing as the land is being reclaimed by its formerly long absent inhabitants.

The fact that something amazingly unique has been going on in the land of Israel for over thirty-five hundred years is undeniable. As a people, Israel is a nation that has been scattered across the world for nearly two millennia and then re-assembled again into their *"promised land"*. During those many years of being scattered their homeland was under the control of other nations. And all of this was done according to the word of the Lord who knows the end of all things before they begin, declaring *"My counsel shall stand. I will do all my pleasure"* [Isaiah 46:10]. The re-emergence of that tiny nation in its original homeland is the preeminent miracle of our modern age. Its present existence is nothing less than a historical impossibility. A nation simply cannot survive for over nineteen centuries with no national real estate to dwell upon. But there they are, not only surviving but thriving even though surrounded by enemies who want to erase them and the very memory of their culture from existence. It's mindboggling.

Sometime ago I read a book called *The Temple at the Center of Time* by David Flynn. The primary thought of the book was that the location of the Jewish Temple in Jerusalem seemed to be the focal point for all of history. Moreover, historical events could even be linked to it according to their dates, locations and respective distances from the geographical coordinates of the Temple Mount. That set me to thinking about the Jewish Temple's location and its peculiar preeminence in scripture. I've read through the Bible many times, but I suddenly found myself wondering what I might have overlooked that would explain the Temple's fixed location and the Temple Mount's exalted status. With this thought in mind let's begin to consider what is known about the twice formerly magnificent (but now demolished) Jewish Temple and the setting intentionally chosen in eternity past by the Creator for its location.

THE LOCATION OF THE JEWISH TEMPLE

What do we know about the Temple's location? Well, we know for certain where it was originally built because the scriptures tell us.

> [2 Chronicles 3:1] **Then Solomon began to build the house of the LORD at Jerusalem in mount Moriah,** where the LORD appeared unto David his father, in the place that

> David had prepared **in the threshingfloor of Ornan the Jebusite**.

If you haven't spent much time in the Bible you may not be acquainted with the history surrounding Ornan the Jebusite's threshingfloor. In 1 Chronicles 21:1 we're told:

> **And Satan stood up against Israel, and provoked David to number Israel.**

I realize this short verse doesn't seem like a big deal, but this seemingly minor incident resulted in a deadly plague that burned through David's kingdom like a raging inferno. The problem was that God is a God of order. He has His own methodology and reasons for doing things the way He wants them done. This is an instance where David didn't do things as directed. It seems that Satan not only lured David into the prideful and self-exalting activity of taking a census for no other reason than to see how many people he had under his royal dominion, but in his arrogance he either forgot or neglected to fulfill the following lawful requirements associated with taking a census in Israel.

> [Exodus 30:12] When thou takest the sum of the children of Israel after their number, then shall they give **every man a ransom for his soul** unto the LORD, when thou numberest them; **that there be no plague among them, when thou numberest them.**

The price for David's vanity was the virulent deaths of seventy thousand men within the three short days the plague swept through his kingdom. As is usually the case in this world, the common people paid the heavy price exacted for their leader's mistake. In sorrow, David watched the death toll rapidly mounting around him and his heart moved him to intercede with God on behalf of his people. Accordingly we read:

> [1 Chronicles 21:16-18] And David lifted up his eyes, and saw the angel of the LORD stand between the earth and the heaven, having a drawn sword in his hand stretched out over Jerusalem. Then David and the elders of Israel, who were clothed in sackcloth, fell upon their faces. And David said unto God, Is it not I that commanded the people to be numbered? even I it is that have sinned and done evil indeed; but as for these sheep, what have they done? let thine hand, I pray thee, O LORD my God, be on me, and on my father's house; but not on thy people, that they should be plagued. **Then the angel of the LORD commanded** [the prophet] **Gad to say to David, that David should go up, and set up an altar unto the LORD in the threshingfloor of Ornan the Jebusite.**

The text shows that God, referred to here as *"the angel of the LORD"*, is the one who chose Ornan's threshingfloor as the location for the altar where the sacrifice was made which brought that terrible plague to an end. As you may recall, we previously read that Solomon built the Temple on this same threshingfloor which was located in Mount Moriah. And in the above passage we find that it was the place where God extended mercy to Israel and brought to an end a grievous plague. This is the very same location that the organization *"Temple Mount & Land of Israel Faithful Movement"* identifies as the Holy of Holies. It is believed to be the exact position where the ark of the Covenant was placed, upon which rested the Mercy Seat of Almighty God. It was both the most sacred place inside the Jewish Temple on mount Moriah and the highest point of elevation on the entire temple mount, which mount is also known as Zion *[spelled "Sion" in the New Testament books of the Authorized Version].* The following is an excerpt from an article found on the Temple Mount Faithful website detailing the Temple location.

The Location of the Temple and the Holy of Holies on the Temple Mount

"The conclusion that I immediately want to place before you and for which I will later bring the evidence is that the location of the Temple is in the same location as that of the present Dome of the Rock and that the rock itself is the rock which was in the Holy of Holies and on which the ark of the Covenant was situated in the First Temple. I will also show that Rabbi Shlomo Goren, who was the Chief Rabbi of the Israeli Defense Force during the Six Day War and later became the Chief Rabbi of Israel, brought a unit of military engineers to the Temple Mount immediately after the war. They surveyed all the Temple Mount according to the Torah, the Mishnah and the Talmud and other sources. His conclusion was that the rock was the rock on which was situated the altar. However, he did not doubt that the rock was in the location of the Temple and that the Dome of the Rock is located there."

The above article can be read in its entirety at the following web address.

http://www.templemountfaithful.org/articles/temple-location.php

Before man was created... before the earth was made... even before the foundation of the earth was laid: somewhere in eternity past God chose Jerusalem,

and more specifically the threshingfloor of Ornan the Jebusite. He undoubtedly had a reason for choosing that particular location because God has a purpose in everything He does! As James, the Lord's half-brother said:

> [Acts 15:18] **Known unto God are all his works from the beginning of the world.**

Jewish tradition also insists that this is the very same spot where many centuries before king David was born, Abraham was commanded to take Isaac and offer him as a sacrifice to the Lord.

> Mishneh Torah, Sefer Avodah, Beit Habechirah, Chapter Two
>> "It is universally accepted that the place on which David and Solomon built the Altar, the threshingfloor of Ornan, is the location where Abraham built the Altar on which he prepared Isaac for sacrifice."

>> [Genesis 22:2] And he said, Take now thy son, thine only son Isaac, whom thou lovest, and **get thee into the land of Moriah**; and offer

> him there for a burnt offering **upon one of
> the mountains** which I will tell thee of.

Jewish tradition is exactly that - tradition. Tradition isn't always right, and their assertion may, or may not, be correct. I'll discuss the traditional teaching regarding this passage in more detail later, but for the moment it is sufficient to say that the Bible does indeed tell us Abraham offered Isaac in the *"land of Moriah"*. However, it does not specifically say it was on *"Mount Moriah"*, the Temple Mount. This aspect of the teaching seems to be conjecture on the part of the Jewish Sages. And as with all seemingly minor details in the scriptures, this point may well be worth noticing. Either way we have now journeyed back beyond 2,000 B.C. and the questions still remain, *"Why this spot when there is an entire world to choose from? What is its original significance? What makes this location so special in the eyes of God?"*

Unbeknownst to most people, there are other ancient Jewish teachings about this area which also carry a profound biblical significance. Some of the ancient Jewish Sages taught that the Temple Mount is also the place where Noah built his altar after the global flood centuries before Abraham was born.

> Mishneh Torah, Sefer Avodah, Beit Habechirah, Chapter Two
>> "Noah built [an altar] on that location when he left the ark."

>> [Genesis 8:20-21] And **Noah builded an altar unto the LORD**; and took of every clean beast, and of every clean fowl, and offered burnt offerings on the altar. And the LORD

smelled a sweet savour; and the LORD said in his heart, I will not again curse the ground any more for man's sake; for the imagination of man's heart is evil from his youth; neither will I again smite any more every thing living, as I have done.

And going back in time further still, the Sages tell us that it's the same place where Cain & Abel offered their sacrifices.

Mishneh Torah, Sefer Avodah, Beit Habechirah, Chapter Two

"It was also [the place] of the Altar on which Cain and Abel brought sacrifices."

[Genesis 4:3-5] And in process of time it came to pass, that **Cain brought of the fruit of the ground an offering unto the LORD. And Abel, he also brought of the firstlings of his flock and of the fat thereof.** And the LORD had respect unto Abel and to his offering: But unto Cain and to his offering he had not respect. And Cain was very wroth, and his countenance fell.

By taking one very small step backwards in time from here we arrive at the original progenitor of the human race, Adam, the father of Cain and Abel. The Jewish Sages have their traditional teaching regarding Adam as well.

Mishneh Torah, Sefer Avodah, Beit Habechirah, Chapter Two

> "[Similarly,] Adam, the first man, offered a sacrifice there and was created at that very spot, as our Sages said: "Man was created from the place where he [would find] atonement.""

Through their traditional teachings, the Sages bring our attention to the Garden of Eden. But can their assertions regarding all of these alleged sacrificial offerings be correct?

Their claim regarding the place of Noah's altar seems highly unlikely since Noah's family got off the ark in the mountains of Ararat, which are nearly a thousand miles from Jerusalem. Yet because of their extended lifespans there remains the possibility (though a remote one) that they travelled to a new distant location before such a sacrifice was made. And if it be objected that Noah and his family were forbidden to enter the garden and could not have sacrificed there, we must point out that the world had been washed clean by the flood before they disembarked, and so the garden was no more. Only the geographical location of the garden remained regardless of whether it was Jerusalem or not. So Noah's journey to Jerusalem is possible though seemingly unlikely.

On the other hand, the claims regarding Cain and Abel's location being on the Temple mount would be impossible if the Temple Mount was actually the location of the Garden of Eden. Why? Because mankind's entrance into the garden was forbidden after Adam and Eve had sinned and obviously remained off limits until the garden was destroyed in the flood of Noah's day. The same prohibition would have prevented their father Adam from sacrificing in the garden as well; unless it is supposed that Adam was offering sacrifices even before he fell into sin. But why sacrifice the life of an animal when there is no sin that would require atonement? This idea seems more than unreasonable. It even appears absurd at face value when one considers that the first animal sacrifice in the Bible was performed by God to clothe the fallen man and his wife by covering their nakedness with coats of skins.

> [Genesis 3:21] Unto Adam also and to his wife did the LORD God make coats of skins, and clothed them.

The question might arise, "If some of these ancient Jewish teachings are unscriptural why include them in this book?" The answer is simple. First, Jewish traditions cannot be unreservedly relied upon for biblical insight. This must be made clear since much of Christianity routinely accepts a great many of their teachings as gospel truth without bothering to compare them to the actual scriptures. Secondly, whether accurate or not, the traditional teaching of the Sages serves to highlight the significance, as well as the continued importance, of the Temple Mount in the Jewish religion.

THE GARDEN OF EDEN

Some time ago I happened across the documentary *"Return to Eden"*, by Jimmy DeYoung. When I saw the title, I wondered *"How can a person return to a place where they had never been and had no idea where it might be found?"* Still, the title intrigued me so I decided to watch the video. At some point in the show Jimmy made the startling statement that the Jewish Sages taught the original location of the Garden of Eden was present day Jerusalem. That statement took me by surprise and I immediately balked at the idea. After all, Genesis chapter two shows that the garden was associated with four rivers. One of them was the Euphrates which runs through modern day Iraq; and another, the Hiddekel, is identified as the Tigris River and is located there as well. The whereabouts of the other two rivers, Pison and Gihon, are thought by many scholars to be unknown. Consequently, all of the available information places the location of the Garden a significant distance east of Israel. Or does it?

Early in my Christian life I developed two very important traits that have served me well over the years. First, I developed an insatiable curiosity regarding why different Christian groups believe the various things they do. This curiosity arose from a naïve assumption I had when I first got saved. I assumed that all Christians believed exactly the same things. I was more than just a little wrong! As time went by I discovered that Christians disagreed about a great many doctrines, and I wanted to know why that was, and what was the truth. In other words, I wanted to know what I was supposed to believe. Accordingly, whenever I heard a new or different belief I asked the proponent to teach it to me so I could understand why he, or she, believed it.

In time I discovered that by simply considering how the logical conclusion of a belief would interact with other scriptures I could usually sort out whether it was true, false, or a little of both. This has allowed me to hone my belief system over the years to a pretty fine point. I don't profess to have figured everything out, but I'm no longer a Bible novice either! On most Bible topics I know what I believe and why I believe it, and I can teach it in pretty short order.

These two characteristics have left me teachable and flexible enough to tweak my beliefs if I encounter a new piece of

Christianity's doctrinal puzzle that better fits the context of the scriptures. Jimmy DeYoung seemed like a pretty intelligent guy, so I was willing to listen for a while and hear what he had to say. I knew at some point he would have to try and justify his statements, and I wanted to hear how he was going to do it. What he said stopped me in my tracks. He quoted the following passage in Joel.

> [Joel 2:1-3] **Blow ye the trumpet in Zion**, and sound an alarm in my holy mountain: let all the inhabitants of the land tremble: for the day of the LORD cometh, for it is nigh at hand; A day of darkness and of gloominess, a day of clouds and of thick darkness, as the morning spread upon the mountains: a great people and a strong; there hath not been ever the like, neither shall be any more after it, even to the years of many generations. A fire devoureth before them; and behind them a flame burneth: **the land is as the garden of Eden** before them, and behind them a desolate wilderness; yea, and nothing shall escape them.

Jimmy pointed out something to the effect of Jerusalem being associated with the Garden of Eden in this messianic prophecy about the second coming of Christ. True, it was a negative association, but the association was there nonetheless. I've been through the Bible enough times to understand that God has a few preferred methods of teaching. He teaches by repetition of patterns; He teaches by contrast [opposites]; and He teaches by similitudes, and this passage was definitely a contrasting similitude. God declares:

> [Hosea 12:10] **I have** also spoken by the prophets, and I have multiplied visions, and **used similitudes**, by the ministry of the prophets.

A *similitude* is simply something *similar* to something else in one or more ways. For instance, Jesus said "whosoever heareth these sayings of mine, and doeth them, I will <u>liken</u> him unto a wise man, which built his house upon a rock:" [Matthew 7:24]

And Peter tells us that *"<u>as</u> newborn babes"* we should desire the sincere milk of the word [1 Peter 2:2]. When you see words such as *"liken"*, *"like"* or *"as"* in the scriptures, a similitude is being employed to teach something by way of comparison.

In addition to the passage in Joel cited above, Jimmy also mentioned one in Ezekiel and another in Isaiah.

> [Ezekiel 36:32-35] Not for your sakes do I this, saith the Lord GOD, be it known unto you: be ashamed and confounded for your own ways, **O house of Israel**. Thus saith the Lord GOD; In the day that I shall have cleansed you from all your iniquities I will also cause you to dwell in the cities, and the wastes shall be builded. And the desolate land shall be tilled, whereas it lay desolate in the sight of all that passed by. And they shall say, **This land that was desolate is become like the garden of Eden**; and the waste and desolate and ruined cities are become fenced, and are inhabited.

> [Isaiah 51:3] For **the LORD shall comfort Zion**: he will comfort all her waste places; and **he will make her wilderness like Eden, and her desert like the garden of the LORD**; joy and gladness shall be found therein, thanksgiving, and the voice of melody.

In the aforementioned verses, we find the land of Israel, and specifically Mount Zion, likened unto the Garden of Eden in a positive context. It turns out Israel is the *only* place in the world the scriptures associate with the Garden of Eden in any manner, either positive or negative.

The Jewish Sages make a lot of claims regarding the significance of the Temple Mount. Some of those claims are obviously true and others are far less convincing. But all of them have one thing in common; they emphasize the significance of the Temple Mount as being a place chosen by God. But again I ask, what's so special about that specific location that God would choose to put his name there above all other places on Earth? Why not the Rock of Gibraltar or Mount Everest?   Why not anywhere else for that matter? Surely there must be more to the story.

THE FOUNDATION STONE

Another interesting teaching the ancient Sages have regarding the Temple Mount, the threshing floor of Ornan the Jebusite, is that it's the **"foundation stone of the world"**.

Midrash Tanchuma, Kedoshim, Siman 10:1

The Land of Israel sits at the center of the world; Jerusalem is in the center of the Land of Israel; the sanctuary is in the center of Jerusalem; the Temple building is in the center of the sanctuary; the ark is in the center of the Temple building; and the foundation

stone, out of which the world was founded, is
before the Temple building.

Wikipedia: "Foundation Stone"
"The Foundation Stone is the name of the rock at
the center of the Dome of the Rock in Jerusalem. It
is also known as the Pierced Stone because it has a
small hole on the southeastern corner that enters a
cavern beneath the rock, known as the **Well of
Souls**. There is a difference of opinion in classical
Jewish sources as to whether this was the location
of the Holy of Holies or of the Outer *[i.e. Brazen]*
Altar. According to those that hold it was the site
of the Holy of Holies, that would make this the
holiest site in Judaism."

When I heard this teaching I wondered, *Could this be true? If so,
it would seem to explain much. And if it is, what are the biblical
implications that would follow such a teaching?* I was fascinated
by the idea so I decided to pursue it further and found the
following scriptures.

[Zechariah 12:1-2] The burden of the word of the LORD for
Israel, saith **the LORD, which stretcheth forth the
heavens, and layeth the foundation of the earth, and
formeth the spirit of man within him.** Behold, I will make
Jerusalem a cup of trembling unto all the people round
about, when they shall be in the siege both against Judah and
against Jerusalem.

[Isaiah 48:12-13] Hearken unto me, O Jacob and **Israel**, my
called; I am he; I am the first, I also am the last. **Mine hand
also hath laid the foundation of the earth,** and my right

hand hath spanned the heavens: when I call unto them, they stand up together.

Perhaps the most interesting thing about the previous verses is that the words *"like"* or *"as"* do not appear in them. There is no signal that they are only a similitude. Quite the contrary, for instance the formation of man's spirit as shown in Zechariah 12:1 above is presented as a fact throughout the entire Bible.

[Genesis 2:7] And **the LORD God formed man of the dust of the ground, and breathed into his nostrils the breath of life; and man became a living soul.**

So, the question arises, did God *actually* lay *"the foundation of the Earth"?* Or is He simply speaking metaphorically?

[Psalms 102:25-27] **Of old hast thou laid the foundation of the earth:** and the heavens are the work of thy hands. They shall perish, but thou shalt endure: yea, all of them shall wax old like a garment; as a vesture shalt thou change them, and they shall be changed: But thou art the same, and thy years shall have no end.

Will the heavens one day perish as the above passage indicates? *Revelation 20:11 and 2 Peter 3:10-12, shows they will.*

Will God make a new heaven and new earth? *According to Revelation 21:1 and 2 Peter 3:13 - He will.*

Will God endure forever? *Obviously the answer is yes, He will, as we can see below.*

[Hebrews 1:10-12] And, Thou, Lord, in the beginning hast laid the foundation of the earth; and the heavens are the works of thine hands: They shall perish; **but thou remainest**; and they all shall wax old as doth a garment; And as a vesture shalt thou fold them up, and they shall be changed: **but thou art the same, and thy years shall not fail.**

[Psalm 45:6] **Thy throne, O God, is for ever and ever**: the sceptre of thy kingdom is a right sceptre.

If all of these statements are literally true, why would we think the laying of Earth's foundation would be metaphorical? These statements all appear together. What if the scriptures mean exactly what they say? This is worthy of our consideration. Let's begin by looking at the construction of the temple.

[1 Kings 5:17] And [Solomon] the king commanded, and **they brought great stones, costly stones, and hewed stones, to lay the foundation of the house** [of the LORD].

When the temple was built *"great stones"* were laid upon the bedrock of Mount Zion to form a foundation on which to build. The first stone put down is called the *"chief corner stone"*. Care is taken about where to place it. It is set plumb and level, and every other stone in the building is set in relation to it. The entire structure is formed according to the position of that one stone. It is the structure's singular, primary, point of reference. Interestingly enough, this is the same way that God speaks regarding His creation of the church.

[Ephesians 2:19-20] Now therefore ye are no more strangers and foreigners, but fellowcitizens with the saints, and of **the household of God**; And are **built upon the foundation of the apostles and prophets, Jesus Christ himself being the chief corner stone;**

We are told that Jesus Christ is the chief corner stone and the apostles and prophets were positioned in relation to Him. All the building (all of the church) is built in relation to a singular point of reference which is the Lord Jesus Christ. He is the original starting place for the rest of the entire building. This being the case, why should we think that God would make the world differently? He is a wise master builder. He knows that to build correctly you must have a single point of reference from which to begin.

> [1 Peter 2:6] Wherefore also it is contained in the scripture, Behold, **I lay in Sion a chief corner stone**, elect, precious: and he that believeth on him shall not be confounded.

But how can we know if God actually did the same thing on Mount Sion when He created the world? How could we tell if He had literally laid a *"chief corner stone"* or a *"foundation stone"* as it's called?

We would know because everything else would be done in relation to that single point of reference. Everything else would continually point back to that one place. This was the premise of David Flynn's book, *"The Temple at the Center of Time"*. This was the original thought that opened my mind to this investigation.

The book of Job is thought by many to be the oldest book of the Bible. It's a remarkable book in its own right for many reasons, but my primary interest in it at the moment is for the light it sheds on our inquiry into the *"foundation stone"* of the world. In this book God demands answers from Job to a series of difficult questions; the following of which are pertinent to this discussion. God asks:

[Job 38:4-7] Where wast thou when **I laid the foundations of the earth?** declare, if thou hast understanding. Who hath laid **the measures** thereof, if thou knowest? or who hath **stretched the line** upon it? **Whereupon are the foundations thereof fastened?** or **who laid the corner stone** thereof; When the morning stars sang together, and all the sons of God shouted for joy?

By these questions God is letting Job know that he is just a man. On the other hand, God is the Creator. He laid the foundation of the earth. He measured it. He leveled it and dropped the plumb line on it. He marked out the original point of reference and set the very first stone, the chief corner stone. And He fastened the foundations to make it secure.

Are we to believe what God has said? I do! And it answers some nagging questions; but it also raises a few more of them. For instance, the fact that Mount Zion may contain the original *"foundation stone"* of the entire world certainly answers the question of why it's so significant. It answers the questions about why things in the Bible always seem to point back to Jerusalem. It's the original reference point for all things on earth.

But knowing that Zion is Earth's foundation stone also raises some intriguing questions, for example: *Is that all there is to the story, or is there more? Do the scriptures reveal a larger narrative connected with Jerusalem that we're still not seeing?*

To answer these questions we must go back in time farther still. We'll have to go back before the Garden, back even before God set in motion the first atom that was summoned into existence.

PART 2

A GOOD PLAN GONE BAD

IN THE BEGINNING GOD

Let's start by taking another look at our previous passage in Job. God asked him:

> [Job 38:4-7] **Where wast thou when I laid the foundations of the earth?** declare, if thou hast understanding. Who hath laid the measures thereof, if thou knowest? or who hath stretched the line upon it? Whereupon are the foundations thereof fastened? or who laid the corner stone thereof; **When the morning stars sang together, and all the sons of God shouted for joy?**

In the above passage, we see that when God laid the foundations of the earth the various angelic host of heaven were present, and they *"sang"* and *"shouted for joy"* as they witnessed the omnipotent powers of the mighty Creator. Undoubtedly it was an awe-inspiring sight to behold, and I'm quite certain that mere words cannot do it justice, but what about before that? What about before the foundation was laid and before the sons of God were created? What was it like *"in the beginning"* when it was just God? As mere humans, we can't grasp what it was like to be God before space existed, before matter was created, before time could be reckoned. God is an eternal being. A virtual eternity had passed before the spiritual beings called *"sons of God"* and *"morning stars"* were created or before the first atom was commanded to appear. What must it have been like to dwell in eternity alone? The human mind simply cannot comprehend that type of solitude; no space, no time, no matter... just self. Men, as lesser beings, have lost their minds as a result of isolation imposed in far smaller measures and of much shorter duration. Humanity has a need for fellowship, for companionship, for relationships. It's not unreasonable to suppose that an intelligent Creator would desire the same things, though He would not necessarily need them. Life is simply better when its joys are shared with others. Literal eons passed as the triune God existed in solitude; but He had a plan.

> [Isaiah 46:9-10] ...I am God, and there is none else; I am God, and there is none like me, **Declaring the end from the beginning, and from ancient times the things that are not yet done**, saying, My counsel shall stand, and I will do all my pleasure:
>> *For an interesting contemplation of the above passage see "The Berisheet Passover Prophecy" video on YouTube.*

IN THE BEGINNING GOD CREATED THE HEAVEN AND THE EARTH

We don't know for certain when, but at some point in the ancient past the Creator made *"the sons of God"* who were present and rejoicing when God laid the foundations of the earth. They came into existence in a time prior to the creation of man and the shaping of the once formless planet we now inhabit. Evidently they are the beings we know as angels. They are celestial beings that are both physical like men and yet sometimes not physical like fire or perhaps a form of pure energy. In a sense, they are what some people refer to as *"shape shifters"*. God apparently transforms them into what He needs them to be.

[Hebrews 1:7] **And of the angels he saith, Who** <u>maketh</u> **his angels spirits, and his ministers a flame of fire.**

And yet they are capable of taking on the corporeal form of human physiology.

[Hebrews 13:2] Be not forgetful to entertain strangers: for **thereby some have entertained angels unawares.**

In fact, whenever the sons of God appear in scripture as humans they always look like men. Accordingly the masculine gender is indicated in the following passages.

[Daniel 9:21] Yea, whiles I was speaking in prayer, **even the man Gabriel,** whom I had seen in the vision at the beginning, being caused to fly swiftly, touched me about the time of the evening oblation.

[Luke 1:19] And **the angel answering said unto him, I am Gabriel,** that stand in the presence of God; and am sent to speak unto thee, and to shew thee these glad tidings.

[Luke 1:12] And **when Zacharias saw him**, he was troubled, and fear fell upon him.

[Luke 1:26-27] And in the sixth month **the angel Gabriel was sent from God** unto a city of Galilee, named Nazareth, To a virgin espoused to a man whose name was Joseph, of the house of David; and the virgin's name was Mary.

[Luke 1:29] And **when she saw him**, she was troubled...

[Acts 1:9-11]   And when he [Jesus] had spoken these things, while they beheld, he was taken up; and a cloud received him out of their sight.   And while they looked stedfastly toward heaven as he went up, behold, **two men stood by them in white apparel;**   Which also said, Ye men of Galilee, why stand ye gazing up into heaven? this same Jesus, which is taken up from you into heaven, shall so come in like manner as ye have seen him go into heaven.

But how many of these sons of God are there?   And where do they live?

[Hebrews 12:22]   But ye are come unto mount Sion, and unto the city of the living God, **the heavenly Jerusalem**, and to **an innumerable company of angels**,

Scripture tells of a heavenly Jerusalem, a city located on a mount called Sion that is far above this earthly sphere.   A great number of angels are its inhabitants, as well as some creatures called cherubim and seraphim.   It is the celestial city of the living God that will one day come down from heaven so that God may dwell with men.

[Revelation 21:2-3]   And **I John saw the holy city, new Jerusalem, coming down from God out of heaven**, prepared as a bride adorned for her husband.   And I heard a great voice out of heaven saying, **Behold, the tabernacle of God is with men, and he will dwell with them, and they shall be his people, and God himself shall be with them, and be their God.**

A person might say, *"Hey that sounds great, but why doesn't God just dwell with people now? What's He waiting for?"*

As it turns out, there is literally something in His way. Like the veil in the Jewish temple separating God in the Holy of Holies from the daily activity of the priests; there is a literal barrier between the habitation of God in heaven and the physical creation of the universe where humanity dwells. Sin has infected the entire universe, and God has separated a part of Himself from it. He has done this because He is *"...of purer eyes than to behold evil, and canst not look on iniquity".* [Habakkuk 1:13]

That's why when Jesus was bearing the sins of the world on Calvary, when He was made *"to be sin for us"* [2 Corinthians 5:21], the Father turned His back and Jesus cried out:

> [Mark 15:34] …Eloi, Eloi, lama sabachthani? which is, being interpreted, **My God, my God, why hast thou forsaken me?**

It appears that in order for the unrestricted holiness of God in all His glory to dwell with men, sin must be completely eliminated and this tainted universe must be destroyed and made anew. This is exactly what we find happening at the end of the Bible once Satan is finally cast into the lake of fire forever.

> [Revelation 21:1] **And I saw a new heaven and a new earth: for the first heaven and the first earth were passed away; and there was no more sea.**

I can imagine someone saying, *"Sure, I see the need for a new earth, but why must the heaven be destroyed as well? We haven't even left our own solar system yet. The rest of the universe is untouched. It's still pristine."*

Is it? That's not what the Bible says. Scripture tells us something quite the opposite.

> [Job 25:5] Behold even to the moon, and it shineth not; yea, **the stars are not pure in his** [God's] **sight.**

> [Job 15:15] Behold, he [God] putteth no trust in his saints; yea, **the heavens are not clean in his sight.**

Understandably, the question may arise; *"How could the rest of the universe be unclean if humanity hasn't even been there yet? How could it have gotten so messed up?"*

Before I give you a biblical explanation, allow me to give you a human one.

My father worked at a Department of Energy high security research lab in Miamisburg, Ohio for many years. Mound Laboratory was originally an Atomic Energy Commission facility for nuclear weapons research during the Cold War and later became a research facility at the leading edge of the Nuclear Age in the United States. Components built at Mound Lab went with NASA to the sun, moon, Mars, Jupiter, Saturn, Uranus and Neptune. Their nuclear Radioisotope Thermoelectric Generators [RTG's] powered many satellites and deep space probes and kept their instruments at operational temperatures in the dark cold of space. When dad worked there in the 1980's and 90's, he was the chief welder that fabricated the nuclear power cores for the Ulysses Solar Polar and Galileo Space Probes. He told my brothers and me that when he assembled and welded the core, he couldn't resist the temptation to take a Needle Plasma Welder and write his name, ever so tiny, on the bottom of the RTG's since he knew the satellites were going into deep space. But, as it turned out, one of the engineers noticed the small inscription, and dad was forced to buff his name off the part. After all, if the engineers weren't allowed to put their names on it they weren't going to let him do it either! Once they saw him buffing his name off and were satisfied, they left; at which time he promptly turned the RTG's over and inscribed his initials in a different place. This time they didn't notice and the satellites were sent on their spaceward journey. As a result, the Galileo space junk now laying on the surface of Jupiter still has my father's initials on it, as does the Ulysses Solar Polar Probe that has become a permanent man made asteroid orbiting the sun. Why did I bother to tell this story? Because, I KNOW there's SIN out there in space, far from planet earth! Dad always chuckled how he got one over on them. His initials are out there – *and theirs aren't!*

That's the human explanation. But there's a biblical one that gets more to the point of our discussion. You may recall the following biblical passage.

> [Matthew 16:21-23] From that time forth began Jesus to shew unto his disciples, how that he must go unto Jerusalem, and suffer many things of the elders and chief priests and scribes, and be killed, and be raised again the third day. Then Peter took him, and began to rebuke him, saying, Be it far from thee, Lord: this shall not be unto thee. But **he turned, and said unto Peter, Get thee behind me, Satan: thou art an offence unto me:** for thou savourest not the things that be of God, but those that be of men.

In the above section of scripture Jesus rebuked Peter and referred to him as Satan. But was Peter really Satan? Of course he wasn't. Jesus was rebuking the influential spirit behind Peter. The wicked spirit known as Satan was influencing Peter to rebel against the will of the Father which had just been revealed in Christ's statement.

In the book of Ezekiel we find a similar type of passage, where God addresses Satan through the person of the king of Tyrus. In this text we will find the answer to the question, _"How did the universe get messed up?"_

> [Ezekiel 28:12-15] Son of man, take up a lamentation upon the king of Tyrus, and say unto him, Thus saith the Lord GOD; Thou sealest up the sum, full of wisdom, and perfect in beauty. **Thou hast been in Eden the garden of God**; every precious stone was thy covering, the sardius, topaz, and the diamond, the beryl, the onyx, and the jasper, the sapphire, the emerald, and the carbuncle, and gold: the workmanship of thy tabrets and of thy pipes was prepared in thee in the day that **thou wast created. Thou art the anointed cherub** that covereth; and I have set thee so: **thou wast upon the holy mountain of God**; thou hast walked up and down in the midst of the stones of fire. **Thou wast perfect** in thy ways from the day that thou wast created, **till iniquity was found in thee.**

We know God is not really addressing the historical person known as the King of Tyrus by what appears in the passage. For instance, we know from Genesis that the king of Tyrus was not in Eden. Adam and Eve were the only humans there. We know that the earthly King of Tyrus was not _"created"_. Adam and Eve were the only people created. All other people were born. We know that humans do not have precious stones and musical instruments as part of their physical bodies. And we know that no human being is a _"cherub"_.

However, there was another being in the Garden of Eden besides God, Adam & Eve. It was identified as *"the serpent"*.

[Revelation 20:2] …the dragon, that old serpent, **which is the Devil**, and Satan…

LUCIFER, THE FIRST ANOINTED (BUT CORRUPT) KING OF EARTH

Ezekiel 28:15 tells us that *"iniquity was found"* in Lucifer. This is the fountain of sin. He is the source from which corruption flows, spreading its infection throughout the entire physical universe. Knowing this, now the prophet Isaiah can help us to understand why the heavens are not clean in God's sight. He will tell what happened when the first act of iniquity was conceived, giving birth to sin in a previously undefiled universe.

[Isaiah 14:12-14] How art thou fallen from heaven, O Lucifer, son of the morning! How art thou cut down to the ground, which didst weaken the nations! **For thou hast said in thine heart, I will ascend into heaven, I will exalt my throne above the stars of God:** I will sit also upon the mount of the congregation, in the sides of the north: I will ascend above the heights of the clouds; **I will be like the most High.**

Much has been written about the fall of Lucifer and it is not the intention of this book to re-plow a well tilled field. So I will simply give a brief synopsis of his history to make certain that the blanks are filled in for those who may still be unaware.

In a nutshell, Lucifer was apparently a kind of heavenly choir director. His physical composition contains musical instruments (pipes and tabrets) and beautiful gems. The name Lucifer means *"light bearer"*. It seems he was a walking musical laser light show. Lucifer was never an angel. He was *"the anointed cherub"*. The appearance of a cherub can be found by examining the descriptions of the four cherubims (plural) found in Ezekiel chapters 1 and 10, and in Revelation chapter 4. Those four cherubims are described as having the likeness of a man with the following exceptions. Their feet were like the split hooves of a calf. They had the arms of a man but also had wings. And each of them had four faces: lion, eagle and man were the first three faces. The remaining face is described three different ways. It is said to be an ox [Ezekiel 1]. It is said to be a calf [Revelation 4] which is a young ox. And it is also called the face of a cherub [Ezekiel 10]. Through simple comparison we can discover that the face of a cherub is the face of a young ox. Getting it all together we find that Lucifer's created appearance is in some ways like that of a man but with legs that go down into strait feet like a calf. He has the body of a man with a man's arms but he also has wings, and his face is that of a young ox. Also, in his body are precious stones and musical instruments. He is the only non-human *"anointed"* royal creature mentioned in the Bible. And his position of *"covering cherub"* was apparently above the throne of God where he led worship services with music and a glittering light show as he reflected the radiant glory of God across the universe like a cosmic aurora borealis. According to Hebrews chapter 12:22 an innumerable company of angels would have been in attendance. It's easy to realize that all eyes would have been on him as he directed the heavenly worship service. Apparently, Lucifer became dissatisfied with his job and decided he was destined for bigger things! His ambition included seizing rulership of the universe.

We also know that he was a king. How do we know this? We know it because he had a throne and he was determined to exalt it. But where was this throne? In Isaiah 14:13, Lucifer is recorded as saying in his heart *"I will ascend into heaven, I will exalt my throne above the stars of God.* So his throne must have been below the stars. He also said *"I will ascend above the heights of the clouds"* so his throne was not only below the stars, but it was also below the clouds. His throne was obviously on earth. But where on earth would his throne be located? The Bible reveals only one place in which Lucifer (now Satan) has shown any real interest. It seems evident that his throne was originally located on none other than the foundation stone of the world. It was located on earthly mount Zion, the place now referred to as the Temple Mount. It is the only proper location of the Holy of Holies inside the Jewish Temple which means it is also the earthly location for the throne of Almighty God. However, that location is presently occupied by the Islamic Dome of the Rock. Whose idea do you suppose it might have been to build an idol's temple on that location? Consider this. The world's greatest dispute over a national boundary encompasses the tiny nation of Israel and the city of Jerusalem is at the center of that controversy. But the very source of contention, the focal point and most heated part of the debate is the dispute over the ownership of the top of Mount Zion, the area of the ancient Jewish temple which is presently the site of the Islamic Dome. What are the odds of that? Could a cosmic controversy over the location of a throne explain the history of this unlikely phenomenon? I believe it does!

A ROYAL SEARCH

We have travelled a long way back. We have crossed the millennia of human history. We have spanned the age of the creation of spiritual beings. We have traversed beyond the dawn of space and matter and even past the creation of time to the eternity of:

> **In the beginning God...** [Genesis 1:1]

Much of this we cannot comprehend. We are simply incapable. The knowledge of it is hidden in the heart and mind of God.

> [Deuteronomy 29:29] The secret things belong unto the LORD our God:

Some things may be hidden from the mind of man. Other knowledge is available for the benefit of all humanity.

> [Deuteronomy 29:29] The secret things belong unto the LORD our God: **but those things which are revealed belong unto us and to our children for ever,** that we may do all the words of this law.

Some people, because of the condition of their hearts, are kept from certain knowledge. Our Lord will not reveal it to them.

> [Matthew 13:34-35] **All these things spake Jesus unto the multitude in parables; and without a parable spake he**

not unto them: That it might be fulfilled which was spoken by the prophet, saying, **I will open my mouth in parables; I will utter things which have been kept secret from the foundation of the world.**

[Matthew 13:10-11] And the disciples came, and said unto him, **Why speakest thou unto them in parables?** He answered and said unto them, **Because it is given unto you to know the mysteries of the kingdom of heaven, but to them it is not given.**

There is also knowledge God enjoys revealing to people whom no one would suspect.

[Luke 10:21] In that hour Jesus rejoiced in spirit, and said, **I thank thee, O Father, Lord of heaven and earth, that thou hast hid these things from the wise and prudent, and hast revealed them unto babes: even so, Father; for so it seemed good in thy sight.**

Other information is only dispersed at certain times or in limited measures to specific people, according to the prerogative of God.

[Daniel 12:9] And he said, Go thy way, Daniel: **for the words are closed up and sealed till the time of the end.**

Then there are things concealed by God for the very purpose of compelling His people to search them out. Such secrets are hidden so that we might seek them with excitement and find them with joy. They are hidden to create a curiosity and a hunger in our hearts for the things of our Creator and to satisfy our souls with the knowledge of His ways.

> [Proverbs 25:2] **It is the glory of God to conceal a thing:** but **the honour of kings is to search out a matter.**

> [Psalms 119:18] **Open thou mine eyes, that I may behold wondrous things out of thy law.**

But this honour is not reserved for earthly priests or kings. It is reserved for those people whom our Lord sees as a royal priesthood in this world. It is an honor graciously extended to the blood bought people of the Lord Jesus Christ.

> [1 Peter 2:9] But ye are a chosen generation, **a royal priesthood,** an holy nation, a peculiar people; that ye should shew forth the praises of him who hath CALLED YOU OUT OF DARKNESS INTO HIS MARVELLOUS LIGHT:

The Apostle John writes:

> [Revelation 1:5-6] **...Unto him that loved us, and washed us from our sins in his own blood, And hath made us kings and priests unto God and his Father;** to him be glory and dominion for ever and ever. Amen.

THREE HEAVENS

Having followed the trail of history back to eternity past, let us now begin to move forward in time looking for details we can add to the things we have already discussed. We must search deeper still if we're to gain the right understanding. But where do we begin? Let's start with what we know so far. We know that eternal God must have existed for a virtual eternity without time, space or matter before the process of creation began. Then, the first thing we are told is:

> [Genesis 1:1] In the beginning God created **the heaven** and the earth.

Did you notice that heaven is used in the singular when creation begins? Just one heaven at that time, yet the apostle Paul tells us there are now three heavens.

> [2 Corinthians 12:2] I knew a man in Christ above fourteen years ago, (whether in the body, I cannot tell; or whether out of the body, I cannot tell: God knoweth;) such an one **caught up to the third heaven.**

As a matter of fact, in Revelation chapter four we find the Apostle John being called up to that third heaven where he receives from Jesus Christ a revelation of future events.

> [Revelation 4:1] After this I looked, and, behold, **a door was opened in heaven**: and the first voice which I heard was as it were of a trumpet talking with me; which said, **Come up hither, and I will shew thee things which must be hereafter.**

Naturally, the questions arise, *1) "When did God make the three heavens"*, and *2) "Why did He make three of them?"*

Actually, there is a great deal of controversy surrounding those two questions. So let me begin by answering the first one. *"When did God make the three heavens?"*

Genesis Chapter 1

1 In the beginning God created the heaven and the earth.

2 And the earth was without form, and void; and **darkness was upon the face of the deep.** And the Spirit of God moved upon **the face of the waters.**

3 ¶ And God said, Let there be light: and there was light.

4 And God saw the light, that it was good: and God divided the light from the darkness.

5 And God called the light Day, and the darkness he called Night. And the evening and the morning were the first day.

6 ¶ And God said, **Let there be a firmament in the midst of the waters,** and let it divide the waters from the waters.

7 And **God made the firmament, and divided the waters which were under the firmament from the waters which were above the firmament**: and it was so.

8 And **God called the firmament Heaven**. And the evening and the morning were the second day.

In the previous text we see that the heaven and earth were created. Then we read that Earth was without form and void and existed submerged in darkness and water until light was created in verse three. The creation of light began the first day; and verses four and five tell us that the light being separated from darkness was *"good"*. In verse six the second day started as a *"firmament"* was made which divided the waters so there were waters above and waters below the firmament. Oddly enough, the second day is the only day in the entire narrative that God did not specifically designate as being *"good"*. A person can either look at this as an accidental oversight on God's part or they can understand it as an intentional exclusion designed to draw the reader's attention to an important fact by way of omission. The passage describing the firmament is expanded upon below.

14 And God said, **Let there be lights in the firmament of the heaven to divide the day from the night;** and let them be for signs, and for seasons, and for days, and years:
15 And **let them be for lights in the firmament of the heaven to give light upon the earth**: and it was so.
16 And **God made two great lights; the greater light to** **rule the day, and the lesser light to rule the night: he made the stars also.**
17 And God set them in the firmament of the heaven to give light upon the earth,
18 And to rule over the day and over the night, and to divide the light from the darkness: and **God saw that it was good.**
19 And the evening and the morning were the fourth day.

We can clearly see that the *"firmament of the heaven"* is what we refer to as outer space. It is the universe where the sun, moon and stars are located. If we are to believe the Bible record, and I do, then we must believe that there is a body of water above the universe just as there is on planet earth below it. We now know where one of the heavens can be found and when it was made. It is the cosmos, outer space; and it was made on day two and called the firmament. But what about the other two heavens, where are they?

Another *"heaven"* found in the Bible is simply earth's atmosphere, as we can see in the following verses. It's the sky where clouds float along from horizon to horizon bringing rain and snow.

[Psalms 147:7-8] Sing unto the LORD with thanksgiving; sing praise upon the harp unto our **God: Who covereth the heaven with clouds, who prepareth rain for the earth,** who maketh grass to grow upon the mountains.

[Isaiah 55:10] For as **the rain cometh down, and the snow from heaven,** and returneth not thither, but **watereth the earth,** and maketh it bring forth and bud, that it may give seed to the sower, and bread to the eater:

Standing here on earth and looking up, the first heaven is the sky, which is actually Earth's atmosphere. The second heaven would then be outer space, or in other words the universe. Both of these were made during the creation week. So what is the third heaven and where is it located?

[Nehemiah 9:6] Thou, even thou, art LORD alone; **thou hast made heaven, the heaven of heavens,** with all their host, the earth, and all things that are therein, the seas, and all that is therein, and thou preservest them all; and the host of heaven worshippeth thee.

The third heaven is *"the heaven* [singular] *of heavens* [plural]*"*. It is heavenly Mount Sion where new Jerusalem is presently located.

LOOKING NORTH

[Hebrews 12:22] But ye are come unto mount Sion, and unto the city of the living God, **the heavenly Jerusalem,** and to an innumerable company of angels,

[Galatians 4:26] But **Jerusalem which is above** is free, which is the mother of us all.

And we are told that new Jerusalem will not always be in the third heaven, but will one day descend to earth so God may dwell with mankind.

> [Revelation 21:2-3]   And **I John saw the holy city, new Jerusalem, coming down from God out of heaven**, prepared as a bride adorned for her husband. And I heard a great voice out of heaven saying, Behold, the tabernacle of God is with men, and he will dwell with them, and they shall be his people, and God himself shall be with them, and be their God.

The day it comes to earth will be a day of rejoicing.

> [Psalm 48:2]   Beautiful for situation, the joy of the whole earth, is **mount Zion, on the sides of the north**, the city of the great King.

Moreover, the scriptures reveal that new Jerusalem is located on heavenly mount Sion which is evidently due north when leaving this planet. Apparently Satan knew exactly where to find it and he was headed that direction when he launched his initial rebellion.

> [Isaiah 14:12-14] How art thou fallen from heaven, O Lucifer, son of the morning! How art thou cut down to the ground, which didst weaken the nations! For thou hast said in thine heart, I will ascend into heaven, I will exalt my throne above the stars of God: **I will sit also upon the mount of the congregation, in the sides of the north:** I will ascend above the heights of the clouds; I will be like the most High.

And lest there be any doubt about the location of the third heaven, notice how the following scripture substitutes God for the direction of north.

[Psalm 75:6-7] For promotion cometh neither from the <u>east</u>, nor from the <u>west</u>, nor from the <u>south</u>. **But <u>God</u> is the judge**: he putteth down one, and setteth up another.

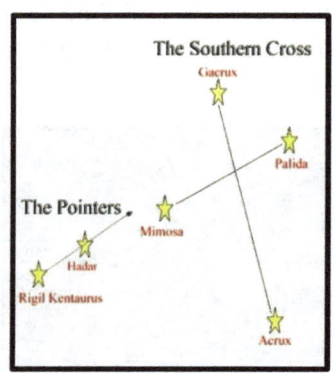

In the above passage, the cardinal points of the compass are used to identify the location of **God** in the universe. Historically, all ships in the northern hemisphere have sailed with an eye towards the **North Star** which is the biblical direction for the Creator. But that's not all, because in the southern hemisphere the North Star cannot be used as a point of reference for sailing. So in the bottom half of the world ships look to a star group called **The Southern Cross** to plot their courses. This illustrates the scriptural truth that Heaven is up and Hell (as in the cross of Christ) is down. But astronomy's corroboration of biblical truth goes even further than this; because it is also significant to note that the stars of The Southern Cross were last visible on the edge of the horizon from Jerusalem, which is in the northern hemisphere, around the time of Christ's crucifixion. Since the time of His resurrection this *"cross"* can no longer be seen from Jerusalem. For confirmation of this fact see the work of *Richard Hinckley Allen, Star-Names and Their Meanings*. Some would label this observation as a mere coincidence, and perhaps the label might be justified if it were the only such occurrence associated with the scriptures. But there are literally hundreds of such coincidences, perhaps even many thousands, and this puts them all well beyond the realm of mathematical probability. At some point reason requires that a person take notice of the staggering magnitude of such unlikely phenomenon which is found only within the pages of the Bible. Our God is also the Creator of mathematical probabilities!

THE DEEP

It has been rightly said: *We can see the first heaven by day and the second heaven by night; but the third heaven can only be seen with the eye of faith.* The apostle Paul comments on the matter saying:

> [1 Corinthians 13:12] **For now we see through a glass, darkly**; but then face to face: now I know in part; but then shall I know even as also I am known.

At this time, the Lord Jesus Christ is physically in the third heaven but one day we will see Him face to face. For the time being, He remains on the other side of *"the deep"* that was first mentioned in the beginning of Genesis. The deep is a physical divider located between the second and third heaven. John stood on top of it when he was called to the third heaven, and he described it for us.

> [Revelation 4:6] **And before the throne there was a sea of glass like unto crystal:**

John's imagery agrees with that of Moses and Job who described a body of water, literally a sea above the top of the universe, and they referred to it as *"the deep"*.

[Genesis 1:2]   And the earth was without form, and void; and darkness was upon **the face of the deep**. And the Spirit of God moved upon **the face of the waters**.

[Job 38:30]   **The waters are hid** as with a stone, and **the face of the deep is frozen**.

King David chimes in as well.

[Psalm 148:4]   Praise him, ye heavens of heavens, and **ye waters that be above the heavens**.

Here we see David giving his assent to the understanding that there are waters above the "*heavens*", which is plural. That is, there is water above the first and second heaven. But this doctrine is not new. Job's friend Elihu looks up into the sky a thousand years before David and confirms the same truth as he drills Job regarding God's creative powers, asking him:

[Job 37:18]   Hast thou with him [God] spread out **the sky, which is strong, and as a molten looking glass?**

These are all different ways of expressing the same idea. Unfortunately, many professing Christians are apparently unaware of how the Bible describes the cosmos, even though they may sing about it in church. Consider the lyrics to the following old hymns that have been historically sung by Christians for many decades.

I Am Bound For The Promised Land

On Jordan's stormy banks I stand,
And cast a wishful eye,
To Canaan's fair and happy land,
Where my possessions lie.
No Chilling winds or poisonous breath,
Can reach that healthful shore.
Sickness and sorrow, pain and death,
Are felt and feared no more.
I am bound for the promised land.
I am bound for the promised land.
O who will come and go with me?
I am bound for the promised land.

[In this song, the Christian is viewed as standing on the bank of the Jordan River and looking across the water to his home in heaven.]

I Will Sing The Wondrous Story

I will sing the wondrous story,
Of the Christ Who died for me.
How He left His home in glory,
For the cross of Calvary
Yes, I'll sing the wondrous story,
Of the Christ Who died for me.
Sing it with the saints in glory,
Gathered by the crystal sea.

[Here the believer sings about standing on the crystal sea in heaven described by John in Revelation 4:6]

Moreover, God teaches His people this truth in various other ways as well. For instance, did you ever notice that the scriptures tell of three different types of arks? On a global scale surely the most famous of the three is Noah's ark. It was the huge boat he was commissioned to build in Genesis chapter six that preserved his family and the animals during the flood. Later, in Exodus chapter two, we are introduced to baby Moses and his little ark of bulrushes. It was the tiny boat that carried him down the Nile to the safety of Pharaoh's daughter. Then we are told about the legendary ark of the Covenant in Exodus twenty-five that was brought to the world's attention by the popular Indiana Jones movie "Raiders of the Lost Ark". But have you ever wondered why that wooden box covered with gold was called an "*ark*"? The reason for this is simple. The ark is representative of the throne of God, and God's throne sits upon the face of the watery deep, which is frozen crystal sea. In this odd way it's like a boat. Isn't it strange that when Jesus begins His ministry, the first four men He chose to follow Him were commercial fishermen? He even told them:

> [Mark 1:17] …Come ye after me, and **I will make you to become fishers of men.**

Why does He call them *"fishers of men"*? It's because they are given the task of getting people into the throne room of God, to the true ark which is located in the third heaven on the other side of the great deep. And what do you suppose those fishermen were to use for bait as they were fishing for men? Well, when you think of fishing what's the first bait that comes to your mind? We can find the answer in one of the most famous messianic passages in the Bible concerning the sufferings of Christ.

> [Psalm 22:6-8] But **I am a worm**, and no man; a reproach of men, and despised of the people. All they that see me laugh me to scorn: they shoot out the lip, they shake the head, saying, **He trusted on the LORD** that he would deliver him: **let him deliver him,** seeing he delighted in him.

And just so we didn't miss the messianic connection, Matthew tells us our Lord's detractors fulfilled the thousand years old prophecy as they railed on Him, saying:

> [Matthew 27:43] **He trusted in God; let him deliver him** now, if he will have him: for he said, I am the Son of God.

So, as we can plainly see, scripture definitely reveals that there are three heavens and that there is a body of water, a veritable cosmic sea, separating the second heaven from the third heaven. We passively acknowledge this truth when we send up a **space-ship** that contains **astro-nauts**. The prefix *"astro"* means star or space; and the suffix *"naut"* (as in *"nautical"*) has to do with water and sailors. Astronauts are sailors in a ship that travels through the *"sea"* of space.

But why is *"the deep"* up there?

NOT GOOD

As previously mentioned, the *"second day"*, introduced in Genesis chapter one, is the only day not specifically said to be *"good"*. This was not an oversight on God's part, but rather a sentiment that was being expressed in a subtle manner. What was wrong with day two that compelled the Creator to withhold His pronouncement of *"good"*? It was the creation of *"the deep"*. It was the need for a barrier to be placed between the second and third heaven. Though God did not desire it, it was necessary that a barrier be placed between the unrestrained glory of His holy righteousness and the defiled physical universe that had been messed up by the king of corruption, Lucifer. As we pointed out before, there is a part of God that is: ***"of purer eyes than to***

behold evil, and canst not look on iniquity" and this is why Christ, apart from the rest of the Godhead, bore the penalty of sin on the cross alone. It's the whole reason why He cried out:

[Mark 15:34] **My God, my God, why hast thou forsaken me?**

One of the eight great mysteries of the church age is *"the mystery of Godliness"* [1Timothy 3:16] *"God was manifest in the flesh"*. And yet a part of God was not exposed to the humiliation of the cross but was kept back and not *"made to be sin for us"*. This is a mystery. It's something we can't really comprehend but rather we accept it by faith because the scriptures tell us it is true. There is a part of God that must be kept pure, must be kept righteous, must be kept *"separate from sinners"* and must even be kept back from a defiled universe. More could be said at this time, but I will not belabor this subject now since I believe it will become increasingly self-evident as we proceed.

The fact that the deep was created prior to man is very revealing. Not only was it created prior to man, but it was also made before the plants and animals, before the sun moon and stars and even before light was separated from darkness. This tells us that something in the universe was already amiss. Lucifer's coup had already been launched and he had suffered a serious reversal of fortune. But if that is so, then there must have been a previous earth from which he launched his failed rebellion. In other words, it becomes apparent that the earth was not created in a state of chaos *"without form and void"*, but rather had come into that condition as a result of the upheaval that ultimately accompanied Lucifer's ill-conceived attempt at a power grab.

If all of this is correct then there was an earth created in Genesis 1:1 that was perfect, complete and functional at its creation. For all intents and purposes it seems that it must have been, in many ways, like the one Adam and Eve experienced at the time of their creation. It likely would have been even better because sin had not yet been introduced into the universe. The cosmos at that time would have well fit Peter's description of what is promised to us in the future; a heaven and earth *"wherein dwelleth righteousness".* [2 Peter 3:13]

It would have been a creation not yet blackened by sin and rebellion. It would have been a universe where all was right at all times. It would have been a place where the wolf could lay down to rest with the lamb without the lamb being nervous; and the serpent would never strike or spit its venom. The newspapers, if there were any, would have been filled with good news every day. War and suffering would never appear in print. Our experiences here on earth have left us ill equipped to imagine such a veritable utopia.

But the first paradise came to a catastrophic end. Earth's original king, Lucifer, became filled with ambitious self-will and made an assault against the throne of God. He found the throne he was given insufficient to fulfill his heart's vain desire to be worshipped as a god. Two thrones existed at that time just as they do now. God Almighty was seated upon one of them. The throne occupied by God was the throne of the *"kingdom of God"*, which is NOT a physical kingdom. It is a kingdom governed by a spiritual condition; the spiritual nature and personal character of God Himself.

[Romans 14:17] For **the kingdom of God is** not meat and drink; but **righteousness, and peace, and joy in the Holy Ghost.**

Jesus proclaimed that the kingdom of God could not be seen with the human eye, and that a person must be spiritually born into it, or he will never see it.

[Luke 17:20-21] And when he was demanded of the Pharisees, when the kingdom of God should come, he answered them and said, **The kingdom of God cometh not with observation:** Neither shall they say, Lo here! or, lo there! for, behold, **the kingdom of God is within you.**

[John 3:3] Jesus answered and said unto him, Verily, verily, I say unto thee, **Except a man be born again, he cannot see the kingdom of God.**

The second throne was the seat of authority over the physical creation. It was called *"the kingdom of heaven"* because the earth was suspended in the heaven, in space, just as it is now. People often mistake heaven for a spiritual condition. But heaven is always a physical location in the Bible even though spiritual beings live there. Authority over the kingdom of heaven was graciously extended to Lucifer just as God has, on various occasions, given it to others. (More will be said about this later.) It seems that scripture tells us very little about Lucifer's rebellion and the events that surrounded it. But we do know he somehow convinced an untold number of the angelic host to follow his lead. Moreover, knowing the context of the book of Revelation points to *future* events, we are told his rebellious persuasion will yet draw a third of the remaining angelic host (represented as *"stars"* in the following passages) into his ongoing rebellion.

[Revelation 12:3-4]   And there appeared another wonder in heaven; and behold a great red dragon, having seven heads and ten horns, and seven crowns upon his heads. And **his tail drew the third part of the stars of heaven, and did cast them to the earth:** and the dragon stood before the woman which was ready to be delivered, for to devour her child as soon as it was born.

[Revelation 12:7-8] And there was war in heaven: Michael and his angels fought against the dragon; and **the dragon fought and his angels, And prevailed not; neither was their place found any more in heaven.**

More will be said later about this subject as well. But for now, if the reader has any question about the tribulation context of Revelation chapter twelve, notice how verses six and fourteen reference the last three and half years of the *"70ᵗʰ week of Daniel"* which is understood to contain the great tribulation, also known as *"the time of Jacob's trouble"* [Jeremiah 30:7].

Apparently the days of Noah were a microcosm, a kind of repeat of an earlier event. In Genesis 1:2 God flooded out the creation to bring Lucifer's original treasonous uprising to a halt. But his rebellion left a lingering problem to be dealt with – SIN. Sin was left circling the gift of free-will like a vulture. Now, as long as there is an opportunity to do wrong, someone will do it. Not all of the angels fell into sin. But many of them did and all because *"one sinner* (in this instance Lucifer) *destroyeth much good"* [Ecclesiastes 9:18]. A world was destroyed, and quite possibly an entire cosmos. But the all-knowing Creator was prepared for this eventuality. It would take time, but He would solve this problem, and in the process He would gather to Himself a people who would willingly choose Him. Not just because His power is awe inspiring; but because He would demonstrate His love toward them and in so doing provide a compelling reason for them to love Him in return.

A NEW EARTH FROM CHAOS

[Genesis 1:1] **In the beginning God created the heaven and the earth.**

Things were good for a while, after the initial creation, when Lucifer was given rulership over the physical kingdom. How long did it last? I don't know. But the scripture seems to indicate there was at least a block of time spanning two thousand years. Later I'll provide some detailed substantiation for that supposition. At this point, suffice it to say that things didn't end as well as they started. Lucifer gave birth to sin. The physical creation was defiled and it appears a great number of celestial beings had been corrupted right along with it. Genesis chapter one verse two (the very next verse) presents us with a formless world engulfed in a dark watery deluge.

[Genesis 1:2] And **the earth was without form**, and **void**; and **darkness was upon the face of the deep**. And the Spirit of God moved upon **the face of the waters**.

Next, God turns on the light.

[Genesis 1:3-5] And God said, Let there be light: and there was light. And **God saw the light, that it was good:** and God divided the light from the darkness. And God called the light Day, and the darkness he called Night. And the evening and the morning were the first day.

The light was good, but what kind of light was it? We can't be certain, but we do know that it wasn't sunlight because the sun, moon and stars weren't made until the fourth day. Maybe it was a magnetic form of light like the aurora borealis. Or perhaps there are exotic kinds of light that we have yet to discover. We aren't told, but we know it was "*good*". Next, God created the firmament which separated the water into two parts. There was water above and water below the firmament, and the firmament was called Heaven.

> [Genesis1:6-8] And God said, **Let there be a firmament in the midst of the waters, and let it divide the waters from the waters.** And God made **the firmament, and divided the waters which were under the firmament from the waters which were above the firmament:** and it was so. **And God called the firmament Heaven.** And the evening and the morning were the second day.

But wait a minute! Why did God make a "*Heaven*" out of the firmament when a heaven already existed in verse one before the firmament was made? It is because the firmament of the heaven was going to be holding the contents of a tainted universe that He would form on the other side of the barrier called "*the deep*", which is a frozen expanse that separates God, in the third heaven, from the physical creation in the second heaven. Consequently, the Creator was not pleased with the undesirable, but necessary, separation He had made. The sun, moon and stars created on the fourth day to populate the firmament are spectacularly good, and He calls them all by name. But the very presence of the deep puts a vital part of the Godhead OUTSIDE of the "*fish tank*", and He doesn't appreciate it. Just like anyone who has ever had an aquarium, He longs to be in there swimming with the fish. Snorkeling is ok. Scuba diving is better because you can stay under longer and do more. But to truly be one of them would be something altogether different. What could match that experience?!!! In the final analysis – day number two forfeited the proclamation that it was "*good*"! Even to this day, it imposes a limitation on the Almighty that must eventually be eliminated in order to satisfy the divine desire for heartfelt human fellowship. Why? Because, at this point, no man can see the face of the full glory of God and live [Exodus 33:20]. So, until the problem of sin is finally ironed out:

[Psalm 29:10] **The LORD sitteth upon the flood;**

PART 3

RE-ESTABLISHING THE KINGDOM

ADAM, SECOND KING OF EARTH, THE IMAGE OF GOD

Lucifer, the anointed cherub, the first king of earth was a washout. A second king was made, Adam. Like Lucifer, Adam was made, not born; but unlike Lucifer, Adam was made in the image of God.

> [Genesis 1:26] And **God said, Let us make man in our image**, after our likeness: **and let them have dominion** over the fish of the sea, and over the fowl of the air, and over the cattle, and over all the earth, and over every creeping thing that creepeth upon the earth.

Notice the passage says, *"Let us"* and *"our likeness"*. In this wording, we see the three-part nature of the Godhead expressed. This three-part nature is stamped on the creation in a great many ways. The following chart lists a sampling of instances where this imprint can be observed in nature rendering man's rejection of God *"without excuse"* [Romans chapter 1].

> **NOTE:** Although creation bears the three-part nature of the Godhead, it is not always evident what part would best be associated with which particular member of the Trinity. It may be that some of the items in the following list could be arranged in a more suitable order. Even so I believe each category, being composed of three complete parts, is sufficiently demonstrated throughout the list.

➢ **The 3 Part Imprint of the Godhead on Creation**

	FATHER	**SON**	**HOLY SPIRIT**
Space	Length	Width	Depth
Matter	Liquid	Solid	Gas
Time	Past	Present	Future
Reality	Time	Matter	Space
Atom	Neutron	Proton	Electron
Humanity	Japheth	Shem	Ham
The Mind	Thoughts	Emotions	Choices
Family	Father	Child	Mother
Condition	Saviour	Lost	Saved
Destiny	Heaven	Earth	Hell
Location	Sea	Land	Sky
Kingdoms	Animal	Mineral	Vegetable
Color	Yellow	Red	Blue
Value	Greater Than	Less Than	Equal To

Like the rest of nature, the three-part image was stamped upon Man at his creation. Adam was made as a body, soul and spirit. He was a three part being made in the image of his Creator - Who is Father, Son and Holy Spirit.

[Genesis 2:7] And the LORD God formed man of the **dust** of the ground, and breathed into his nostrils the **breath** of life; and man became a living **soul**.

Genesis gives us a peek at the creation of man, but it is

only a peek. It is a fleeting glimpse that can leave us with the wrong impression unless we search out the whole counsel of God. Genesis tends to persuade us that the Creator scooped up a handful of dirt from the top of the ground and formed a man. But is this mental image accurate? Could it be the result of a preconceived idea based on illustrated messages we have seen or heard, or maybe just a lack of pertinent information we have yet to consider? What if the latter is true and there are things which should be added to the equation? Could a little additional information actually change our view of things on such a basic subject? Let's venture forth and see.

As previously mentioned, Adam's beginning was radically different than that of all other people, with the exception of Eve. She was individually fashioned as well although the manner of her making differed from Adam's. Neither of these two people were conceived and born whereas everyone else was. Theirs was a *"special creation"*. I would like to consider this fact in the light of David's statements in Psalm 139. He says:

> [Psalm 139:13-14] For thou hast possessed my reins: **thou hast covered me in my mother's womb**. I will praise thee; for **I am fearfully and wonderfully made**: marvellous are thy works; and that my soul knoweth right well.

This statement is quite accurate. David was formed in the womb just like all people with the exception of humanity's original parents. Eve was made from Adam's rib and Adam was formed from the dust of the ground. But look at David's next statement.

> [Psalm 139:15] My substance was not hid from thee, when **I was made in secret**, and curiously wrought **in the lowest parts of the earth**.

This statement is NOT accurate — at least it isn't if it's applied to David. But what if David's reflections have gone deeper? We see this type of message occurring in many messianic prophecies. The discussion is about someone else; then suddenly a prophetic verse or two about Jesus is suddenly inserted. For instance:

> [Psalm 69:5-9] **O God, thou knowest my foolishness; and my sins are not hid from thee.** Let not them that wait on thee, O Lord GOD of hosts, be ashamed for my sake: let not those that seek thee be confounded for my sake, O God of Israel. Because for thy sake I have borne reproach; shame hath covered my face. I am become a stranger unto my brethren, and an alien unto my mother's children. **For the zeal of thine house hath eaten me up;** and the reproaches of them that reproached thee are fallen upon me.

In Psalm 69 we know that David, speaking of himself, acknowledges his foolishness and sins, but this same thing cannot be said about Christ. Yet we also know that the statement *"the zeal of thine house hath eaten me up"* definitely applies to Christ because the Apostle John quotes it as such.

> [John 2:17] And his [Jesus] disciples remembered that it was written, **The zeal of thine house hath eaten me up.**

It is much the same in Psalm 139. David was clearly not *"made in secret, and curiously wrought in the lowest parts of the earth."* David was born of a woman like the rest of us; but there was a man in David's lineage that was made differently — Adam.

If, in fact, we are correct that David was at that point reflecting on the creation of Man and not himself, then we have picked up some interesting pieces of information. First of all, we discover that Adam was *"made in secret"*.   This raises three obvious questions. *"Why would God make him in secret? Who was He keeping the secret from? And why was He keeping it secret?"* We'll return to these questions shortly, but let's set them aside for the moment.

Next we discover this secret operation was conducted *"in the lowest parts of the earth"*. This seems like an odd place to make a human! Is there any reason why God would go to a place inside the earth to make the man, and where would that place likely be? At this point, I'll bring to your remembrance the teachings of the Jewish Sages regarding the *"foundation stone"* of the Earth.

> Mishneh Torah, Sefer Avodah, Beit Habechirah, Chapter Two
>> "It is universally accepted that the place on which David and Solomon built the Altar, the threshing floor of Ornan, is the location where Abraham built the Altar on which he prepared Isaac for sacrifice. Noah built [an altar] on that location when he left the ark. It was also [the place] of the Altar on which Cain and Abel brought sacrifices. [Similarly,] **Adam, the first man,** offered a sacrifice there and **was created at that very spot**, as our Sages said: "Man was created from the place where he [would find] atonement."

Again, I do not take the teachings of Jewish Sages as gospel truth. Like all men, they are fallible in their understanding concerning the things of God. But here they do bring up a point of interest. Was Adam actually created at the place of the Foundation Stone? Let's take the question to a much deeper level. **Was Adam**

created in secret, under the foundation stone of the world, deep within the lowest parts of the earth? This is a provocative question. And if the answer is yes, then the scriptures, like a chain of dominoes, may well fall in a different direction than we had previously supposed.

What are we to make of this verse?

> [Isaiah 51:1] Hearken to me, ye that follow after righteousness, ye that seek the LORD: **look unto the rock whence ye are hewn, and to the hole of the pit whence ye are digged.**

Now it's time to raise the three questions we put on hold earlier in this section.

1) **Why would God make Adam in secret?**
   The answer to that question would seem to be obvious. If it was done in secret, it must have been to keep someone from seeing Him do it.

2) **If so, from whom was God keeping the "secret" of Adam's creation?**
   By now, this answer should be obvious as well. If God was hiding when He made Adam, He must have been hiding from Lucifer who had already lost the earthly throne of the kingdom of heaven in his failed attempt to oust God. Ultimately, Lucifer would come to be known as Satan the adversary.

3) **Finally, why was God keeping the secret of Adam's creation from Lucifer?**
   I can think of only one logical reason that God would hide from Satan when He made Adam. He didn't want Satan to

see how He made him. But I can hear someone objecting, *"Wait a minute, doesn't that imply Satan could have possibly learned how to make a living creature from inorganic materials by watching God create Adam?"* Well, yes, it seems like that could be a possible implication, but is it really a possibility? After all, we know that this is the very point where Pharaoh's magicians dropped the ball in their contest against Moses. During the Exodus plagues, Moses miraculously made living lice that were created out of the dust. Pharaoh's men failed to duplicate the miracle with their satanic powers, and they openly admitted it.

> [Exodus 8:19] Then the magicians said unto Pharaoh, **This is the finger of God:**

Just so we're on the same page with all of this, let's put a few of the pieces together and see what they look like. Suppose it's true that the top of Mount Zion is the Foundation Stone of the world just as the Jewish Sages have indicated. And suppose the Foundation Stone was the location of Lucifer's throne before he launched his ill-conceived rebellion against God and brought the universe to ruin. If such be the case, are you able to imagine what may have transpired on that spot between God and Lucifer at the beginning of human history? The following is one possible, perhaps even likely, scenario.

> God, the King of Glory, goes to the Foundation Stone, the place of authority for the kingdom of heaven in the newly re-formed earth. It's the place where Lucifer's throne would have sat before the would-be usurper was unseated. Once there, God orders Lucifer to *"stand at attention"* like a Five Star General commands a slick sleeve Army grunt.

He stares at him eye to eye for a moment, and then says: *"Your rebellion has failed. Now, you just keep standing right there at attention, and don't move a muscle. I'm going somewhere, but I'll be back in a few minutes with a surprise."*

Suddenly God disappears, diving right underneath the Foundation Stone of the world. He plunges deep underground, travelling instantaneously to the lowest parts of the earth. There, the Creator scoops up some dust and using the *"just add water method"* [think clay] He fashions the figure of a man and breathes into his nostrils the breath of life. Then just as quickly as He left, He returns to the Foundation Stone on the surface of the Earth and by His side stands Adam - made in the image of his Creator.

The fallen cherub looks at the man and says to God, *"What's this? It smells like dirt."*

The Almighty replies with a smile, *"This is the surprise I mentioned. He's your replacement. YOU'RE FIRED!"* And Adam, who Luke's genealogy refers to as *"the son of God"*, becomes the second created being to receive dominion over the physical *"kingdom of heaven"*. All of Eden's creatures bend the knee to acknowledge their new Sovereign *–All Hail King Adam!*

[Luke 3:38] ...**Adam, which was the son of God.**

But Lucifer, now Satan, is a rebel. And all rebels, when they hear one of God's pronouncements, murmur within their hearts *"We'll see about that!"* The fifth cherub, whom we now call *"the devil"*, hated Adam instinctively. Why? Isn't it obvious? It's because Adam was his replacement. What was once Satan's now belongs to Adam's race. But he also hates him because the man is an inferior creation. He is not a celestial being; he is a lesser creature made of dirt. And not just any dirt but seemingly it was the dirt which came from under the place of authority, the Foundation Stone, the very place where Lucifer believes his throne should sit.

[Hebrews 2:6-7]   But one in a certain place testified, saying, **What is man**, that thou art mindful of him? or the son of man, that thou visitest him?   **Thou madest him a little lower than the angels; thou crownedst him with glory and honour, and didst set him over the works of thy hands:**

Satan's snarl reveals that the changing of the crown will not be accepted without a fight. He reasons within himself, *"A plan must be devised that will cause Adam to abandon his throne so I can regain my lost dominion over the kingdom of heaven."*

Of course, all of the preceding drama is mere logical supposition based on the possibility that the major points of interest we have reviewed concerning these events have been considered correctly. More information will need to be gathered. More meat will need to be added to the bone before we can reach a judicially logical *"preponderance of the evidence"*.

JUST PASSING THROUGH

[Genesis 2:8]   **And the LORD God planted a garden eastward in Eden; and there he put the man whom he had formed.**

We don't know how long Adam was in the garden. But because Adam was a type of Christ in some respects, and Christ is called the last Adam, I would tend to guess that the amount of time Adam spent in the Garden before he was given Eve was about three and a half years. Why? Because one of the things God uses to teach us is repeating patterns. I see that not only did Christ's ministry last three and a half years before He got His bride, but the rule of the antichrist (the false Christ) will last three and a half years as well. Why is that important? Because, he will be posing as Christ so he can deceive the nations. Anyway, I don't know for sure, but if I were going to hazard a guess based on the pattern in the scriptures, I would say Adam was in the Garden three and a half years naming the animals and enjoying fellowship with God before Eve was created. Incidentally, if his time with Eve was short before their expulsion, it would explain why Eve had not yet gotten pregnant. After all, having been given the commission to *"be fruitful and multiply"*, I would assume they were both created quite fertile.

Regardless of how long Adam inhabited the garden, this we know for certain; he had dominion over the creation. He was the king. And in the process of time he shared the Garden with his bride, Eve. Together, they were to *"replenish"* and have *"dominion"*, not just in the garden but over the whole earth.

> [Genesis 1:28] And God blessed them, and **God said unto them, Be fruitful, and multiply, and <u>replenish</u> the earth, and subdue it: and have dominion** over the fish of the sea, and over the fowl of the air, and over every living thing that moveth upon the earth.

This is the same commission that was later given to Noah after the earth had been destroyed by water in the global flood that occurred in his days.

> [Genesis 9:1-2] And God blessed Noah and his sons, and said unto them, **Be fruitful, and multiply, and replenish the earth.** And the fear of you and the dread of you shall be upon every beast of the earth, and upon every fowl of the air, upon all that moveth upon the earth, and upon all the fishes of the sea; **into your hand are they delivered.**

In fact, most of the water for Noah's flood apparently came from *"the deep"* which had washed out the previous creation that was recorded in Genesis 1:1-2.

> [Genesis 7:11-12] In the six hundredth year of Noah's life, in the second month, the seventeenth day of the month, the same day were all the **fountains of the great deep** broken up, and the **windows of heaven were opened.** And the rain was upon the earth forty days and forty nights.

I know that many people frame an argument over the word *"replenish"*. Some define it to mean *"fill"*, and others say it means *"refill"* and both do it to prove their respective doctrines. I have even heard both sides cite *"the Hebrew"* as their evidence. A methodology such as that seems to solve nothing. I prefer to simply look and see how the word fits into the broader context of scripture. I am persuaded that one word, verse or passage in the Bible cannot be properly understood if it is seen as doing damage to another verse. Scripture does not destroy the harmony of scripture. Or as Jesus said, *"The scripture cannot be broken"* [John 10:35]. Since the entire Bible is the word of God, I must be able to believe one verse as surely as I believe another. In a way, it's a kind of spiritual Hippocratic Oath which directs the believer to "*First do no harm*" to the scriptures. But, for now, let us reserve judgment on the definition of *"replenish"* until we have collected more evidence.

Our Lord loves a garden. He made a garden for Adam and Eve as a means of bringing pleasure to their lives. And let's face it; there is a peace inspiring atmosphere in a beautiful garden. Evidently the Creator feels the same way and enjoyed walking with Adam in the garden during the cool of the day. And it shouldn't surprise us to find that the *"last Adam"*, the Lord Jesus Christ, often enjoyed the peaceful serenity of a garden as well.

> [John 18:1-2] **When Jesus had spoken these words, he went forth with his disciples over the brook Cedron, where was a garden,** into the which he entered, and his disciples. And Judas also, which betrayed him, knew the place: for **Jesus ofttimes resorted thither** with his disciples.
>
> [1 Corinthians 15:45] And so it is written, The first man Adam was made a living soul; **the last Adam was made a quickening spirit.**

But the idea of a garden holds greater significance in the scriptures than just the enjoyment of peace and tranquility. We must take care to notice that the first Adam lost his kingdom in a garden, without prayer. And the last Adam gained his kingdom in a garden with prayer. You may recall that Christ's first blood laden drops of sweat fell in the garden as He began the atonement process and prayed His way to victory the night He was betrayed.

> [Luke 22:44] **And being in an agony he prayed more earnestly: and his sweat was as it were great drops of blood falling down to the ground.**

Moreover, if our contemplations regarding the world's foundation stone being the location of Lucifer's throne are correct, then Lucifer lost his kingdom from a garden as well! At this point we are able to see the beginnings of a pattern developing. If such a pattern continues to recur it must simultaneously gain doctrinal credibility. But the evidence of that being the case remains to be seen at this point.

THE PARADISE THAT WAS LOST

What do we really know of this garden paradise? We know it had trees in it. Two of them were very special and possessed supernatural properties.

> [Genesis 2:9] And out of the ground made the LORD God to grow every tree that is pleasant to the sight, and good for food; **the tree of life** also in the midst of the garden, and **the tree of knowledge of good and evil.**

The tree of knowledge of good and evil was the instrument used by the serpent, Satan, to bring about the downfall of King Adam and his wife. Through their sin they allowed the kingdom to fall back into the hands of the previously dethroned king. And we know it didn't take long for the kingdom to acquire the devil's nature since the first child born on this planet ended up murdering his younger brother, who is thought by many to have been his twin.

The tree of life was there as well, and both of these supernatural trees are said to have been *"in the midst of the garden"*. When reading the Genesis account we can see how the decision to seek knowledge at any cost ended in disaster. And we observe that the first couple's misguided quest still plagues our world today. It is also irrefutably evident that the tree of life was equally capable of imparting its supernatural property, which was everlasting physical life. Because of this, after the fall of the first man, access to the tree was blocked to prevent the corrupted couple from attaining physical immortality.

> [Genesis 3:22-24] And the LORD God said, Behold, the man is become as one of us, to know good and evil: and now, **lest he put forth his hand, and take also of the tree of life, and eat, and live for ever**: Therefore the LORD God sent him forth from the garden of Eden, to till the ground from whence he was taken. So he drove out the man; and **he placed at the east of the garden of Eden Cherubims, and a flaming sword which turned every way, to keep the way of the tree of life.**

It is assumed by most Christians that Adam and Eve possessed *"physical"* immortality before the unwary couple partook of the forbidden fruit. But is that a safe assumption? Are there other thoughts regarding this matter? And what are the logical conclusions which follow each of them?

In order to provide a small window with which to peer into these intriguing questions, the following four scenarios are presented for your thoughtful consideration. The first two scenarios suggest that they ate of the tree of life before they ate of the tree of the knowledge of good and evil. The last two scenario's support the notion they had not yet eaten of the tree of life before tasting the forbidden fruit.

THEY ATE OF THE TREE OF LIFE BEFORE THEY SINNED:

1) *Some people believe that Adam and Eve had already eaten of the tree of life and were immortal as a result; but when they ate of the tree of the knowledge of good and evil the effect of the tree of life was cancelled out and they were withheld from future access to the tree that would renew its effects.* The problem I see here is that this understanding is based on at least one of two unsubstantiated presumptions. First, it presumes they ate of the tree of life even though we are never told this happened. And second, it presumes the tree of the knowledge of good and evil would cancel the effects of the tree of life and end their immortality. Scripture would seem to suggest the opposite. We find that after they had sinned they were kept from the tree of life specifically because it would not cancel the effects of the tree of the knowledge of good and evil. It is apparent that if they had eaten of the tree of life, after having sinned, they would have been under the influence of the properties of both trees. They would have then physically lived forever as immortal sinners. I see no scriptural or logical indication that simply by reversing the order in which they're eaten, one tree would cancel out the

supernatural effects of the other. Rather, it seems logical that if they had eaten of both trees they would be under the influences of the supernatural properties of both trees as well.

2) **There are others who believe the first couple had eaten of the tree of life before they sinned, but it had no effect upon them at all since they already had everlasting physical life.** The problem with this position is that it assumes the tree of life had no properties to offer Adam and Eve until after they had sinned. It suggests that as far as man in his created state was concerned, this tree was no different than any other tree that was good for food. The problem here is that the biblical text definitely sets the two trees in contrast to each other, thereby offering the man and his wife a choice: obedience and eternal life, or disobedience and death. And again, there is no statement that they ever ate of the tree of life. That is simply conjecture.

THEY HAD NOT YET EATEN
OF THE TREE OF LIFE BEFORE THEY SINNED:

3) **Here, the supposition is that the man and his wife had not eaten of the tree of life yet, but they were already immortal and didn't need it.** This is in many ways like point number two, above. It is the equivalent of saying that the tree of life had nothing supernatural to give them. It offered no more than a snack or a meal. But how then can this tree be set in contrast to the tree of the knowledge of good and evil which DID have a

supernatural impartation in its fruit? The scripture plainly sets the two in contrast against each other, both vying for the attention of the new couple.

4) **This last scenario presents Adam and Eve as sinless mortals who had not yet eaten of the tree of life.** Both trees had a supernatural property to offer them and a decision would ultimately be made on their part that would determine the state of their future, one way or the other. This of course accepts the fact that, as mortals, they would need the tree of life to gain immortality. But this possibility raises new questions. For instance: What if they did not indulge in the forbidden fruit but also did not eat of the tree of life? What would happen to their mortal bodies then? Having not eaten of the tree of the knowledge of good and evil, they would not be under sin's curse and so would not suffer death as we understand it today. Would their soul somehow absorb their body one day? Or would their soul eventually step out of its mortal shell and just keep walking as if nothing had happened? Would stepping out of their body cause them to become something greater than they had previously been? Would such an event be the opposite of the way things are for an unregenerate man when he leaves his body as a sinner? When a lost person leaves their body they become less. They lose a part of themselves in the grievous process of death, and that part will never be regained.

All are good questions, but these are scenarios for which I have so far been unable to find a fully formed answer. And, in truth, it's not the objective of this book to untangle this particular theological knot. Having identified the knot, I am now content to leave the reader to pull the thread of his/her choice and see what unravels. As for myself, I think it now best to follow David's wise advice. He said:

> [Psalms 131:1] LORD, my heart is not haughty, nor mine eyes lofty: **neither do I exercise myself in great matters, or in things too high for me.**

So moving on, I have no doubt things were pretty good in the garden before sin. And as was pointed out previously, the Lord enjoys the ambiance of a peaceful garden. Four thousand years passed between the events in the garden and John's writing of Revelation, yet apparently God hadn't changed His mind. John discovered that the Lord still likes to keep the tree of life *"in the midst"* of a well-dressed garden.

> [Revelation 2:7] He that hath an ear, let him hear what the Spirit saith unto the churches; **To him that overcometh will I give to eat of the tree of life, which is in the midst of the paradise of God.**

Returning back to Genesis chapter two, we're told the garden was *"eastward in Eden"* and that a river flowed *"out of Eden to water the garden"*.

> [Genesis 2:8] And **the LORD God planted a garden eastward in Eden**; and there he put the man whom he had formed.

[Genesis 2:10] And **a river went out of Eden to water the garden**; and from thence **it was parted, and became into four heads.**

We also know that the river which flowed into the garden was *"parted, and became into four heads"*, which also became rivers.

[Genesis 2:11-14] The name of the first is **Pison**: that is it which compasseth the whole land of Havilah, where there is gold; And the gold of that land is good: there is bdellium and the onyx stone. And the name of the second river is **Gihon**: the same is it that compasseth the whole land of Ethiopia. And the name of the third river is **Hiddekel**: that is it which goeth toward the east of Assyria. And the fourth river is **Euphrates**.

This is quite a bit of information, but there is a problem with it. It's certain that Noah's flood had to significantly alter the surface of the earth, as raging flood waters always do. For example, today no one knows anything about the Pison River. It is apparently lost to us. The Hiddekel is said to be the Hebrew name for the Tigris. We know where the Euphrates is located, and it's in pretty much the same area as the Tigris, but we don't know where their original courses ran because of the changes that were likely made in topography by Noah's flood. But the Gihon River seems to be a different matter entirely. It's mentioned only six times in the Bible. It appears once in the Garden of Eden passage we just discussed, and it appears five times in connection with Jerusalem. Moreover, three of those occurrences are of great significance when considered in connection with the subject matter of this book. But this topic will be more appropriately addressed in a future section, so I'll table this discussion until then.

While escorting the fallen pair out of the garden, God provided for the ultimate defeat of the evil king who was once again ruling in the kingdom of heaven. A prophecy was issued telling of the serpent's future defeat by the *"seed of the woman"*. God said:

> [Genesis 3:15] And I will put enmity between thee and the woman, and between thy seed and **her seed; it shall bruise thy head**, and thou shalt bruise his heel.

But in the meantime, the downward trend continued until finally:

> [Genesis 6:12] ...God looked upon the earth, and, behold, it was corrupt; for **all flesh had corrupted his way upon the earth.**

KING NOAH

Life on earth took a serious downward turn after Mr. and Mrs. Adam were expelled from the garden. And to make matters worse, the fallen angelic *"sons of God"* contributed to the moral decline. Some of them developed a taste for the pleasures of earth women and the resulting offspring were a hybrid race of angel/human chimera that were giants. Here we find the origin of beings like the giants Goliath and Og King of Bashan as well as other strange but notable chimeric creatures found within the pages of the Bible.

> [Genesis 6:1-5] And it came to pass, when men began to multiply on the face of the earth, and daughters were born unto them, That **the sons of God saw the daughters of**

men that they were fair; and they took them wives of all which they chose. And the LORD said, My spirit shall not always strive with man, for that he also is flesh: yet his days shall be an hundred and twenty years. **There were giants in the earth in those days;** and also after that, when the sons of God came in unto the daughters of men, and they bare children to them, the same became mighty men which were of old, men of renown. And **GOD saw that the wickedness of man was great in the earth, and that every imagination of the thoughts of his heart was only evil continually.**

I do not take the ancient Book of Enoch to be a "lost book of the Bible" as some like to claim. But its antiquity is without question and it does raise some interesting considerations about the days of Noah. For instance, the book of Enoch, in chapters six through eight, says that of the angels which rebelled with Lucifer only two hundred committed fornication with the *"daughters of men"*. But that wasn't the end of their corruption. It's said that they caused a similar corruption of the animal kingdom as well. There would seem to be something to this story since *Genesis 6:12 tells us that "all flesh had corrupted his way upon the earth"*. We are also told in Genesis 6:9 that Noah *"was perfect in his generations"*. That is, Noah was of a pure, human, genetic stock. His DNA was not corrupted, which the scriptures seem to indicate had become an increasingly rare condition, even among the animal population. Apparently this biblical account is the source of the legendary chimera contained in the lore of every culture in the ancient world. And if that weren't problem enough, the book of Enoch also tells of the giants exhausting the food supply and turning to human cannibalism in order to satisfy their hunger, much like the giants of the ancient Celtic fable who bellowed: *"Fe fi fo fum, I smell the blood of an Englishman"*. Moreover, those fallen angels are said to be responsible for providing humanity with all manner of knowledge in warfare, the crafting of armaments, astrology, and occult magic of various forms, etc. If we have understood even half of this correctly then the need to wash this planet off was critical, which is exactly what the Lord did with the flood in Noah's day.

After the flood, Noah was given dominion over the earth just like Adam – he became king of the physical earthly realm. God pronounced a blessing on him and his family, allowing them to start off in a fresh world with a clean slate.

> [Genesis 9:1] And **God blessed Noah and his sons**, and said unto them, Be fruitful, and multiply, and replenish the earth.

> [Genesis 9:20] And **Noah** began to be an husbandman, and he **planted a vineyard**:

It turns out that the blessing God speaks over Noah's sons gathers additional significance as the narrative progresses. The washed off world is dramatically altered from what it was before the flood. It appears that entropy on earth became accelerated causing lifespans to decrease and allowing fermentation to occur. These developments seem to be new changes that somehow resulted from the flood. The adversary, Satan, could not rest content with a new king presiding over what he considered his domain. It's interesting to note that there are only two forbidden fruits in the Bible; one is the fruit of the tree of knowledge of good and evil, and the other is the fruit of the _"vine tree"_ _[grape vine]_ which was forbidden in any form to those under the vow of a Nazarite _[Numbers 6]_ and forbidden in its fermented form to those who were ministering in the priests office _[Leviticus 10:8-10]_. Like a serpent, the wild grape vine crawls across the ground, climbing where it can, and the scriptures present its fermented concoction as a viper's venom.

[Proverbs 23:29-32] Who hath woe? who hath sorrow? who hath contentions? who hath babbling? who hath wounds without cause? who hath redness of eyes? They that tarry long at the wine; they that go to seek mixed wine. **Look not thou upon the wine when it is red,** when it giveth his colour in the cup, when it moveth itself aright [indicating fermentation]. **At the last it biteth like a serpent, and stingeth like an adder.**

[Deuteronomy 32:31-33] For **their rock is not as our Rock,** even our enemies themselves being judges. For **their vine is of the vine of Sodom,** and of the fields of Gomorrah: **their grapes are grapes of gall,** their clusters are bitter: **Their wine is the poison of dragons, and the cruel venom of asps.**

Recall, for a moment, some of the specifics spoken of Lucifer in Ezekiel 28.

[Ezekiel 28:12-15] Son of man, take up a lamentation upon **the king of Tyrus...** **Thou hast been in Eden the garden of God...** **Thou art the anointed cherub that covereth...** **...iniquity was found in thee.**

Lucifer was called *"king of Tyrus"*, and the word Tyrus means *"a rock"*. Moses was correct in Deuteronomy 32 above when he said, *"**their rock is not as our Rock**"* and *"**their wine is not as our wine**"*. That being the case, who do you suppose showed up and whispered in Noah's ear that he should start a vineyard? It may be that Noah wasn't even aware of fermentation yet. But someone was aware, and that was all it took.

What's the bottom line here? Noah got a full dose of snake venom from that old serpent, the devil; and the crown to the kingdom fell off his head as he tumbled to the ground in a drunken stupor just before everything went black. Unfortunately, Noah did not yet know the royal admonition spelled out for kings.

> [Proverbs 31:4] **It is not for kings, O Lemuel, it is not for kings to drink wine; nor for princes strong drink:**

Noah got more than just a little buzz going. He wound up passed out naked in his tent and then something BAD happened. We aren't given all the details of what his son did to him, but hints abound when you follow the biblical trail of Ham's descendent forward from this point. However, we are told exactly what happened afterwards, so there's no need to guess.

> [Genesis 9:24-25] And **Noah awoke from his wine, and knew what his younger son** [Ham] **had done unto him.** And he said, **Cursed be Canaan**; a servant of servants shall he be unto his brethren.

Whatever happened while Noah was *"under the influence"* was so heinous that he cursed his grandson over it. I have been asked before, *"Why did Noah curse Canaan when it was his father Ham that did whatever it was?"* As I pointed out before, when they got off the ark, God blessed Noah and his sons [Genesis 9:1], and who can curse someone whom God has blessed? But this cursing of his grandson is a thought-provoking situation. At this time I have ten grandchildren, and I can't even imagine one of my kids doing something so terrible to me that I felt the need to curse one of my grandkids in order to settle the score, unless POSSIBLY one of the grandkids was somehow personally involved. It may be Ham learned some evil ways in the world before he got on the ark, and he passed them on to his son many years after the ark had landed. I don't know. But this much is certain, Noah's dominion was toppled by wine and the world fell into darkness once again. The fallen crown rolled back to the serpent and no son of Adam was given dominion over the whole world again for a very, very long time. Even so, it must be recognized that the Bible is a book about kings and kingdoms from the beginning to the end.

THE FATHER OF OUR FAITH

History has shown that no man can properly hold on to his earthly crown for very long. The enemy is too crafty, and his temptations are too strong. The Creator knows this and has provided for it in His plans. But it was first necessary to demonstrate that even the best of fallen men did not possess the personal character required to maintain a truly righteous kingdom. Paul was correct when he penned one of the great truths of the ages.

[Romans 3:23] **For all have sinned, and come short of the glory of God;**

There would need to be a BETTER man. One who was able to keep hold of the crown, and a family line had to be selected for His birth. Here's where we're introduced to a man named Abram and his barren wife Sarai. When God calls Abram to leave Ur of the Chaldees and go to what is known as *"the promised land"*, He made him a promise saying:

> [Genesis 12:3] And **I will bless them that bless thee, and curse him that curseth thee: and in thee shall all families of the earth be blessed.**

Egypt, Babylon, Persia, Greece, Rome, Germany, Niger, Chad, Ethiopia, Mauritania, Senegal, Mali, England, Iran, and many others - what do all of these countries have in common? They all chose a political position contrary to the nation of Israel and are paying the price for it. Why? Because about 4,000 years ago God made a promise to a man named Abram, saying: *"I will bless them that bless thee, and curse him that curseth thee".* As any student of the Bible knows, Abram is the man God chose to begin the lineage that would ultimately bring forth the Righteous King that would successfully rule the kingdom of heaven. That righteous King is, of course, the Lord Jesus Christ and it may be that Abram met Him almost two millennia before Christ's earthly birth when he encountered an extraordinary individual named Melchizedek *[spelled Melchisedec in the New Testament].*

> [Genesis 14:18-19] And **Melchizedek king of Salem** brought forth bread and wine: and he was the priest of the most high God. And he blessed him, and said, Blessed be Abram of the most high God, possessor of heaven and earth:

In Hebrews chapter seven, the apostle Paul makes some interesting observations about Melchisedec. In that chapter we learn that Salem means *PEACE*, so he is the King of Peace. And his name, Melchisedec, means *KING OF RIGHTEOUSNESS*. There is much controversy over whether this man is a type of Christ or an actual pre-incarnate appearance of Him. Many have failed to consider the possibility that both of these positions may be true. He may have actually been Christ but appearing only in type. In other words, He may have appeared as the future crucified, risen and glorified King, which He wasn't yet but would ultimately become. In His millennial reign, the resurrected Christ will be King over Jerusalem, which is Hebrew for City of Peace. And of course, the priestly Melchisedec provided bread and wine, typifying Christ at the last supper. Here we have Jerusalem singled out as the location of a person known as the King of Righteousness and King of Peace who was also a priest of the Most High God. And this takes place nearly a thousand years before David makes an offering on the threshing floor of Ornan the Jebusite where the temple would eventually be built and about two thousand years before Jesus (the King of Glory) was born of a woman. So we see that Jerusalem, very early in the scriptures, is rising in prominence as compared to the other cities of the world.

Moreover, as every student of the Bible also knows, because of Abram's willingness to believe the promises of God, the Lord changed his name to Abraham.

[Genesis 17:5] Neither shall thy name any more be called Abram, but **thy name shall be Abraham; for a father of many nations have I made thee.**

This name change typified the promise that all the families of the world would be blessed through him as a result of his willingness to believe and obey God. The seal of the covenant between Abraham and God was circumcision. When a man is circumcised, his flesh is removed revealing the source of life. Once removed it is gone forever. It cannot grow back. This physical surgery is explained in Colossians chapter two as representing the "operation of God" which is "the circumcision made without hands, in putting off the body of the sins of the flesh by the circumcision of Christ". What Abraham did with his hands to the physical bodies of the males under his authority, God does without hands, in a spiritual way, to the Christian at the moment of salvation. He removes the flesh to reveal the source of life. In this way Abraham is the father of our faith.

Abraham's faith and obedience is made even more evident when he is tested by the command to offer his son upon the altar. As we discussed earlier, Abraham was directed to go to the land of Moriah, to a mountain God would indicate, and there he was to make an offering of Isaac his son. That offering was interrupted by God once it was apparent that Abraham was willing to obey and a substitutionary offering was provided.

[Genesis 22:13-18] **And Abraham lifted up his eyes, and looked, and behold behind him a ram caught in a thicket by his horns: and Abraham went and took the ram, and offered him up for a burnt offering in the stead of his son.** And Abraham called the name of that place Jehovahjireh: as it is said to this day, In the mount of the LORD it shall be seen. And the angel of the LORD called unto Abraham out of heaven the second time, And said, By myself have I sworn, saith the LORD, for because thou hast done this thing, and hast not withheld thy son, thine only son: That in blessing I will bless thee, and in multiplying I will multiply thy seed as the stars of the heaven, and as the sand which is upon the sea shore; and thy seed shall possess the gate of his enemies; **And in thy seed shall all the nations of the earth be blessed;** because thou hast obeyed my voice.

Perhaps the most important thing about this Biblical passage is the prophetic answer of Abraham when Isaac questioned what was happening.

> [Genesis 22:7-8] And Isaac spake unto Abraham his father, and said, My father: and he said, Here am I, my son. And he said, Behold the fire and the wood: but where is the lamb for a burnt offering?   And Abraham said, My son, **God will provide himself a lamb** for a burnt offering: so they went both of them together.

As we can see in the above passage God provided a lamb for sacrifice in place of Isaac. That, however, is just one way to read the text because in a prophetic sense the text also indicates that God would provide "*himself*" manifested in the flesh as a sacrificial Lamb. This was ultimately accomplished on Calvary, and it is unlikely Abraham understood the prophetic implication of his actions. Earlier in the chapter "THE LOCATION OF THE JEWISH TEMPLE" I mentioned how the Jewish Sages have taught that Abraham offered Isaac on the foundation stone at the top of the Temple mount. But is this teaching reliable? That's a good question; but I would remind the reader that Calvary is also located on a mountain in "*the land of Moriah*" and it is very near the Temple Mount, just outside the gates of Jerusalem. I suggest that this is the most likely location where Abraham and Isaac built their altar since it is the very place where God did "*provide himself a lamb*" for a sacrifice. [See Genesis 22, John 1:29 and 1 Corinthians 5:7]

MOSES vs. MAGICIANS

In a previous section we touched on Moses' showdown with Pharaoh's magicians.   It must be admitted that they

demonstrated an impressive array of powers, matching Moses miracle for miracle initially. Accordingly, many people have been drawn into occult practices in an attempt to gain similar powers for themselves. But there came a point where the powers of the magicians failed, and the power of God, under the hand of Moses and his brother Aaron, did not. The magicians were not able to transform lifeless dust into organic life, specifically lice.

[Exodus 8:16-19] And the LORD said unto Moses, Say unto Aaron, Stretch out thy rod, and smite the dust of the land, that it may become lice throughout all the land of Egypt. And they did so; for **Aaron stretched out his hand with his rod, and smote the dust of the earth, and it became lice** in man, and in beast; all the dust of the land became lice throughout all the land of Egypt. And **the magicians did so with their enchantments to bring forth lice, but they could not:** so there were lice upon man, and upon beast. **Then the magicians said unto Pharaoh, This is the finger of God**: and Pharaoh's heart was hardened, and he hearkened not unto them; as the LORD had said.

We are told in Exodus chapter 7 that the magicians were able to turn their rods into serpents much like Aaron and Moses did. As I said, this is impressive, but what were their limitations? They were able to transform one form of organic life into another form: plant life (a rod) into animal life (a serpent). But they were stopped cold when it came to creating life, which was lice, from non-living dust. At this point the contest was over for the magicians, but Moses and Aaron continued on with additional miracles. Even so, the place marking the limitation of the magicians raises some interesting contemplations. Why were they not able to make lice from dust? It would seem this was the limit of their satanic powers. But WHY was it the limit? Was it because Satan does not possess the power to do it? Or is it that he does not possess the KNOWLEDGE to do it? Previously we discussed the implications of Psalm 139 which indicates that God made Adam in *"secret …in the lowest parts of the earth"*. Could it be this is why He made Adam secretly? It is reasonable to suppose that Satan, whose desire it is to *"be like the most high"* [Isaiah 14:14], would feel a compulsion to create life so he could *"show… himself that he is god"* [2 Thessalonians 2:4]. Perhaps he is capable of making a life form, if he can get the knowledge required to do it. After all, Revelation 13:15 says he has *"power to give life to the image of the beast"*. It may be that the Almighty, in His infinite wisdom, has prevented Satan from obtaining that knowledge prematurely.

We are presented with a peculiar passage in Jude that seems to have, what is at least, a peripheral relationship to this subject.

> [Jude 9] Yet **Michael the archangel, when contending with the devil he disputed about the body of Moses,** durst not bring against him a railing accusation, but said, The Lord rebuke thee.

For some undisclosed reason we find Michael and the devil arguing over who's taking the body of Moses. It seems logical to suppose that this controversy arose relatively soon after Moses' death. But prior to that, the last thing we read about Moses was that God personally buried him.

[Deuteronomy 34:5-6] So **Moses the servant of the LORD died there in the land of Moab, according to the word of the LORD.** And he buried him in a valley in the land of Moab, over against Bethpeor: but **no man knoweth of his sepulchre unto this day.**

Here we find another instance where God acted in secret. But who was he keeping the secret from this time? Evidently it was from Satan since Moses' body was the source of the later dispute with Michael. It would appear that God buried the body of Moses Himself so that Satan couldn't use it for some nefarious purpose. Moreover, at some point God sent Michael to fetch the body and bring it to the third heaven. Accordingly, we find it documented in the gospels that Moses, fifteen hundred years after he died, appeared resurrected on the mount of Transfiguration with Elijah and Jesus. But what could the devil have wanted with Moses' body? We aren't specifically told what his intentions were, but it seems that he intended to reanimate it and use it to lead the Hebrew people astray. After all, a living puppet would certainly seem to be of more use to him than a rotting corpse. Admittedly, these contemplations contain some amount of speculation, but we do know three things for certain about Satan that appear related to this discussion.

1) He definitely thought he could get some use out of Moses' corpse.

2) He does have the power to turn a dead stick into a living serpent, as we saw in the case of Pharaoh's magicians. [Exodus 7:11-13]

3) And we know that he is able to enter the body of another person, because we are told he did that very thing to Judas Iscariot. [John 13:26-27]

During the last supper Jesus informed the disciples that one of them would betray him that night. At the prompting of Peter, the apostle John asked Jesus who was going to be the betrayer, and His answer follows.

> [John 13:26-27] Jesus answered, He it is, to whom I shall give a sop, when I have dipped it. And **when he had dipped the sop, he gave it to Judas Iscariot**, the son of Simon. And after the sop Satan entered into him. Then said Jesus unto him, That thou doest, do quickly.

As a side note, it has been observed that, with the exception of the antichrist, Judas is the only man in the Bible referred to as *"the son of perdition"*. We find this reference in Jesus' prayer just before His suffering.

> [John 17:12] While I was with them in the world, I kept them in thy name: those that thou gavest me I have kept, and **none of them is lost, but the son of perdition**; that the scripture might be fulfilled.

Now, if you were paying attention, you may have noticed a very subtle connection between the above two passages regarding Judas. He was called the **S**on **O**f **P**erdition, and the sign he was the betrayer was a **SOP**. Betrayal is Satan's *"**S**tandard **O**perating **P**rocedure"!* The Bible is a strange book. It's literally filled with peculiar phenomenon which typically goes unnoticed. The presence of this type of phenomenon, which is so abundant in our historic Authorized Version of the Bible, is one of the evidences of its supernatural origin. It is an attribute that seems to be greatly lacking in modern translations.

Before we move on past Moses, it's important to point out that in some ways he typifies the Lord Jesus Christ. For instance, Jesus was prophesied to come as the prophet like Moses, a great miracle worker. Moses told the Israelites:

> [Deuteronomy 18:15] The LORD thy **God will raise up unto thee a Prophet** from the midst of thee, of thy brethren, **like unto me;** unto him ye shall hearken;

And like Joseph the son of Jacob, Moses also had a gentile bride. Both were from Africa.

> [Genesis 41:45] And **Pharaoh called Joseph's name Zaphnathpaaneah; and he gave him to wife Asenath the daughter of Potipherah priest of On.** And Joseph went out over all the land of **Egypt.** [Egypt is in North Africa]

> [Numbers 12:1] And Miriam and Aaron spake against **Moses** because of the Ethiopian woman whom he had married: for he **had married an Ethiopian woman.** [Ethiopia is also in Africa]

The significance of these men having a gentile bride will become more apparent later.

PART 4

OH' THEM SHEKELS!

KING DAVID, THE SWEET PSALMIST OF ISRAEL

[2 Samuel 23:1-5] Now these be the last words of David. David the son of Jesse said, and the man who was raised up on high, the anointed of the God of Jacob, and the sweet psalmist of Israel, said, The Spirit of the LORD spake by me, and his word was in my tongue. **The God of Israel said, the Rock of Israel spake to me, He that ruleth over men must be just, ruling in the fear of God.** And he shall be as the light of the morning, when the sun riseth, even a morning without clouds; as the tender grass springing out of the earth by clear shining after rain. **Although my house be not so with God;** yet he hath made with me an everlasting covenant, ordered in all things, and sure: for this is all my salvation, and all my desire, although he make it not to grow.

David saw the true need within the kingdom – proper ruling requires righteousness. But he also saw the problem, saying *"Although my house be not so with God"*, and he was right. David himself was guilty of at least two capitol offences where the death penalty was required. But like Nathan the prophet said, *"the LORD also hath put away thy sin; thou shalt not die"*. And David's sons, Amnon, Absalom and Adonijah were like rotten apples that didn't fall far from the tree of David's sin. But David was different in that he did value spiritual things. He had a real heart for God, but he also had the kind of power and authority that few humans ever experience. People lived and died according to David's spoken word as king. It's easy for one who is relatively powerless to judge his few abuses harshly. But having never commanded such unrestrained power, we have no idea what our own cruelties might be in that dark moment when fallen human nature raises its evil head. At such a moment we see in David the truthful axiom *"Power corrupts, and absolute power corrupts absolutely"*. For on a few occasions in his life, David's heart gave way to the corrupting influences of power allowing its corruption to flow unrestrained. Yet God saw in David something exceptional, and from the tribe of Judah, He chose him to be the king of Israel.

> [Psalms 78:67-72] Moreover he [God] refused the tabernacle of Joseph, and chose not the tribe of Ephraim: But **chose the tribe of Judah, the mount Zion which he loved.** And he built his sanctuary like high palaces, like the earth which he hath established for ever. **He chose David also his servant,** and took him from the sheepfolds: From following the ewes great with young he brought him to feed Jacob his people, and Israel his inheritance. So he fed them according to the integrity of his heart; and guided them by the skilfulness of his hands.

Moreover, the LORD made with him an everlasting covenant. Through David's lineage the promised Messiah King would come and Zion would be the place of His throne.

> [Psalm 132:11-14] **The LORD hath sworn in truth unto David;** he will not turn from it**; Of the fruit of thy body will I set upon thy throne.** If thy children will keep my covenant and my testimony that I shall teach them, their children shall also sit upon thy throne for evermore. **For the**

LORD hath chosen Zion; he hath desired it for his habitation. This is my rest for ever: here will I dwell; for I have desired it.

[Acts 2:29-30] Men and brethren, let me freely speak unto you of the patriarch **David**, that he is both dead and buried, and his sepulchre is with us unto this day. Therefore **being a prophet, and knowing that God had sworn with an oath to him, that of the fruit of his loins, according to the flesh, he would raise up Christ to sit on his throne;**

ORNAN OR ARAUNAH?

In an earlier section I mentioned the teaching of the Jewish Sages regarding the threshingfloor of Ornan the Jebusite where David offered a sacrifice to stop the plague. I discussed their teaching, that the Garden of Eden was a large area surrounding Jerusalem and that the Temple Mount was actually the location of the Foundation Stone of the entire world. But here we must discuss another interesting detail about Mount Zion which is the place God has chosen to put His name and the location from where the Messiah will rule when He returns to this earth.

Previously Jerusalem *"the city of peace"* was known as Jebus *"a threshing place"*.

[1 Chronicles 11:4] And David and all Israel went to **Jerusalem, which is Jebus**; where the Jebusites were, the inhabitants of the land.

To *"thresh"* is to beat small or trample under foot. We see the word used this way in the following scriptures.

[Isaiah 41:15] Behold, I will make thee a new sharp threshing instrument having teeth: thou shalt **thresh** the mountains, and **beat them small**, and shalt make the hills as chaff.

[Micah 4:13] Arise and **thresh**, O daughter of Zion: for I will make thine horn iron, and I will make thy hoofs brass: **and thou shalt beat in pieces many people**:

And, of course, we know that the highest point on the Temple Mount is the threshing floor David bought from Ornan the Jebusite. The problem is that the scriptures give what seems to be conflicting accounts of the purchase. There appears to be a discrepancy regarding how much he paid for the property and who he bought it from. Did he buy it from Ornan for 600 shekels of gold or was it a guy named Araunah for 50 shekels of silver?

[1 Chronicles 21:25] So David gave to **Ornan [וְנָ‎א]** for the place **six hundred shekels of gold by weight.**

[2 Samuel 24:24] And the king said unto **Araunah, [הַנּוּרָא]** Nay; but I will surely buy it of thee at a price: neither will I offer burnt offerings unto the LORD my God of that which doth cost me nothing. So David bought the threshingfloor and the oxen for **fifty shekels of silver.**

If you were to check with the various Old Testament commentaries on these passages you would discover that Araunah and Ornan are actually the same word with a slight alteration. The idea the commentators attempt to convey is that the scriptures were originally correct, but in the process of copying them, someone made a mistake, and now they contain a *"minor"* copying error. But this conclusion introduces some questions of its own. For instance, on what authority did they make this determination? Have any ancient Hebrew texts been found that do not contain the alteration? If so, then why is it still spelled different in our English translations? It's because the answer is NO, there are no Hebrew texts without the alteration. The commentators thought it was a spelling mistake and they were attempting to protect God's reputation for the "*error*" they found in the scriptures. Apparently, the reasoning was that God couldn't have made a mistake, so it must be a copy error. The problem is that this line of reasoning doesn't really solve the dilemma. There are numerous passages in EVERY Bible version that clearly demonstrate God's intention to preserve the scriptures in a pure form. And if He failed to do so then He still made a mistake. He made a promise and didn't keep it. He lied. That is, UNLESS the alteration is intentional. What if it's not a mistake? What if it's still exactly as it was supposed to be? What if it's a subtle message, and the commentators are just missing the point because they are willing to accept the idea of "*minor*" mistakes in the biblical text? What might we find if we decided to believe the biblical text instead of believing the commentators? To answer these questions we'll first have to take a trip down the rabbit hole and try to understand the biblical definition for the value of a shekel. But it seems unbelief may have *shackled* the minds of the commentators on this subject as well.

SHACKLES OR SHEKELS

One day, as I was doing my daily Bible reading, I encountered a passage that set me to thinking about the value of a shekel. I wondered what exactly a shekel was. What was it worth? So I checked Google to see if I could find a decent answer, and here's what I found.

> *"As with many ancient units, the **shekel** had a variety of values depending on era, government and region; weights between 7 and 17 grams and values of 11, 14, and 17 grams are common."*

Let's face it, that response is less than satisfying. The values proposed by Google, between 7 and 17 grams, vary by 240%. That's a pretty big margin for error. Accepting that statement as biblical truth shackles a believer's mind and renders the idea of a shekel's value completely unusable for the purpose of biblical study. But then it dawned on me that I wasn't interested in the fluctuating values ascribed by governments or regions. I just wanted to know what value God put on it! After all, He must have had something in mind when He included shekels in the scripture, or they wouldn't even be in the Bible. Then I remembered that the scriptures tell of a shekel that is associated with the sanctuary.

> [Exodus 30:13] This they shall give, every one that passeth among them that are numbered, half a shekel after **the shekel of the sanctuary**: (a shekel is twenty gerahs:) an half shekel shall be the offering of the LORD.

I realized that the *sanctuary shekel* was my primary interest. Obviously God had a specific value in mind in the above verse. That's when I decided to try and plug in a few numbers to see  how they worked out from a biblical perspective. Google mentioned 7, 11, 14 & 17 grams. The number 11 was the closest figure to midrange between 7 and 17 so I decided to start with that. But where should I apply it? I reasoned that since everything in the Bible centers around the Lord Jesus Christ, I should start with Him. I recalled Zechariah's prophecy about the thirty pieces of silver involved in Christ's betrayal, and how Matthew told of its fulfillment.

[Zechariah 11:12-13] And I said unto them, If ye think good, give me my price; and if not, forbear. So they weighed for my price **thirty pieces of silver.** And the LORD said unto me, Cast it unto the potter: a goodly price that I was prised at of them. And **I took the thirty pieces of silver, and cast them to the potter in the house of the LORD.**

[Matthew 27:3-8] Then Judas, which had betrayed him, when he saw that he was condemned, repented himself, and **brought again the thirty pieces of silver to the chief priests and elders**, Saying, I have sinned in that I have betrayed the innocent blood. And they said, What is that to us? see thou to that. And **he cast down the pieces of silver in the temple**, and departed, and went and hanged himself. And the chief priests took the silver pieces, and said, It is not lawful for to put them into the treasury, because it is the price of blood. And **they took counsel, and bought with them the potter's field**, to bury strangers in. Wherefore that field was called, The field of blood, unto this day.

This seemed like the right place to begin. After all, the gnat straining Pharisees could no doubt be safely relied upon to use nothing but official Jewish currency, which is the sanctuary shekel. So, here's the math.

30 shekels x 11 grams per shekel = **330** grams

This is interesting! Why? Because anyone who has ever studied Bible numerology knows that there is a solid connection between the number three and God. Just as Satan's incarnate number is

666, God in the flesh can be associated with the number 333. So I figured a little tweaking appeared to be in order. My revised figure was 11.1 grams per shekel.

30 shekels x 11.1 grams = **333** grams

This looked promising. But I wondered if it would hold up under scriptural examination? I believe it does, but since it is not the purpose of this book to delve into numerology I will just give a couple more examples demonstrating the appropriateness of my calculations using 11.1 grams per shekel.

GOLIATH OF GATH

Almost everyone knows the story of David the underdog and his legendary triumph over the evil giant. Goliath's height was six cubits and a span. That's 9 feet 6 inches at a minimum. He would likely tower 3 feet above most of the tallest people you have ever met. He was an imposing figure for sure! But my present interest lies in this satanic soldier's weaponry. Regarding his spear we are given some information. Its shaft was like a weaver's beam. Large and solid no doubt, but its weight was not given. But then, for some strange reason God wants us to know the actual weight of the spears head. This seems like an odd detail to be so specific about, but the Lord always has His reasons, so let's read the passage and do the math.

> [1 Samuel 17:7] And the staff of his spear was like a weaver's beam; and **his spear's head weighed six hundred shekels of iron:** and one bearing a shield went before him.

600 shekels of iron x 11.1 grams per shekel = **6,660** grams of iron; just over 14 ½ pounds in the spear's head alone!

Several things are important to note about this passage and its calculation.

1) The number 666 is indisputably connected to Satan.

2) Iron in the Bible is always cast in a negative light, being connected to the giant offspring of fallen angels.

3) Iron tools were forbidden to be used in the building of any altar or during the assembly of the Temple.

4) According to Daniel 2:43, the *"iron"* will once again attempt to mingle their seed with the seed of men in the tribulation period.

[Daniel 2:43] And whereas thou sawest iron mixed with miry clay, **they shall mingle themselves with the seed of men**: but they shall not cleave one to another, even as iron is not mixed with clay.

5) The value of 11.1 grams per shekel works perfectly in this passage.

NAAMAN THE SYRIAN

[2 Kings 5:5-6] And the king of Syria said, Go to, go, and I will send a letter unto the king of Israel. And he departed, and took with him **ten talents of silver**, and **six thousand pieces of gold**, and **ten changes of raiment**. And he brought the letter to the king of Israel, saying, Now when this letter is come unto thee, behold, I have therewith sent

> Naaman my servant to thee, that thou mayest recover him of his leprosy.

Naaman the Syrian was a gentile, in other words not a Jew, and he was a leper. Leprosy is a picture of sin in the Bible, which should give you some idea of what God thinks about sin. You'll notice that the king of Syria, for Naaman's cleansing from leprosy, was willing to give ten changes of clothes, and ten is the number representing gentiles in the Bible. He was also offering six thousand pieces of gold. Six is the number of man, and gold represents deity, but we don't know the value of the Syrian gold pieces. Now let's pay attention to both: the ten talents, because ten is the number for gentiles; and the silver, because in the Old Testament the price of atonement was paid in silver.

> [Exodus 30:13-15] This they shall give, every one that passeth among them that are numbered, half a shekel after the shekel of the sanctuary: (a shekel is twenty gerahs:) an half shekel shall be the offering of the LORD. Every one that passeth among them that are numbered, from twenty years old and above, shall give an offering unto the LORD. **The rich shall not give more, and the poor shall not give less than half a shekel,** when they give an offering unto the LORD, **to make an atonement for your souls**.

The king of Syria was offering ten talents of silver, but how much is a talent? According to the Bible, a talent, which is a Jewish measure, was three thousand shekels. That fact can be corroborated by examining the figures given in the redemption of the men of Israel and how afterwards that silver was used in the tabernacle.

[Exodus 38:25-28] And **the silver of them that were numbered of the congregation was an hundred talents, and a thousand seven hundred and threescore and fifteen shekels,** after the shekel of the sanctuary: A bekah for every man, that is, half a shekel, after the shekel of the sanctuary, for every one that went to be numbered, from twenty years old and upward, for **six hundred thousand and three thousand and five hundred and fifty men.** And of the hundred talents of silver were cast the sockets of the sanctuary, and the sockets of the vail; an hundred sockets of the hundred talents, a talent for a socket. And of the thousand seven hundred seventy and five shekels he made hooks for the pillars, and overlaid their chapiters, and filleted them.

In the above passage we are told that 603,550 men each gave [0.5] half a shekel, which equals 301,775 shekels in total. Verse 25 says that this amount equaled 100 talents with 1,775 shekels left over. That being the case, 300,000 shekels equates to 100 talents, or 3,000 shekels per talent.

So, the king of Syria was offering ten talents of silver [30,000 shekels] for the person who could heal Naaman of his leprosy, a type of the sinful corruption in a man.

30,000 shekels x 11.1 grams per shekel = **333**,000 grams
Did you notice the three 3's, the number for God incarnate, in the calculation. What happened to Naaman in the rest of the story? God's prophet Elisha told him what to do to be cleansed of his leprosy, and in the process He discovered that the God of Israel was the only real God.

[2Kings 5:15] And he returned to the man of God, he and all his company, and came, and stood before him: and he said,

> Behold, now I know that there is no God in all the earth, but in Israel...

Just as 666 points to the antichrist, Satan incarnate; 333 points to Jesus Christ, which was God incarnate. We see that 11.1 grams per shekel works flawlessly here as well. There are many other passages I could point to that would demonstrate the same thing if I were to continue. But now it's time to exit the rabbit hole and resume our contemplations regarding Ornan/Araunah the Jebusite, the ancient owner of Mount Moriah; otherwise known as the Temple Mount.

ORNAN OR ARAUNAH? *[REVISITED]*

As you may recall, the scriptures give what seems to be conflicting accounts of David's purchase of the Temple Mount. There appears to be a discrepancy regarding how much he paid for it and who sold it to him. Did he buy it from Ornan for 600 shekels of gold; or was it a man named Araunah for 50 shekels of silver?

> [1 Chronicles 21:25] So David gave to **Ornan** for the place **six hundred shekels of gold by weight.**

> [2 Samuel 24:24] And the king said unto **Araunah,** Nay; but I will surely buy it of thee at a price: neither will I offer burnt offerings unto the LORD my God of that which doth cost me nothing. So David bought the threshingfloor and the oxen for **fifty shekels of silver.**

As I mentioned previously Ornan and Araunah are essentially the same Hebrew word with the spelling slightly altered. Personally, I don't know enough Hebrew to fill a thimble, but I'm going to make an outrageous claim right now, and you can decide when

I'm finished whether you agree with me or not. I'm going to say that Araunah is the genuine rendering of the name in question, and Ornan is the alteration: it is the counterfeit. Someone might ask, *"How can you come to that determination if you don't know Hebrew?"* First, let me point out that a firm knowledge of the Hebrew language didn't provide any insight to the commentators on this subject, so why bother to look there? Secondly, my approach is different. I arrived at my understanding by believing the Bible I hold in my hand is a supernatural book that is PURE. I approach it that way because that's the biblical methodology. Bear with me and I'll show you what I've found.

Over the years I've had a lot of people ask me: *"Brother Mark, what do you think about the hidden Bible Codes?"*

I always answer them the same way. I tell them: *"I'm sure there's something to it, but I think you ought to get used to reading the Bible straight through before you start trying to read it sideways!"* If you think about it, there's some pretty flawless logic in that statement. Yet at the same time, there is something truly fascinating about the source of their question. It was an article published in the magazine Statistical Science, August 1994, called *"Equidistant Letter Sequences in the Book of Genesis"*; more commonly referred to as the *"Bible Codes"*.

Many years ago, I was given a book on encryption and subsequently became curious about various types of codes and how they work. In the process of reading the book I discovered that the Bible contained a few types of Hebrew substitution ciphers. In one such cipher, called **Atbash**, the first letter of the Hebrew alphabet is substituted for the last letter; the second letter is substituted for the next to last, and so on. You can find an example of this in Jeremiah 51:41 where the word *"Babel"* is encrypted using the Atbash cipher and is then rendered as *"Sheshach"*.

Another Hebrew substitution cipher is called **Albam**. This method splits the 22 letters of the Hebrew alphabet into two groups of eleven letters. Then the first group of letters is placed directly above the second set of letters. In this cipher the first letter is substituted for the twelfth letter under it; the second letter for the thirteenth, and so on. An example of a modified version of Albam can be seen in Isaiah 7:1-6 where *"Remaliah"* is encrypted as *"Tabeal"*.

Why did God use encryption on occasion? I'm afraid I can't answer why He chose to do it. Maybe it's to stimulate human curiosity, or perhaps to hide the information from one person and reveal it to another like Jesus did with the parables. Why God did it no one knows for sure. But the fact remains that He definitely did it! Knowing this, what if Ornan and Araunah are not just a sloppy alteration resulting from a scribal error? What if it is, in fact, a premeditated alteration cipher with a hidden meaning intended to reveal information to someone who will simply believe the word of God is pure? Dare we believe that the Jewish and Christian commentators have been self-blinded to an, as yet undiscovered scriptural cipher? Did they unwittingly forfeit its revelation simply because they were willing to believe it was a mistake in God's word instead of admitting they didn't understand it? Could they have unwittingly transformed themselves into *"doubting Thomas's"* by not considering that the difference between their acceptance of a *"few minor errors"* in the Bible, and the position of a Christ rejecting atheist who believes the Bible is 99% wrong, is simply a matter of degree? Did they not notice that both positions find agreement on the principal that the Bible isn't perfect, and that it contains mistakes; only disagreeing on how many mistakes there are? Is the acceptance of errors in the biblical text the same faith taught by the apostles, prophets, or even Christ Himself? NO – IT IS NOT! Then what might we find if we actually believe the text like a Christian is supposed to do? What will we find if we are truly willing to believe God's word is still perfectly pure?

As I mentioned earlier, I believe Araunah is the proper spelling of the name, and if I'm correct then Ornan may be an intentional alteration cipher. That being the case, it seems fitting to start with the scriptural account containing Araunah, whose name is said to mean *"joyful shouting of JAH"* - JAH being short for Jehovah, as in Psalm 68.

> [Psalm 68:4] **Sing unto God,** sing praises to his name: extol him that rideth upon the heavens by **his name JAH,** and rejoice before him.

However, even if Araunah and Ornan are the same name, an alterational cipher wouldn't explain the difference in the amounts David paid for the property. How are we to account for the difference in the purchase price?

> [2 Samuel 24:24] And the king [David] said unto **Araunah,** Nay; but I will surely buy it of thee at a price: neither will I offer burnt offerings unto the LORD my God of that which doth cost me nothing. So David bought <u>the threshingfloor and the oxen</u> for **fifty shekels of silver.**

> [1 Chronicles 21:25] So David gave to **Ornan** for <u>the place</u> **six hundred shekels of gold** by weight.

If you read the texts carefully, you'll see that David paid Araunah fifty shekels of silver for the *"oxen"* and the *"threshingfloor"*; which, if you recall from our earlier discussions, the threshingfloor fits inside the Temple. But he paid Ornan 600 shekels of gold for the *"place"*, the entire mount where Solomon would eventually build the first Temple to the God of Israel. That is easy enough to sort out. It's the same type of supposed *"problem"* we find in 1 Kings 4:26 / 2 Chronicles 9:25 where one passage says *"Solomon had forty thousand stalls of horses for his chariots"* and the other says *"Solomon had four thousand stalls for horses and chariots"*. There we find one writer counting individual horse stalls and the other counting the overall stall for each chariot that had ten horses. Again, not a problem if you read the text carefully. So, we see that what appears to be a numerical discrepancy is actually just a matter of differing methods of computation.

Can we learn anything from the fact that one passage mentions silver and the other gold? I believe we can. Gold in the Bible is associated with deity. The insides of the Tabernacle and the Temple were literally covered with gold. And it was common to make idols out of gold as well. For instance, in Daniel chapter three Nebuchadnezzar, king of Babylon, set up an image of gold that was sixty cubits tall, six cubits wide and they worshipped it with six musical instruments. You couldn't miss the 666 connected with that golden image if you tried; shades of Revelation chapter 13.

And the scriptures connect silver with atonement.

> [Exodus 30:13-15] This they shall give, every one that passeth among them that are numbered, half a shekel after the shekel of the sanctuary: (a shekel is twenty gerahs:) an half shekel shall be the offering of the LORD. Every one that passeth

among them that are numbered, from twenty years old and above, shall give an offering unto the LORD. **The rich shall not give more, and the poor shall not give less than half a shekel,** when they give an offering unto the LORD, **to make an atonement for your souls.**

In Exodus 38:25-28 the tally given for this collection was paid in silver. Does the price of atonement that each man was to pay, which was half shekel of silver, tell us anything? It may, if we look at the math.

½ shekel [.5] x 11.1 = **5.55** grams of silver

What was the price that David paid to Araunah to purchase the threshingfloor so he could make an atonement for Israel to deliver the nation from the plague? David paid 50 shekels of silver.

50 shekels x 11.1 grams per shekel = **555** grams of silver

You may not be aware of it but there is some disagreement over the number five in Bible numerology. Some people say it represents *"death"* and others that it speaks of *"grace"*. I tend to agree with the former, but the truth is, in some ways there is very little difference between the two. There can be no grace, no unmerited favor of God, without the death of the Lord Jesus Christ to atone for sin. In the Exodus passage we saw that half a shekel *(which is .5 shekels)* was the price to atone for one of the sons of Israel, but in 2 Samuel 24 the price of atonement for the nation was **many** times greater; 100 times greater to be exact.

[Hebrews 2:9-10] But we see **Jesus**, who was made a little lower than the angels for the suffering of death, crowned with glory and honour; that he **by the grace of God should taste**

death for every man. For it became him, for whom are all things, and by whom are all things, in **bringing <u>many sons unto glory</u>**, to make the captain of their salvation perfect through sufferings.

What of Ornan? Are there any buried treasures we can uncover through the examination of his passage? Ornan is said to be the same name as Araunah, but because of the change made by an alteration, the name is changed to mean *"light was perpetuated"*. This is worth noting because perpetuated means that it was *"made perpetual"*. 1st John 1:5 tells us that *"God is light"* He wasn't *"made"* light. It is His nature; it is part of His essence. He has always been light. However, there was a created being in who *"light was perpetuated"*. His name was Lucifer, which means *"light-bearer"*.

It is indisputable that English is the language of the world in the last days, and one of the beautiful things about the English language is a vocabulary that consists of nearly half a million words. Many of them are borrowed from other languages, such as the word Lucifer, which is a Latin word [LUX – *light*; and, FERO – *to bring*] meaning light-bringer or light-bearer. It's the perfect word to use in Isaiah 14, because it not only identifies the fallen cherub as a person, Lucifer (now Satan), but it describes his attributes as well. Yet, what does this have to do with Ornan? In our text we're told that David paid Ornan 600 shekels of gold for *"the place"* that would later come to be known as the Temple Mount. We also know that gold has to do with deity, whether speaking of God or an idol. And remember, Satan likes to pass himself off as a god. So let's do the math.

600 shekels x 11.1 = **6,660** grams of gold

What are we to make of this? This is odd because it connects the Temple Mount with Satan and the antichrist. However, we know that the temple is associated with God and Jesus Christ. But that isn't all there is. Look at the following verses.

> [2 Samuel 24:1] And again the anger of **the LORD** was kindled against Israel, and he **moved David against them to say, Go, number Israel and Judah.**

> [1 Chronicles 21:1] And **Satan** stood up against Israel, and **provoked David to number Israel.**

Here we have two seemingly contradictory records of the event that led David to number Israel. Does one of these passages contain a mistake? We now have two accounts of the reason for the same plague. In one account God is said to cause David to number Israel and the other passage says Satan pushed David to do it. And we know that in both instances, an area of the Temple Mount was purchased to offer a sacrifice to stop the plague.

Let's take a moment and consider what we have. In 2 Samuel 24, the passage associated with God, we find a man named Araunah whose name means *"joyful shouting of JAH"*. In that passage the area was purchased with silver which is linked with redemption and atonement. The amount of silver paid is 555 grams. The number 5 is understood to mean either death or grace, both of which are associated with the atoning death of Jesus Christ.

On the other hand we have Ornan, whose name means *"light was perpetuated"*. The meaning of his name is associated with Lucifer, the Light Bearer, and we are told in 1 Chronicles 21 that Satan provoked David to number Israel. David paid Ornan in gold, which is connected to deity, and this is what Satan wants to be. And

finally, the amount of gold David paid was 6,660 grams which screams the mark of the beast.

These accounts are literally polar opposites. Surely you can see this is beyond the realm of coincidence. Ancient historians writing different accounts could not have conspired to create this phenomenon. Why? Because three thousand years ago no one on this planet had any idea what a GRAM was, except God, Who knows the end of all things from the beginning. Nor did anyone understand the workings of the still future antichrist during the tribulation period. Like Pharaoh's magicians said, *"This is the finger of God"!* How are we to understand this amazing revelation? I can think of three possible scenarios where this encoded revelation could play out.

1) The texts could be like two guys describing opposite ends of an elephant. It's the same event seen from different perspectives. Consider this: Daniel's 70th week is seven years long, and it is divided into two periods of three and one-half years. In the first half the antichrist looks like some kind of Saviour of the world. People think he's the Messiah and crown him king of planet earth; this would be Araunah. In the middle of the tribulation he goes into the temple and proclaims himself God, and at that point the mark of the beast [666] is instituted, and here we have Ornan. In this way, they could represent the two personas

of the antichrist during the last seven years before Christ returns.

2) Scenario number two suggests that in the dispute over who has the right to put their throne on the top of Mount Zion, the Lord Jesus Christ is characterized by Araunah vs Lucifer, who is symbolized by Ornan. In this contemplation, Lucifer's tribulation throne would sit in a temple made after the pattern of Herod's, who was a type of the antichrist and a persecutor of Israel. The Jews currently say the temple must be built on *"the threshingfloor of **Ornan** the Jebusite"* that was purchased for 6,660 grams of gold, and which is consistent with the counterfeit pattern since Ornan means *"light perpetuated"*, a good description of Lucifer. When Christ returns he will defeat the devil, bring redemption to Israel (represented by the 555 grams of silver) and build Messiah's Temple on the *"threshingfloor of **Araunah"*** according to the pattern described in Ezekiel. Here, both Christ and Lucifer are represented in their respective biblical passages.

3) The third explanation, which I find to be the most favorable, concedes that both of the interpretations may be equally valid. It's possible that the alteration cipher allows us to look into the scriptures as though they were a diamond with multiple facets. Each facet you look into presents you with a different but unique and totally accurate view of a future prophetic truth.

I view these revelations as absolutely astonishing, and they are the product of a very simple thing, belief that the word of God, the age-old book I have in my hand (my old KJV) is something truly remarkable. In my estimation the word of God is nothing less than a mind-boggling miracle. Its prophecies, numerology and cyphers are absolutely astounding. And since I can't sum this issue up any better than Solomon, I'll just use his words.

> [Proverbs 16:11] A just weight and balance are the LORD'S: **all the weights of the bag are his work.**
> *Apparently this would include grams as well!

Now, before I leave off of numerology there is one more text I would like to present for your consideration. Even though it does not use the previous 11.1 grams per shekel in its calculation, I think you'll still find it interesting. But what may possibly be its greatest significance will be reserved for inclusion in a future section.

PART 5

HE WAS WARNED!

THE QUEEN OF SHEBA

This time let's take a look at the gentile Queen of Sheba from the African land of Ethiopia. She heard of the wisdom of Solomon, the son of king David, and went to test him with hard questions. His answers were apparently more than convincing. And her response to his answers follows.

> [1 Kings 10:9-10]   Blessed be **the LORD thy God, which delighted in thee, to set thee on the throne of Israel**: because the LORD loved Israel for ever, therefore made he thee king, to do judgment and justice. And she gave the king **an hundred and twenty talents of gold**, and of **spices** very great store, and **precious stones**: there came no more such abundance of spices as these which the queen of Sheba gave to king Solomon.

Ok, what do we see in this passage? The queen's offering to Solomon, whose name means *"peace"*, is listed in chapter 10 verse 10 hinting at her gentile origin since 10 is the number for gentiles in the Bible. She brings to the son of David precious stones, which is how Paul, the apostle to the gentiles, describes the believer's works in 1st Corinthians chapter 3. She also brings spices. We aren't told what the spices were, but we do know that spices are used

to make the temple incense, which is a type of prayer [Revelation 8:3], and she brings a *"very great store"* of them; the same way believers should bring their prayers. But the most significant aspect of the text, as it relates to our subject, is the 120 talents of gold. When the calculations for Naaman were performed, I demonstrated from the scriptures that a talent was equal to 3,000 shekels. With this in mind, let's run the numbers on the queen of Sheba.

> 120 talents of gold x 3,000 shekels per talent = 360,000 shekels
>
> 360,000 divided by 360 days in a prophetic year = **1,000 years**
>
> > **NOTE**: A biblical prophetic year is calculated as 12 months of 30 days each. SEE: 3 ½ years [James 5:17] = 42 months [Revelation 11:2], and = 1,260 days [Revelation 11:3].

Anyone who has spent any real time studying the Bible knows that Solomon, the son of David, the king whose name means *"peace"* and who rules over Jerusalem *[the city of peace],* is a type of Christ during His 1,000-year earthly kingdom. He will reign with a predominantly gentile queen [the church] who will bring Him gold, precious stones and the fragrant incense of prayers. Again, the math and the similitude work out perfectly.
*See: 1 Corinthians 3 and 1 Thessalonians 5:17.

But there's also an interesting Ethiopian tradition most people are unaware of that intersects with the biblical account of Solomon's reign. Ethiopia's national epic called *"Kebra Nagast"*, which means *"Glory of Kings"*, insists that the queen of Sheba, Makeda of Axum, was impregnated by Solomon during her visit there.

Their child was claimed to be Emperor Menelik who founded the *"Solomonid Dynasty"*. It is said that when Menelik grew up he went to Jerusalem to meet his father and returned to Ethiopia with the Ark of the

Covenant. The Ethiopians maintain that the ark has remained there under the protective guard of a celibate priest class ever since and is presently in the Church of Our Lady of Zion in Axum. Is there a possibility that this legend is accurate? That may depend upon the answer to the following questions. How many arks are there? And which ark might be involved in such a legend?

Many people do not realize that the scriptures seem to tell of two different arks when speaking of the ark of the Covenant. The most famous ark is the elaborate golden ark made by Bezaleel the son of Uri.

> [Exodus 37:1-2] And **Bezaleel made the ark of shittim wood:** two cubits and a half was the length of it, and a cubit and a half the breadth of it, and a cubit and a half the height of it: **And he overlaid it with pure gold within and without, and made a crown of gold to it round about.**

But the lesser-known ark is the one Moses seems to have personally made. In the following text Moses is in the process of recalling Israel's history. He talks about the first set of Ten Commandments, which were made by God and how God wrote them on stone tablets. Moses also tells how he personally threw them down and broke them because of the golden calf that Israel had made; and in the passage below he's telling of the second set of tablets which he made to replace them.

> [Deuteronomy 10:1-5] At that time **the LORD said unto me, Hew thee two tables of stone like unto the first,** and come up unto me into the mount, **and make thee an ark of wood.** And I will write on the tables the words that were in the first tables which thou brakest, and thou shalt put them in the ark. And **I made an ark of shittim wood,** and hewed two tables of stone like unto the first, and went up into the mount, having the two tables in mine hand. And he wrote on the tables, according to the first writing, the ten commandments, which the LORD spake unto you in the mount out of the midst of the fire in the day of the assembly: and the LORD gave them unto me. **And I turned myself and came down from the mount, and put the tables in the ark which I had made; and there they be, as the LORD commanded me.**

 Is it possible there are two arks? And if so, did one of them end up in Ethiopia in the Church of Our Lady of Zion in Axum? And if one of them ended up there, which one was it, the one Moses made or the one made by Bezaleel? Why would there be two of them? Could it be because there are two sets of the Ten Commandments? If so, which ark contains the broken set of commandments? *You can be absolutely certain they didn't toss the broken commandments in the rock heap because they were PERSONALLY made by God and written with His finger!* But do any of these contemplations even matter?   These are all good questions that deserve consideration. Perhaps we can provide

some possible answers for them in the remaining pages of this book.

SOLOMON, THE SON OF DAVID

We saw previously that the location for the Temple Mount was the threshingfloor of Ornan [Araunah] the Jebusite. It was the place chosen by God where David was to build an altar and offer a sacrifice to stop the plague that was ravaging Israel, a plague which resulted from David's decision to number the people.

[2 Chronicles 3:1] Then **Solomon began to build the house of the LORD** at Jerusalem in mount Moriah, where the LORD appeared unto David his father, **in the place that David had prepared in the threshingfloor of Ornan the Jebusite.**

Although the Temple is actually the "*house*" of the Lord God of Israel, it is typically referred to as "*Solomon's Temple*" since he was the builder of it. And just like the Tabernacle that was made under the leadership of Moses after Israel's exodus from Egypt, the architect of the Temple was God Almighty and a specific pattern was given for its construction and for its contents. But as we have seen, the requirements for the Temple go a bit further. The Tabernacle was intentionally portable so it could be moved from place to place, but the Temple was given a very permanent location in the mountains of Moriah, specifically on Mount Zion. And the Temple itself was situated on the mountain in such a way that the highest point on the mount, Ornan's threshingfloor, often called "*the foundation stone*", would be the one and only fixed location for the Holy of Holies within the Temple. This specific orientation was decided by God and the temple can be situated no other way and still be in compliance with His plans.

[1 Chronicles 28:19]   All this, said David, **the LORD made me understand in writing by his hand upon me, even all the works of this pattern.**

SOLOMON, A TYPE OF CHRIST

By far, the main character in the Bible is Israel's Messiah, the Lord Jesus Christ. The scriptures present Him to the reader in more ways than I could possibly enumerate. Jesus articulated this point perfectly on the road to Emmaus when the disciples were relating the facts concerning His death and expressing their doubts about the stories of His resurrection. Though He was actually walking with them, they did not recognize Him. We are told *"their eyes were holden that they should not know him."* [Luke 24:16]

[Luke 24:25-27]   Then he [Jesus] said unto them, O fools, and slow of heart to believe all that the prophets have spoken: Ought not Christ to have suffered these things, and to enter into his glory?   And **beginning at Moses and all the prophets, he expounded unto them in all the scriptures the things concerning himself.**

Students of the Bible have long recognized that Solomon is in many ways one of the greatest pictures of Israel's Messiah. The following is a small sampling of their many similarities.
- Both men are referred to as the son of David.
  - o [2 Chronicles 1:1]   And **Solomon the son of David** was strengthened in his kingdom, and the LORD his God was with him, and magnified him exceedingly.
  - o [Matthew 1:1]   The book of the generation of **Jesus Christ, the son of David,** the son of Abraham.

- **Both built a temple.**
  - o [1 Chronicles 6:10] And Johanan begat Azariah, (he it is that executed the priest's office in **the temple that Solomon built in Jerusalem:**)
  - o [John 2:19&21] Jesus answered and said unto them, **Destroy this temple, and in three days I will raise it up.** But he spake of the temple of his body.
- **Both are said to be wise.**
  - o [1 Kings 4:34] And there came of all people to hear **the wisdom of Solomon**, from all kings of the earth, which had heard of his wisdom.
  - o [Luke 11:31] The queen of the south shall rise up in the judgment with the men of this generation, and condemn them: for she came from the utmost parts of the earth to **hear the wisdom of Solomon; and, behold, a greater than Solomon is here.**
- **Both sit on the throne of David.**
  - o [1 Kings 2:12] **Then sat Solomon upon the throne of David** his father; and his kingdom was established greatly.
  - o [Luke 1:31-32] And, behold, thou shalt conceive in thy womb, and bring forth a son, and shalt call his name **JESUS.** He shall be great, and shall be called the Son of the Highest: and **the Lord God shall give unto him the throne of his father David:**
- **Both reign during a time of peace**
  - o [1 Chronicles 22:9] Behold, a son shall be born to thee, who shall be a man of rest; and I will give him rest from all his enemies round about: for his name shall be Solomon, and **I will give peace and quietness unto Israel in his days.**
  - o [Psalm 72:1-8] [A Psalm for Solomon] Give the king thy judgments, O God, and thy righteousness unto the king's son. He shall judge thy people with righteousness, and thy poor with judgment. The

mountains shall bring peace to the people, and the little hills, by righteousness. He shall judge the poor of the people, he shall save the children of the needy, and shall break in pieces the oppressor. **They shall fear thee as long as the sun and moon endure**, throughout all generations. He shall come down like rain upon the mown grass: as showers that water the earth. **In his days shall the righteous flourish; and abundance of peace so long as the moon endureth. He shall have dominion also from sea to sea, and from the river unto the ends of the earth.**

> **This is, of course, prophetic of the Lord Jesus Christ since these things cannot be applied to Solomon.*

- Both Christ and Solomon even appear in the same verse with the Queen of Sheba.
  - [Matthew 12:42] **The queen of the south** shall rise up in the judgment with this generation, and shall condemn it: for she came from the uttermost parts of the earth to hear the wisdom of **Solomon; and, behold, a greater than Solomon** is here.

AN UNCONDITIONAL PROMISE

In 2 Samuel 7, King David looks around and sees how blessed he is. God has exalted him and has given him victory over his many enemies. He has a beautiful home, and the kingdom of Israel is finally enjoying a time of peace and prosperity. In his gratitude, he gets the idea to build God a temple as opposed to the tabernacles Israel had been using since the days of Moses 500 years earlier. The Lord had not asked anyone to build Him a temple, but He was pleased that it was in David's heart to do it. Even so, there was a problem with the idea, and David recounts the details of that problem in the later years of his life. Below he explains what was required to overcome it.

> [1 Chronicles 22:5-10] And David said, Solomon my son is young and tender, and the house that is to be builded for the LORD must be exceeding magnifical, of fame and of glory throughout all countries: I will therefore now make preparation for it. So David prepared abundantly before his death. Then he called for Solomon his son, and charged him to build an house for the LORD God of Israel. And David said to Solomon, My son, **as for me, it was in my mind to build an house unto the name of the LORD my God: But the word of the LORD came to me, saying,** Thou hast shed blood abundantly, and hast made great wars: **thou shalt not build an house unto my name**, because thou hast shed much blood upon the earth in my sight. Behold, **a son shall be born to thee**, who shall be a man of rest; and I will give him rest from all his enemies round about: for **his name shall be Solomon**, and I will give peace and quietness unto Israel in his days. **He shall build an house for my name**; and he shall be my son, and I will be his father; and **I will establish the throne of his kingdom over Israel for ever.**

As we can see from the passage the prophesied son, who would be a man of peace named Solomon, would be the builder of the temple, not his warrior father David. And a promise was made that the throne of Solomon's kingdom would be established forever.

Life is of such a nature that things don't always work out as neatly as intended. The scriptures reveal that one of David's other sons, Adonijah, had ambitions for the throne, and he made a grab for it when David was old and weak. In fact, it seems that Adonijah had actually obtained his desire and many of Israel's most influential leaders attended a coronation party with rejoicing and shouted *"God save king Adonijah"*. Apparently, the throne was all but in Adonijah's hands. [See 1 Kings Chapter 1]

Many years ago when I was a young Christian, my dear pastor and mentor David Burger gently admonished my impatience saying, *"Brother Mark, God is never early, and He's never late. He's always right on-time."* To which I replied, *"I know preacher, but He always looks like He's gonna be late!"* I'm sure the situation with Adonijah looked very much the same to Solomon's loyal friends. It seemed like God was going to be too late. Solomon would not be crowned as king and God's promise would not be kept. Truthfully, it was a VERY close call! If God had not sent in Nathan the prophet when He did in a matter of hours, perhaps even less, it may have been too late. Solomon, Bathsheba his mother, and Nathan the prophet would likely have been slain by the followers of Adonijah in order to secure his claim to the throne. It was a fairly common practice for evil kings and usurpers to do that very thing. But God took action *"right on-time"* just like my pastor said. And it's the surprising elements involved in that action that merit our attention now.

In this book's earlier section *"The Paradise That Was Lost"* I deferred the discussion of Eden's Gihon River until a later time. I pointed out that Gihon was mentioned six times in the Bible, and that we would later see that three of those remaining five occurrences were of great significance. We have just arrived at the appropriate time to renew that discussion. What we find is that David's plan to pry the kingdom from the hands of his son Adonijah involved Solomon making a trip to the Gihon River!

[1 Kings 1:32-35] And king David said, Call me Zadok the priest, and Nathan the prophet, and Benaiah the son of

Jehoiada. And they came before the king. The king also said unto them, Take with you the servants of your lord, and **cause Solomon my son to ride upon mine own mule, and bring him down to <u>Gihon</u>:** And let Zadok the priest and Nathan the prophet **anoint him there king over Israel: and blow ye with the trumpet, and say, God save king Solomon.** Then ye shall come up after him, that he may come and sit upon my throne; for he shall be king in my stead: and I have appointed him to be ruler over Israel and over Judah.

In the above passage we see that Solomon was taken down to Gihon to be anointed king. The situation was desperate and required immediate action because their lives were in peril. From the time that David gave the orders regarding where to go and what to do until Solomon was seated on the mule, taken to Gihon and brought back to sit on the throne as king, could not have been much more than a couple hours. That being the case, it is evident that the Gihon must have been very close. Perhaps even inside the Jerusalem wall.

GOING UPSTREAM

Christians are familiar with the testimony of the blind man Jesus healed in John 9. He said:

> [John 9:11] A man that is called Jesus made clay, and anointed mine eyes, and said unto me, **Go to the pool of Siloam**, and wash: and I went and washed, and I received sight.

The man was told to go to the pool of Siloam and wash away the clay. He did and received his sight. But the pool of Siloam is not a pool in the sense that many people may think of it. In other words, it's not just a depression in the ground that fills with water when it rains. Apparently, it is the visible part of a river which flows underground and comes to the surface as it moves through

the area. The place where the river surfaces is the pool of Siloam. Jimmy DeYoung, whose video I mentioned earlier, also has a book called *"Revelation: A Chronology"*. On page 162 he makes the following statement.

> *"I talked with an archeologist at the city of David, which is the original site of the city of Jerusalem. He and his son (who is the equivalent of a Navy Seal in the Israeli Navy) and a couple of his buddies went on an expedition. They put on their scuba equipment and got down in the pool of Siloam which is in the city of David and is fed by the Gihon River. They swam up underneath the Temple Mount and there they found the headwaters for the Gihon River. The Gihon River flows out from underneath the Temple Mount."*

In Hebrew, the name Gihon means *"gushing or bursting forth"*. And if their story is to be believed, Jimmy's associates apparently found a *"gusher"* down underneath the Temple Mount; and that river is identified as the Gihon. But does this information fit the biblical narrative? It seems that it does. For instance:

- A river flowed out of Eden to water the garden. If Jerusalem is Eden and the Temple Mount is within the area of the garden then there should be a river nearby, and there is.

- When Christ's millennial Temple is established in Jerusalem, a river will flow out of it; and even now a river is under the Temple mount.
  - o [Ezekiel 47:1] Afterward he brought me again unto the door of the house; and, behold, **waters issued out from under the threshold of the house eastward:** for the forefront of the house stood toward the east, and the waters came down from under from the right side of the house, at the south side of the altar.
- The river with headwaters under the Temple mount is said to be the Gihon and it feeds the pool of Siloam.
- Since Solomon went to the Gihon and returned in a short period of time it must be very near Jerusalem, just as is the pool of Siloam.

WHEN MUCH IS GIVEN

Jesus said it best.

[Luke 12:48] **...unto whomsoever much is given, of him shall be much required:** and to whom men have committed much, of him they will ask the more.

Solomon was in many ways a type of Christ during His millennial reign as King of kings and Lord of lords. But types are never perfect. They are only similar in certain respects, and they tend to fall far short in others. David's son was no exception. In all truthfulness, the rules for Israel's kings weren't all that restrictive, but God not only expected a king's compliance, it was REQUIRED of them. From the New Testament we know that Jesus "*the son of David*" successfully fulfilled the law, but Solomon - not so much.

In fact he did quite the opposite. He seemed almost determined to violate every precept of his royal charge. What were some of the *"thou shalt not's"* that a king of Israel was expected to observe? God, speaking through Moses, laid them out for us.

> [Deuteronomy 17:14-17] When thou art come unto the land which the LORD thy God giveth thee, and shalt possess it, and shalt dwell therein, and shalt say, I will set a king over me, like as all the nations that are about me; Thou shalt in any wise set him king over thee, whom the LORD thy God shall choose: one from among thy brethren shalt thou set king over thee: thou mayest not set a stranger over thee, which is not thy brother. But **he shall not multiply horses to himself, nor cause the people to return to Egypt, to the end that he should multiply horses:** forasmuch as the LORD hath said unto you, Ye shall henceforth return no more that way. **Neither shall he multiply wives to himself,** that his heart turn not away: **neither shall he greatly multiply to himself silver and gold.**

These are fairly simple rules, but what do we find Solomon doing?

> ➢ **Solomon multiplied gold** – *Strike 1*
>> [1 Kings 10:21-23] And all king **Solomon's drinking vessels were of gold, and all the vessels of the house of the forest of Lebanon were of pure gold; none were of silver: it was nothing accounted of** in the days of Solomon. For the king had at sea a navy of Tharshish with the navy of Hiram: once in three years came the navy of Tharshish, **bringing gold, and silver**, ivory, and apes, and peacocks. So **king Solomon exceeded all the kings of the earth for riches** and for wisdom.

> **Solomon multiplied horses** – *Strike 2*
>
> [1 Kings 10:28] And **Solomon had horses brought out of Egypt**, and linen yarn: the king's merchants received the linen yarn at a price.
>
> [1 Kings 4:26] And **Solomon had forty thousand stalls of horses** for his chariots, and twelve thousand horsemen.

> **Solomon multiplied wives** – *Strike 3*
>
> [1 Kings 11:1-8] But king **Solomon loved many strange women,** together with the daughter of Pharaoh, women of the Moabites, Ammonites, Edomites, Zidonians, and Hittites; **Of the nations concerning which the LORD said unto the children of Israel, Ye shall not go in to them**, neither shall they come in unto you: for surely they will turn away your heart after their gods: Solomon clave unto these in love. And **he had seven hundred wives, princesses, and three hundred concubines: and his wives turned away his heart.** For it came to pass, when Solomon was old, that his wives turned away his heart after other gods: and his heart was not perfect with the LORD his God, as was the heart of David his father. For Solomon went after Ashtoreth the goddess of the Zidonians, and after Milcom the abomination of the Ammonites. And **Solomon did evil in the sight of the LORD,** and went not fully after the LORD, as did David his father. Then did Solomon build an high place for Chemosh, the abomination of Moab, in the hill that is before Jerusalem, and for Molech, the abomination of the children of Ammon. And likewise did he for all his strange wives, which burnt incense and sacrificed unto their gods.

[Nehemiah 13:26] **Did not Solomon king of Israel sin by these things?** yet among many nations was there no king like him, who was beloved of his God, and God made him king over all Israel: nevertheless **even him did outlandish women cause to sin.**

* OUTLANDISH: women from outside the land of Israel

That's a strike out! But just in case you're thinking T-Ball, I'll give you one more.

[Proverbs 31:4] It is not for kings, O Lemuel, **it is not for kings to drink wine;** nor for princes strong drink:

> ➤ *Solomon went heavy on the wine* - *Strike 4*
> [Ecclesiastes 2:3] **I sought in mine heart to give myself unto wine,** yet acquainting mine heart with wisdom; and **to lay hold on folly,** till I might see what was that good for the sons of men, which they should do under the heaven all the days of their life.

So, how did all of this work out for Solomon?

[1 Kings 11:9] And **the LORD was angry with Solomon, because his heart was turned from the LORD God of Israel,** which had appeared unto him twice,

As a result of these things and others, Solomon got more fouled up than a barn full of sick pigs. It worked out for him just like Moses said it would. His heart was turned away from the LORD and he wound up sacrificing to heathen gods such as Molech and Chemosh. Apparently, the possession of wisdom does not guarantee that obedience will follow. Knowledge can be learned through a variety of methods. Wisdom is the ability to use knowledge that has been gained. Understanding is the practice of using wisdom properly, especially in our relationship to God Almighty. Solomon, like Lucifer the anointed cherub, had volumes of wisdom but they both had a serious lack of understanding in their dealing with the Lord and in both cases it resulted in sin.

If we take careful notice, a valuable lesson is to be found here. Even when God fills a man with wisdom, still his flesh will seek to have its way and use the wisdom for its own purposes if it's not kept in check. Solomon's disobedience brought him dishonor; a nasty stain on a previously sterling reputation. As if to memorialize his rebellion, the Lord flips Solomon's story over and begins to use him as one of the many types of antichrist we find in the scriptures.

SOLOMON AS ANTICHRIST

[1 Kings 10:14-20] Now the weight of gold that came to Solomon in one year was **six hundred threescore and six talents of gold** [666], Beside that he had of the merchantmen, and of the traffick of the spice merchants, and of all the kings of Arabia, and of the governors of the country. And King Solomon made two hundred targets of beaten gold: **six hundred shekels of gold went to one target**. And he made three hundred shields of beaten gold; three pound of gold went to one shield: and the king put them in the house of the forest of Lebanon. Moreover the king made a great throne of ivory, and overlaid it with the best gold. **The throne had six steps**, and the top of the throne was round behind: and there were stays on either side on the place of the seat, and two lions stood beside the stays. And **twelve lions** stood there on the one side and on the other upon the **six steps**: there was not the like made in any kingdom.

Let's take a moment and contemplate what we see in this passage, for there are several indications that information regarding the antichrist is here for our observation.

- Solomon got **666** talents of gold in one year.
- Solomon's throne had **6 steps** with **6 lions** on one side and **6 lions** on the other side of each step. Again 666.
- Each target, which was armor that covers a man's back, had 600 shekels of gold in it.

> 600 shekels x 11.1 grams per shekel = **6,660** grams of gold

Oddly enough, the only person in the Bible who is specifically named as wearing a target is evil Goliath, the satanic offspring of the fallen angels. And if you recall, he is connected to 666 by the weight of his spear's head. The implications abound.

There are ways in which the antichrist will mimic Solomon with all his wisdom. He will be extremely wealthy and present himself as a man of peace. He will make affinity with Egypt where Israel was once enslaved, and he will worship a false god. And of course, he will be connected with 666. These are just a few of the things we

can see by Solomon's sinful example. You may not have noticed, but all of the *"666"* hints of antichrist type behavior appear in the text AFTER Solomon's rebellion against God's prescribed code of conduct for Israel's kings.

PART 6

DEVIL IN THE DETAILS

TEMPLE NUMBER TWO

As we discussed earlier, Solomon was the builder of the temple, but many years later Solomon's temple was destroyed as a result of the national idolatry that began to flourish under his reign. Ultimately, the Temple he built was totally demolished and Jerusalem was burnt to the ground. But God's plan continues its forward motion even when it doesn't look like it. In the process of time another temple was built, and it was constructed in the very same place, the Temple Mount. Why? Because there is only one place where the Temple can be legitimately built, the threshingfloor of Ornan the Jebusite. As with any building project, a point of reference is established so the foundation can be laid. And so it was with the building of the second temple.

[Ezra 3:12] But many of the priests and Levites and chief of the fathers, who were ancient men, that had seen the first house, **when the foundation of this house was laid before their eyes, wept with a loud voice; and many shouted aloud for joy:**

The laying of the foundation was a source of rejoicing just like the first time a foundation was observed being laid. It calls to mind God's conversation with Job many centuries earlier.

[Job 38:4-7] Where wast thou when **I laid the foundations of the earth?** declare, if thou hast understanding. Who hath **laid the measures** thereof, if thou knowest? or who hath

stretched the line upon it? Whereupon are the foundations thereof fastened? or who **laid the corner stone** thereof; **When the morning stars sang together, and all the sons of God shouted for joy?**

The second Temple, built under the leadership of Ezra, Nehemiah and Zerubbabel stood until 70 A.D. when it was destroyed by the armies of Titus. But it did not stand in the same way that those men had constructed it. Around 20 B.C. the Temple underwent extensive, dramatic remodeling as a result of a building project initiated by Herod the Great. Once completed, the former appearance of the second Temple was no longer discernible. The *"renovation"* is the Temple that Jesus frequented in the course of His ministry. Ironically, Herod the Great, the man who had brought splendor and opulence to the previously modest second Temple, was also the same person who attempted to kill the Lord Jesus Christ after His birth by giving the order to murder all the

male children under two years old in all the coasts of Bethlehem. The actual number is not given, but it was without doubt a great tragedy to the many people who lost a child at the hands of Herod's assassins.

[Matthew 2:16] Then **Herod**, when he saw that he was mocked of the wise men, was exceeding wroth, and **sent forth, and slew all the children that were in Bethlehem, and in all the coasts thereof, from two years old and under**, according to the time which he had diligently enquired of the wise men.

Herod the Great is a picture of the antichrist who in his satanic fury will seek to destroy the seed of the woman, which is Israel, in order to prevent the fulfillment of Bible prophecy.

> [Revelation 12:13] And when the dragon saw that he was cast unto the earth, **he persecuted the woman which brought forth the man child.**

> [Revelation 12:17] And **the dragon was wroth with the woman, and went to make war with the remnant of her seed,** which keep the commandments of God, and have the testimony of Jesus Christ.

So then, what do we have? Here we have a satanic figure that helps to build a Jewish Temple but also persecutes the Jewish people. Against impossible odds, this 2,000 year old scene will be played out yet again in a larger scale on a future stage. As Solomon once said, *"There is no new thing under the sun".*

MESSIAH THE PRINCE

Dominion over the earthly kingdom of heaven had been held by Satan for a very long time, ever since the days of Noah. Now it's true that Israel had been given a sliver of the kingdom. But the land grant God gave to Abraham was minuscule when compared to the whole earth, which was given to Adam and Noah. It was only 1/450th of the earth's total surface area. Though limited, it was still quite large and extended from the Euphrates to the Nile River.

> [Genesis 15:18] In the same day **the LORD made a covenant with Abram, saying, Unto thy seed have I given this**

land, from the river of Egypt unto the great river, the river Euphrates:

And though the land grant given to Abraham and his seed was unconditional, the Israelites were unable to stay in possession of it because of sin. To own the title to the property, and then to keep it in possession are two entirely different things. Even the very best of rulers, like King David, are sin flawed men who find it easy to abuse their almost limitless governmental powers when it comes to matters of a personal nature. We recall how David, though a good king, succumbed to sensual temptation in the matter of Bathsheba and then murdered her husband Uriah [2 Samuel 11] . On the other hand, we find that Jeconiah, one of the most wicked kings of Judah, was so evil that our gracious God started calling him *"Coniah"* and wouldn't use the prefix *"Je"* in his name because it stood for Jehovah. It seems the Lord didn't want any more to do with him [Jeremiah 22:24-26]. When we study the history of the kings of Israel and Judah, we see a basic truth in the axiom which says, *"Power corrupts, and absolute power corrupts absolutely"*. And yet David tells us:

> [2 Samuel 23:3] The God of Israel said, the Rock of Israel spake to me, **He that ruleth over men must be just, ruling in the fear of God.**

If we pay attention when we read the history of God's chosen people, we find two major hindrances interfered with their ability to maintain their national position. First, it was a rare thing to have a righteous, God fearing, leader who would actually make an effort to keep himself back from sin and abuse of power. Because of man's fleshly nature it's sometimes easier to justify sinful behavior than it is to do what's right. And second, when they did get a good king, even though a humanly flawed one, they eventually lost him by reason of death. Mortal men don't live forever and the next king in line was often a scoundrel. Unjust leadership would ultimately bring about a national moral decline that would result in severe hardships, slavery and even death.

[Proverbs 14:34] **Righteousness exalteth a nation: but sin is a reproach to any people.**

[Deuteronomy 28:45-48] Moreover **all these curses shall come upon thee, and shall pursue thee, and overtake thee, till thou be destroyed; because thou hearkenedst not unto the voice of the LORD thy God, to keep his commandments and his statutes which he commanded thee:** And they shall be upon thee for a sign and for a wonder, and upon thy seed for ever. Because thou servedst not the LORD thy God with joyfulness, and with gladness of heart, for the abundance of all things; **Therefore shalt thou serve thine enemies which the LORD shall send against thee,** in hunger, and in thirst, and in nakedness, and in want of all things: and he shall put a yoke of iron upon thy neck, until he have destroyed thee.

Over 400 years of Israel's repeated failures to hold their small sliver of the kingdom of heaven teaches an important lesson. There could be no continuing kingdom without a truly righteous king who was able to maintain personal victory  over sin. Such a king as this would be a great national treasure indeed! But even this king could not establish a perpetual kingdom – UNLESS – unless He was able to live forever. If the righteous king was able to live forever no rogue could succeed Him on the throne. This is the ONLY solution to the dilemma. Consequently, a prophecy was proclaimed that would solve the problem.

[Isaiah 9:6-7] **For unto us a child is born, unto us a son is given: and the government shall be upon his shoulder:** and his name shall be called Wonderful, Counsellor, The mighty God, **The everlasting Father**, The Prince of Peace. Of the **increase** of his government and peace **there shall be no end**, upon the throne of David, and upon his kingdom, to order it, and to establish it with judgment and with justice from **henceforth even for ever**. The zeal of the LORD of hosts will perform this.

As we can see from the above prophecy, before the *"government"* of Israel can be upon His shoulder, the child must first be *"born"* and then be *"given"*. Two millennia ago this King of kings was birthed into the world by a virgin woman and the ancient prophecy began to unfurl its glory before the face of all mankind. The gospels give us a holy glimpse of that special night.

[Luke 2:8-14] And there were in the same country shepherds abiding in the field, keeping watch over their flock by night. And, lo, the angel of the Lord came upon them, and the glory of the Lord shone round about them: and they were sore afraid. And **the angel said unto them, Fear not: for, behold, I bring you good tidings of great joy**, which shall be to all people. **For unto you is born this day in the city of David a Saviour, which is Christ the Lord**. And this shall be a sign unto you; Ye shall find the babe wrapped in swaddling clothes, lying in a manger. And suddenly there was with the angel a multitude of the heavenly host praising

God, and saying, **Glory to God in the highest, and on earth peace, good will toward men.**

[John 3:16] **For God so loved the world, that he "gave" his only begotten Son**, that whosoever believeth in him should not perish, but have everlasting life.

This is the One that would fulfill all righteousness. Here is the Prince of Peace, the Melchisedec that could bear the burden of the kingdom of heaven's royal government upon His sinless shoulders FOREVER! This is the *"given"* Son that would offer Himself as a sacrifice for sin and conquer death. He is the solution to the problem of the failing kingdom.

[Ephesians 5:1-2] Be ye therefore followers of God, as dear children; And **walk in love, as Christ also hath loved us, and hath given himself for us an offering and a sacrifice to God** for a sweetsmelling savour.

As was proper among the Israelite priest class, Jesus entered public ministry at *about thirty years of age* [Luke 3:23]. But as Paul points out:

[Hebrews 7:14-16] For **it is evident that our Lord sprang out of Juda**; of which tribe Moses spake nothing concerning priesthood. And it is yet far more evident: for that **after the similitude of Melchisedec there ariseth another priest, Who is made,** not after the law of a carnal commandment, but **after the power of an endless life.**

As our Lord prepared to launch His public ministry, His first duty was to be *"numbered with the transgressors"* which He began to do at John's baptism.

[Mark 1:4-5] **John did baptize in the wilderness, and preach the baptism of repentance for the remission of sins.** And there went out unto him all the land of Judaea, and they of Jerusalem, and **were all baptized of him in the river of Jordan, confessing their sins.**

And though John was reluctant to baptize the sinless Son of God, the desire of the Lord prevailed, and He was baptized like the common people, yet with no sin to confess.

[Matthew 3:13-15] Then cometh Jesus from Galilee to Jordan unto John, to be baptized of him. **But John forbad him, saying, I have need to be baptized of thee, and comest thou to me?** And Jesus answering said unto him, Suffer it to be so now: for thus it becometh us to fulfil all righteousness. Then he suffered him.

Our Lord being *"numbered with the transgressors"* began at John's baptism, but it was ultimately completed at Calvary.

[Mark 15:26-28] And the superscription of his accusation was written over, THE KING OF THE JEWS. And with him they crucify two thieves; the one on his right hand, and the other on his left. **And the scripture was fulfilled, which saith, And he was numbered with the transgressors.**

Two great battles would have to be waged and won before the kingdom of heaven could be torn from the hands of Satan and returned to Adam's race, and the initial battle began after Jesus was baptized and first entered His ministry.

[Matthew 3:16-4:1] And Jesus, when he was baptized, went up straightway out of the water: and, lo, the heavens were opened unto him, and he saw the Spirit of God descending like a dove, and lighting upon him: And lo a voice from heaven, saying, This is my beloved Son, in whom I am well pleased. **Then was Jesus led up of the Spirit into the wilderness to be tempted of the devil.**

The Messiah came to earth to retrieve dominion from the king of pride and rebellion. God's Prince must be tested as a man. He must wear a man's flesh. He must endure a man's hardships and temptations without faltering. The God/Man must bridle His unlimited power with holy righteousness at all times, regardless of His circumstances, and He must be affected by all of the weaknesses and frailties of a man while He does it. He must be tested in all points as a man: lust of the flesh, the pride of life, and the lust of the eyes. He must endure such trials without sin. And His first test came after forty days of self-denial.

[Matthew 4:2] And **when he had fasted forty days and forty nights, he was afterward an hungred.**

1) Hungry and tired, Jesus was tempted by the cravings of His stomach to satisfy the demands of His **flesh.**

[Matthew 4:3-4] And when the tempter came to him, he said, If thou be the Son of God, command that these stones be made bread. But he answered and said, It is written, **Man shall not live by bread alone, but by every word that proceedeth out of the mouth of God.**

2) Satan's next attack was intended to exploit Christ's victory over the first temptation. He tempted Jesus to act in presumption and indulge in worldly **pride** by displaying His divine nature for personal satisfaction. In effect, the devil

said, *"I see you trust in scripture. Let's see you actually PROVE you believe it!"*

[Matthew 4:5-7] Then the devil taketh him up into the holy city, and setteth him on a pinnacle of the temple, And saith unto him, If thou be the Son of God, cast thyself down: for it is written, He shall give his angels charge concerning thee: and in their hands they shall bear thee up, lest at any time thou dash thy foot against a stone. **Jesus said unto him, It is written again, Thou shalt not tempt the Lord thy God.**

3) And the devil's last attack in this battle was an appeal to the physically weakened Lord's exhausted flesh. His tired **eyes** were tempted with the offer of dominion easily acquired by simply bending the knee to unrighteous authority. Satan suggests, *"Why don't we just do this the easy way. Let me give you what you deserve."*

[Matthew 4:8-11] Again, the devil taketh him up into an exceeding high mountain, and sheweth him all the kingdoms of the world, and the glory of them; And saith unto him, All these things will I give thee, if thou wilt fall down and

worship me. **Then saith Jesus unto him, Get thee hence, Satan: for it is written, Thou shalt worship the Lord thy God, and him only shalt thou serve.** Then the devil leaveth him, and, behold, angels came and ministered unto him.

These temptations were but an opening salvo, the first shots fired in a raging war where neither side would EVER consider a truce. Satan had lost the first battle. It was a relatively new experience for Him. His previous skirmishes with men had typically resulted in easy victories. In the past, if he hadn't gotten his way completely, he had usually accomplished it at least in part and if not at the time, then later for certain. This time the outcome would be very different. Satan had long carried the crown and the effects of his rulership had infected the entire earth. Sin, suffering and death had crept into every crevice, every dark corner. But now the long-awaited promise of the Messiah's kingdom was just over the horizon. The Son of God had finally arrived and His forerunner, John the Baptist, had come to proclaim the good news.

> [Matthew 3:1-4] In those days came John the Baptist, preaching in the wilderness of Judaea, And saying, **Repent ye: for the kingdom of heaven is at hand.** For this is he that was spoken of by the prophet Esaias [Isaiah], saying, The voice of one crying in the wilderness, **Prepare ye the way of the Lord,** make his paths straight. And the same **John had his raiment of camel's hair, and a leathern girdle about his loins;** and his meat was locusts and wild honey.

John came bearing Elijah's message, and oddly enough he was even dressed like him. We find this out by way of king Ahaziah's messenger, who met the prophet and described him to the king.

> [2 Kings 1:7-8] And he said unto them, What manner of man was he which came up to meet you, and told you these words? And they answered him, He was an hairy man, and **girt with a girdle of leather about his loins. And he said, It is Elijah the Tishbite.**

The last book of the Old Testament had ended with a prophecy telling of Elijah's future return before the Messiah would come.

> [Malachi 4:5-6] **Behold, I will send you Elijah the prophet before the coming of the great and dreadful day of the LORD:** And he shall turn the heart of the fathers to the children, and the heart of the children to their fathers, lest I come and smite the earth with a curse.

Not only did John dress like Elijah and preach his message, but before John was even conceived, an angel's prophecy associated him with that legendary prophet who left this earth without ever dying. John was to get Israel ready to meet their Messiah.

> [Luke 1:17] And **he** [John] **shall go before him** [Messiah] **in the spirit and power of Elias** [Elijah], to turn the hearts of the fathers to the children, and the disobedient to the wisdom of the just; **to make ready a people prepared for the Lord.**

In some way, the prophecy of John going *"in the spirit and power of Elijah"* qualified (conditionally) as the fulfillment of Malachi's prophecy that Elijah would come. Jesus Himself bears witness to this truth in Matthew's gospel, saying:

> [Matthew 11:12-14] And from the days of John the Baptist until now **the kingdom of heaven suffereth violence, and the violent take it by force.** For all the prophets and the law prophesied until John. **And if ye will receive it, this is Elias** [Elijah]**, which was for to come.**

The prerequisite for Israel obtaining the kingdom was, *"if ye will receive it"*. To have a kingdom they must have a King. While they made up their minds whether Jesus was the Christ or not, the battle for the kingdom continued. Later, the apostles described Christ's ministry, telling people:

[Acts 10:38] **How God anointed Jesus of Nazareth with the Holy Ghost and with power: who went about doing good, and healing all that were oppressed of the devil; for God was with him.**

Day by day Jesus diminished the effects of the Devil's kingdom. Casting out devils, healing the sick, raising the dead, the lame walked, the deaf could hear and the blind received their sight as the gospel of the kingdom was preached to all who had ears to hear it. But what was this kingdom to be? It was to be a kingdom of prosperity and peace, a kingdom of righteousness, deliverance and rest from their enemies for the people of Israel. It was to be a mighty Sabbath, a Sabbath unlike anything that men had ever seen before. It was to be a Sabbath for the earth. Once the Devil and his powers of sin and death were defeated righteousness could reign among men. Speaking of the day when Christ physically defeats the devil, takes His rightful place on the throne of the kingdom of heaven, and establishes His millennial Sabbath, the Bible says:

> [Isaiah 14:5-7] The LORD hath broken the staff of the wicked, and the sceptre of the rulers. He [the devil] who smote the people in wrath with a continual stroke, he that ruled the nations in anger, is persecuted, and none hindereth. **The whole earth is at rest, and is quiet: they break forth into singing.**

Doctrinally speaking, offering the kingdom of heaven to the nation of Israel at this point in time is a bit of a problem. It's a *"sticky wicket"* as the British would say. Why? It's because, as I pointed out previously, the kingdom of Christ is a Sabbath. In fact, it is a great and mighty Sabbath, and all previous Sabbaths are but mere steppingstones leading up to it.

So that I might better explain this problem I'll set aside the discussion of Christ's ministry temporarily and introduce a new subject that will shed some light on this issue.

PART 7

HOW OLD ARE YOU ANYWAY?

EARTH, YOUNG AGAIN

As the title of this section implies, I am doctrinally a *"young Earther"* in regard to the age of the *current earth*. In truth, there is a great deal of controversy within Christianity regarding the age of the earth. On the one hand, I tend to agree with the young earth assessment because of the scriptural evidence which will be presented in the following pages. On the other hand, I also see evidence in the Bible which suggests a version of the earth which predates the one we're living on today. How can both be true? Maybe, like other biblical issues, both views need to be understood in their proper context. For instance: is Messiah God or man? Scripturally, He is both, although there is debate regarding the deity of Christ and the triune nature of the godhead to this present day. And what about Calvinism vs. Armenianism, can a person lose their salvation or are they eternally secure in it? What if both are true, but they must be viewed in their proper dispensational settings? Perhaps they must be *"rightly divided"* as Paul admonishes, if they are to be understood correctly. The truth is salvation is assured at the moment a person receives the imputed righteousness of God, and not until then. However, that moment is not the same in every dispensation. That's why in the Old Testament righteous people went to Abraham's bosom and did not go to heaven. It is because they had not yet received the gift of God's imputed righteousness because Christ had not yet died for them. But in this New Testament period, when a person believes on Christ and then dies he is said to be absent from the body and *"to be present with the Lord"* [2 Corinthians 5:8]. We arrive at this simple, but profound, truth by examining the Bible the way we are told. Paul instructs us to:

> [2 Timothy 2:15] Study to shew thyself approved unto God, a workman that needeth not to be ashamed, **rightly dividing the word of truth**.

Now, the belief in a prior Earth among some professing Christians goes back to at least 400 A.D. and possibly earlier. *[See the appendix in this book for the comments of St Augustine]* Is it possible that the "*old earth vs. young earth*" controversy falls into the same category as the doctrines mentioned in the above paragraph? Perhaps both positions are true, but they must be viewed in their proper dispensational context. Maybe they just need to be rightly divided in order to be properly understood. I think this may be the solution to the controversy, and I arrive at this conclusion by paying attention to one of God's most fundamental teaching methods – Repetition.

First of all, I notice in Genesis chapter one a repeating pattern of statements made by God during the creation week. If you look carefully you will see that each day of the creation begins with the statement *"And God said, Let..."*. That statement is followed by what He did on that particular day. And when He's finished, at the end of each day the passage says, *"And the evening and the morning were..."* thereby identifying on which day those things were accomplished. The only two verses in the entire chapter that do not fit within those brackets are verses one and two. The question is obvious: *Why don't they?* The answer seems apparent to me. I am persuaded that they obviously occurred sometime before He began the six days that follow them in the same chapter.

One cannot read the scriptures without noticing that the Creator has placed significant emphasis on certain numbers found in the Bible. Bible Numerology is an interesting subject and much can be learned from observing God's use of numbers, but numerology has its limits and can't really be used for the purpose of creating doctrine. Even so, it can often help to sort out some sticky doctrinal passages. There are certain numbers with meanings that are almost universally agreed upon. For instance, the number 1 points to God. Number 3 is typically associated with the three-part nature of the Godhead. 4 represents the world. 9 signifies fruitfulness. 666 is the mark of the beast. But it is the number "7" I would bring to your attention now. The use of the number seven indicates that God has finished something; He has completed an act, or process just like He did in the creation week found in Genesis chapters one and two. Seven is a Sabbath, and a Sabbath is a time of rest from one's labors just as the Creator did from His. And let us not forget what Jesus said about it.

[Mark 2:27] ...**The sabbath was made for man, and not man for the sabbath**:

The seventh day was given for a man to rest, to reflect on his Creator, his own mortality and his own eternal destiny. Adam didn't need a Sabbath since his life was not intended to be filled with labor and death. That's why the word "Sabbath" doesn't show up in Genesis. The practice is introduced much later, in Exodus 16. It was delivered to Israel after they were led out of their Egyptian bondage and had crossed the Red Sea.

[Exodus 16:23] And he [Moses] said unto them, This is that which the LORD hath said, To morrow is **the rest of the holy sabbath unto the LORD**: bake that which ye will bake

to day, and seethe that ye will seethe; and that which
remaineth over lay up for you to be kept until the morning.

Israel was *"born in a day"* as a nation when they left Egypt, but
that fledgling band of people lacked national organization. The
Sabbath became part of their organizational structure and was
introduced to them as they were being formed into a nation. It's
some of what set them apart from the other kingdoms around
them. The Hebrew people were chosen to be a light to the world.
They were to be a *"peculiar people"* in many ways, and one of
those ways was the *"sign"* of the Sabbath.

> [Exodus 31:13] **Speak thou also unto the children of Israel,
> saying, Verily my sabbaths ye shall keep: for it is a sign
> between me and you** throughout your generations; that ye
> may know that I am the LORD that doth sanctify you.

And just as the preceding passage indicates, this was only the first
of several types of *"sabbaths"* [plural] that Israel would be
instructed to keep. For instance, Clarence Larkin pointed out in
his book *Dispensational Truth* how the Sabbaths form a chain, a
repetition, a series of events that lead to a greater reality that is
intended to be understood by the child of God. The series is as
follows:

1) **A *"Week"* of Days**, 6 days of work and the 7th day is a
   Sabbath of rest.
2) **A *"Week"* of Weeks**, a period of 7 weeks between the holy
   days of Passover and Pentecost.
3) **A *"Week"* of Months**, with the exception of the weekly
   Sabbath, all of Israel's God ordained original holy days fall
   in the first 7 months of the year.

4) **A "*Week*" of Years**, 6 years they were to plant their fields and in the 7th year the land would rest.
5) **A "*Week*" of Weeks of Years**, 7 groups of 7 years was to be between Israel's Jubilee celebrations.

God has formed an unmistakable pattern here and He has emphasized it by the use of repetition. These repeating cycles of 7 point to the predominant theme of the entire Bible. It is the theme of the Kingdom. The first coming of Christ is a precious event in the heart of every true believer. It's the day we look to for our eternal salvation, and we gladly acknowledge the selfless sacrifice that the Lord Jesus Christ made on our behalf. But the Father often sees things differently than we mortal sinners do. The big day on the Father's calendar isn't the day when wicked men spit in His Son's face and tore His beard out by the hunks. The Father didn't get all warm and fuzzy when the Lord Jesus Christ was whipped until His flesh hung in ribbons - until you could count His rib cage and was then nailed to a cross naked in public humiliation. That was when the Lord Jesus Christ *"became sin for us"* and the Father had to turn His back on His only begotten Son because He's of *"purer eyes than to behold evil"*. It's when Jesus cried out *"My God, my God, why hast thou forsaken me?"* That event was a necessary evil that had to happen for our sakes so we could be saved from the penalty of sin. It was imperative that the precious blood of Jesus be shed for sinners, and that He remain victorious over the Devil, even unto death. That's our big day and we thank God for it! But the Father's big day is when His Son gets what rightfully belongs to Him. It's the day His Son, the Lord Jesus Christ, is crowned King of kings and Lord of Lords. It's the day that Jesus Christ returns to this planet and establishes His Kingdom and will reign on Earth for 1,000 years. There are about 50 prophesies that foretell the first coming of Christ, but there are over 500 that tell about the second coming. By a ratio of ten to one God puts the emphasis on the day Christ reigns as King; and we would do well to remember that the Father's view of things isn't the same as a sinners view, and the Bible is God's book not ours.

All of those previous Sabbaths point to, and build upon the understanding of, what the Bible calls *"the day of the Lord"*. In the scriptures, the day of the Lord begins with Christ coming back at a time when the world does not expect it. He will ultimately seize control of the kingdoms of this world and reign for a thousand years. Then *"the day of the Lord"* ends when the universe is destroyed so the new heavens and new earth can be created, just as Peter spells it out in the following verses.

> [2 Peter 3:10-13] But **the day of the Lord will come as a thief in the night; in the which the heavens shall pass away with a great noise, and the elements shall melt with fervent heat, the earth also and the works that are therein shall be burned up.** Seeing then that all these things shall be dissolved, what manner of persons ought ye to be in all holy conversation and godliness, Looking for and hasting unto the coming of the day of God, wherein the heavens being on fire shall be dissolved, and the elements shall melt with fervent heat? **Nevertheless we, according to his promise, look for new heavens and a new earth, wherein dwelleth righteousness.**

When reading the book of Revelation we find out that *"the day of the Lord"* lasts 1,000 years. The description is emphatic and reads as follows.

Revelation 20

1 And I saw an angel come down from heaven, having the key of the bottomless pit and a great chain in his hand.

2 And he laid hold on the dragon, that old serpent, which is the Devil, and Satan, and bound him a **thousand years**,

3 And cast him into the bottomless pit, and shut him up, and set a seal upon him, that he should deceive the nations no more, till the **thousand years** should be fulfilled: and after that he must be loosed a little season.

4 And I saw thrones, and they sat upon them, and judgment was given unto them: and I saw the souls of them that were beheaded for the witness of Jesus, and for the word of God, and which had not worshipped the beast, neither his image, neither had received his mark upon their foreheads, or in their hands; and they lived and reigned with Christ a **thousand years**.

5 But the rest of the dead lived not again until the **thousand years** were finished. This is the first resurrection.

6 Blessed and holy is he that hath part in the first resurrection: on such the second death hath no power, but they shall be priests of God and of Christ, and shall reign with him a **thousand years**.

7 And when **the thousand years** are expired, Satan shall be loosed out of his prison,

8 And shall go out to deceive the nations which are in the four quarters of the earth, Gog and Magog, to gather them together to battle: the number of whom is as the sand of the sea.

In Revelation chapters 19 and 20 we see how the Lord Jesus Christ returns, defeats the Devil and has him bound for 1,000 years while He reigns as King of kings. Satan is then briefly let loose and is swiftly conquered and cast into the lake of fire forever. Six times John tells us that Christ's earthly kingdom (which Peter refers to as a "day") will last for 1,000 years. Now let's look at what Peter said again.

2 Peter 3

8 ¶ But, beloved, be not ignorant of this one thing, that **one day *is* with the Lord as a thousand years, and a thousand years as one day.**
9 ¶ The Lord is not slack concerning his promise, as some men count slackness; but is longsuffering to us-ward, not willing that any should perish, but that all should come to repentance.
10 But **the day of the Lord will come as a thief in the night; in the which the heavens shall pass away with a great noise, and the elements shall melt with** fervent heat, the earth also and the works that are therein shall be burned up.
11 ¶ *Seeing* then *that* all these things shall be dissolved, what manner *of persons* ought ye to be in *all* holy conversation and godliness,
12 Looking for and hasting unto the coming of the day of God, wherein the heavens being on fire shall be dissolved, and the elements shall melt with fervent heat?
13 **Nevertheless we, according to his promise, look for new heavens and a new earth, wherein dwelleth righteousness.**

Peter's statement is in perfect harmony with John's. Peter says, *"be not ignorant of this one thing"*. The other Sabbath's pointed forward to this magnificent truth. It is the dawning of the great day of Christ's kingdom here on earth. This is the day that is dearest to the Father's heart. It is the day when things begin to be set right. He is rightfully pleased with His Son, and He looks forward to seeing Him get the respect and recognition He deserves [Psalm2]. After all, what loving father wouldn't feel the same way? The millennial kingdom, *"the day of the Lord"*, begins with Christ returning as a thief in the night and continues until He has reigned for 1,000 years and the heavens are dissolved. This recognition adds another piece to the Sabbath pattern.

1) **A *"Week"* of Days**, six days of work and the 7th day is a Sabbath of rest.
2) **A *"Week"* of Weeks**, a period of 7 weeks between the holy days of Passover and Pentecost.
3) **A *"Week"* of Months**, with the exception of the weekly Sabbath, all of Israel's God ordained original holy days fall in the first 7 months of the year.
4) **A *"Week"* of Years**, they would plant their fields for 6 years and in the 7th year the land would rest.
5) **A *"Week"* of Weeks of Years**, 7 groups of 7 years were to be between Israel's Jubilee celebrations.
6) **A *"WEEK"* OF 1,000 YEARS**, six groups of 1,000 years, and the 7th group is the 1,000-year Sabbath of the earth.

Did you see what we have so far? We now have a NEARLY COMPLETED repetitious pattern. Just as John mentions the 1,000 years six times in Revelation chapter twenty; the 1,000 years he tells of occupies the sixth place in the repeating pattern of the Sabbaths. But there is also another interesting phenomenon associated with the millennial reign of Christ. The 1,000 years is mentioned in *exactly* seven verses in the New Testament. In 2nd Peter 3:8 we find the first verse. The next six verses are found in Revelation chapter twenty. The 1,000 years are mentioned the 2nd time in verse 2, the 3rd time in verse 3, the 4th time in verse 4, the 5th time in verse 5, the 6th time in verse 6, and the 7th and final time in verse 7. I wonder; what are the odds of this happening in such perfect order? Quite slim I would imagine!

But is this idea of a week of millenniums scripturally reliable? Some people reject the doctrine of Christ's physical kingdom on earth, but are they right? Surely, this question is worthy of every Christians contemplation.

Many believers are unaware that James Ussher (1581-1656), a highly respected Anglican Archbishop of Ireland in the seventeenth century, created a chronology of the Old Testament by working backwards through the genealogies it contained. By calculating the years and lifespans listed therein he concluded that this present world was created around 4,000 years before the days of Christ. Others have done similar research and have come to comparable conclusions. Their differences comprising less than forty years out of four thousand equate statistically to a 99.99% agreement. From the evidence of the genealogies, the Bible reckons this present world was approximately 4,000 years old at the time of Christ; and since His death and resurrection nearly 2,000 years have passed. In all, about 6,000 years have elapsed since Adam was expelled from the garden because of sin. Of course, this would mean we are very near the arrival of the 1,000-year kingdom we've been discussing. As I mentioned earlier in this book, the "Berisheet Passover Prophecy" will convey this idea in greater detail.

In order to solidify this teaching, allow me to offer two simple examples which demonstrate how this understanding harmonizes with the Sabbath pattern we have discussed.

1) **The future Millennial Kingdom is shown in the Mount of Transfiguration, which Jesus connected to his *"coming in his kingdom"*.** Unknown to most Christians, a very interesting

problem arises when comparing the following Transfiguration accounts in Matthew and Luke.

[Matthew 16:28-17:3] Verily I say unto you, **There be some standing here, which shall not taste of death, till they see the Son of man coming in his kingdom.** And <u>after six days</u> Jesus taketh Peter, James, and John his brother, and bringeth them up into an high mountain apart, And was transfigured before them: and his face did shine as the sun, and his raiment was white as the light. And, behold, there appeared unto them Moses and Elias talking with him.

[Luke 9:27-30] But I tell you of a truth, **there be some standing here, which shall not taste of death, till they see the kingdom of God.** And it came to pass <u>about an eight days after</u> these sayings, he took Peter and John and James, and went up into a mountain to pray. And as he prayed, the fashion of his countenance was altered, and his raiment was white and glistering. And, behold, there talked with him two men, which were Moses and Elias:

We have here two accounts of the Transfiguration. Matthew tells us it was *after six days,* but Luke says it was *about eight.* Is there a contradiction in the Bible? If so, which is correct? I submit to you that both writers are correct. Consider this, what's after six and about eight? The answer, of course, is seven. God is once again teaching by throwing up a red flag. Keeping Ussher's Chronology in mind, look at the following chart where we see approximately 4,000 years in the Old Testament followed by 2,000 years of New Testament Church Age. As we have shown earlier, 2 Peter *3:8 admonishes us saying: "But, **beloved, <u>be not ignorant</u>** of this one thing, that one day is with the Lord as a thousand years, and a thousand years as one day."*

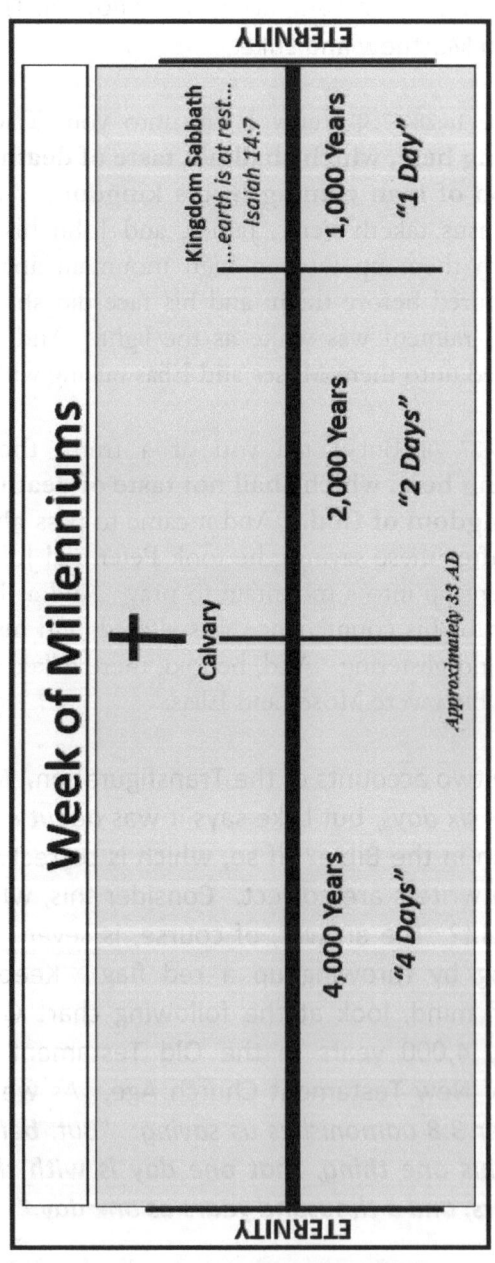

Week of Millenniums

ETERNITY

Kingdom Sabbath
...earth is at rest...
Isaiah 14:7

1,000 Years

"1 Day"

2,000 Years

"2 Days"

Calvary

Approximately 33 AD

4,000 Years

"4 Days"

ETERNITY

Not only do we find the 'one day equals 1,000 years' calculation working out perfectly , but the two tribulation witnesses, Moses & Elijah [Elias] are present with Jesus on the mount, connecting them with His second coming. Surely the 1,000-year Kingdom is even now on the horizon.

2) **The time of Christ's 1,000-year kingdom is echoed by the prophet Hosea as well.** In chapter 6 a prophecy is given where the *'one day equals 1,000 years'* calculation works out perfectly once again, although this time it only includes the Church Age and the Millennium.

> [Hosea 6:1-2] Come, and let us return unto the LORD: for he hath <u>torn</u>, and he will <u>heal</u> us; he hath <u>smitten</u>, and he will <u>bind</u> us up. **After two days** will he revive us: **in the third day** he will raise us up, and we shall live in his sight.

Hosea speaks of two events and two time periods. He tells us that Israel has been torn and smitten by the Lord, but that He will also bind [bandage] and heal them. When did this happen? I suggest to you that it started in earnest when they rejected and crucified their Messiah saying *"we have no king but Caesar"*. Moreover, they even agreed *"his blood be on us and on our children"*. Since that time, Paul tells us that the wrath of God has been upon them *"to the uttermost"* and for the past two millennia they have been made *"a proverb and a byword among all nations."* [Deuteronomy 28:37]

But the prophecy doesn't stop there, because *"after two days he will revive"* them: or in other words, after 2,000 years. And then *"in the third day"* (in the 1,000-year kingdom) he will *"raise"* them up and they *"shall live in his sight"*. In Romans 11:26 we are told that one day *"there shall come out of Sion the Deliverer, and shall turn away ungodliness from Jacob".* In the meantime, they will continue from persecution to persecution until they say *"blessed is he that cometh in the name of the Lord".* This chart reflects the future fulfillment of Hosea's prophecy.

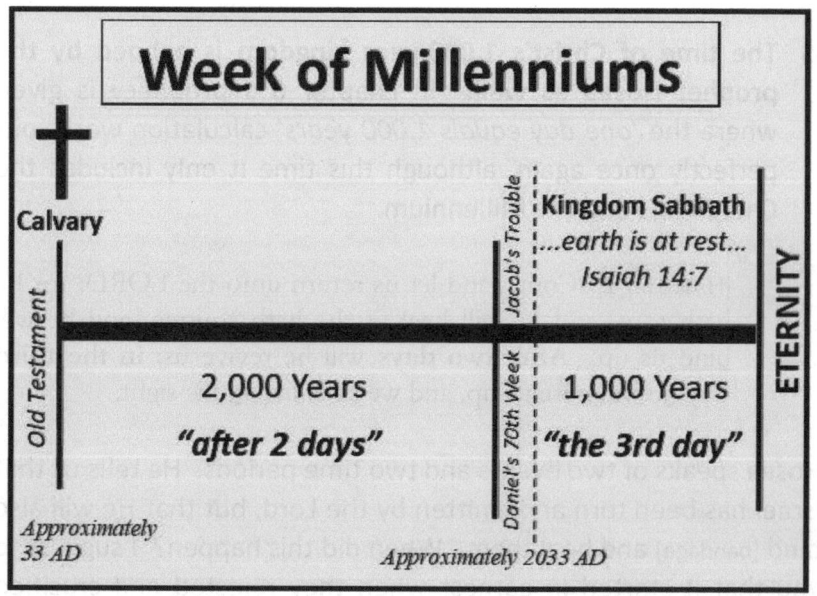

As I said previously, the Week of Millenniums is the sixth repetitive advancement of this teaching on Christ's coming kingdom. Keep this in mind as the 7th and final piece of the pattern will be discussed later.

This is the thought that takes us back to the offer of the kingdom of heaven which was preached by Jesus and John the Baptist. I mentioned previously that there was a snag associated with their preaching of the imminent physical kingdom. Why? What was the problem? Simply put, the kingdom was obviously intended to be a Sabbath for the earth. This means it must be the seventh at the end of a period of six in order for it to follow the proper repetitive pattern for a Sabbath. So the question arises, how can it be at the end of a period of six if the earth was only 4,000 years old at the time? If *"one day is like unto a thousand years"*, that would only count as four days; UNLESS, there is a block of time somehow associated with the first two verses in Genesis that spans 2,000 years. If there was a 2,000-year block of time, and Ussher's chronology going back to Adam is about 4,000 years from Adam to Christ, then the offer of the kingdom preached by both John and Jesus would have been preached at the end of a 6,000 year period. In such a case, the offer of the Sabbath kingdom, which lasts 1,000 years, would have been a legitimate offer. It would have been a Sabbath offered in keeping with the pattern that God had meticulously developed. Moreover, since it does not necessarily add millions of years to this present Earth's creation account it would not bring harm to the biblical narrative. In fact, it seems to solve a few problems. For instance, God creating anything *"without form and void"* is inconsistent with what we see in all of His other creative acts. There is no pattern for this type of creative activity. He always starts by creating an original item in its maturity. Humans and animals that are already capable of reproduction and trees that are capable of bearing fruit because they already have their seeds in them, etc. Why would we think the formation of the earth would be the lone exception to the methods we find in His firmly established creative pattern? We are told on several occasions that when God made the earth He laid the foundation, dropped the plummet, and stretched the line upon it. This would be the exact opposite of making it *"without form and void"*.

PROBLEMS SOLVED BY A RE-CREATED YOUNG EARTH

A 2,000-year block of time in Genesis 1:1-2 also solves the issue of the Devil sinning so quickly after his creation. After all, when he appears as a serpent in Genesis chapter three he has already fallen into sin and accordingly has lost his throne. In fact, both his throne and the dominion it represented were obviously already lost on the sixth day before Adam was created. We know this because Adam's dominion over creation was predetermined before he was brought into existence. It is apparent that he was made for the very purpose of exercising the dominion that Lucifer had lost.

> [Genesis 1:26] And God said, Let us make man in our image, after our likeness: and **let them have dominion** over the fish of the sea, and over the fowl of the air, and over the cattle, and **over all the earth**, and over every creeping thing that creepeth upon the earth.

King David contemplates man's intended authority as well.

> [Psalms 8:3-6] When I consider thy heavens, the work of thy fingers, the moon and the stars, which thou hast ordained; What is man, that thou art mindful of him? and the son of man, that thou visitest him? For thou hast made him a little lower than the angels, and hast crowned him with glory and honour. **Thou madest him to have dominion over the works of thy hands; thou hast put all things under his feet:**

There is no dispute over the fact that Lucifer is a created being, but WHEN was he created? Was he created to rule over a prior Earth or are we to believe that holy Lucifer became unholy Satan before the sixth day of creation? And which of the days was he supposed to have been created on? Was it before the animals on day 5? or before the sun, moon and stars on day 4? or before the plants on day 3? or while the earth was still a mess on day 2? or was it even before there was ANY light on day 1? It's worth noticing that His origin is not listed during the days of creation in Genesis and neither is the origin of the angels. But we do know that the angels, *"the sons of God"*, existed before the earth, because they rejoiced when Earth was created. In a conversation that God had with Job He brought up this very issue in a series of questions. He asked:

> [Job 38:4-7] **Where wast thou when I laid the foundations of the earth?** declare, if thou hast understanding. Who hath laid the measures thereof, if thou knowest? or who hath stretched the line upon it? Whereupon are the foundations thereof fastened? or who laid the corner stone thereof; **When the morning stars sang together, and all the sons of God shouted for joy?**

The recognition of a prior earth existing before Genesis 1:2 also explains why God commissioned Adam to *"replenish"* the earth, which is the exact same commission He gave to Noah. Replenish simply means to fill, but it is accompanied with the understanding that it is not the first filling.

> [Genesis 1:28] And God blessed them, and God said unto them, **Be fruitful, and multiply, and replenish the earth**, and subdue it: and have dominion over the fish of the sea, and over the fowl of the air, and over every living thing that moveth upon the earth.

[Genesis 9:1] And God blessed Noah and his sons, and said unto them, **Be fruitful, and multiply, and replenish the earth.**

If Earth had been previously formed and inhabited by created beings such as Lucifer and the sons of God, then Adam's commission to replenish the Earth would make perfect sense. Especially when you consider the fact that Christ's genealogy in Luke calls sinless Adam, in the day of his creation, *"the son of God"*. In this we see the hint of a prior Earth created for an angelic host to occupy.

[Luke 3:38] Which was the son of Enos, which was the son of Seth, which was the son of **Adam, which was the son of God.**

Apparently Adam, the earthly son of God, was commissioned to replenish the earth with a race of sinless sons of God that would replace the sons of God Lucifer corrupted. However, Adam didn't even get started before Satan beguiled Adam's new queen and brought ruin upon her and her king, making them incapable of properly ruling the kingdom. This was discussed in an earlier section.

I am aware that some people say "The word *replenish* used to mean *'fill'*, not necessarily to *"refill"*. As evidence they show the usage in Webster's 1828 Dictionary, which is as follows.

> **REPLEN'ISH**, verb transitive [Latin re and plenus, full.]
> **1.** To fill; to stock with numbers or abundance. The magazines are replenished with corn. The springs are replenished with water.
> Multiply and replenish the earth. Genesis 1:28.

REPLEN'ISH, verb intransitive To recover former fullness.

The problem with their argument is that this definition serves to support my supposition, not theirs. Consider this, are we to understand that the *"magazines"* (i.e. storehouse) mentioned in the definition above had never before been filled with corn? Were they brand new storehouses that had never been used? And what about the *"springs"*; are those to be understood as holes in the ground that had never gushed with water? If they had never produced water, why were they called a spring and not just a hole in the ground? Why would anyone think they were springs if water had never before flowed from them? Obviously, the context is that springs can run dry occasionally and then be replenished by the rain which fills the ground with water and causes them flow again. And storehouses of corn can be emptied by use during the winter months and then be refilled or *"replenished"* during the next harvest season. This is exactly what storehouses are for, and it is often what springs of water will do.

PART 8

NOW THAT'S A BIG JOB!

BACK TO MESSIAH THE PRINCE

I have pointed out on several occasions that the God of the Bible is a God of repeating patterns. It is His way of teaching and doing things. To be consistent and true to God's established pattern, Christ's offer of a kingdom 2,000 years ago had to be on a *seven* because it was intended as a Sabbath. And as I've shown, if the original Earth in Genesis 1:1-2 contained within it the saga of Lucifer's kingdom, and if that era lasted 2,000 years, and if the Old Testament chronology reflects a 4,000 year period, then the preaching of the kingdom by John the Baptist and Jesus Christ was right on time. A Sabbath of the earth was ready to appear but there was a snag, and it was not a new one. The physical kingdom of Heaven could not function as intended because of sin in the people and their leaders. That kingdom must be ruled in righteousness. But where is a totally righteous, incorruptible king to be found? Man had proven himself incapable of rising to such a holy standard. There is ONLY one solution. God would have to take upon Himself the form of a man, and this He did! Speaking of the Lord Jesus Christ, the Bible says:

> [John 1:1-3 & 14] **In the beginning was the Word, and the Word was with God, and the Word was God.** The same was in the beginning with God. All things were made by him; and without him was not any thing made that was made. **And the Word was made flesh, and dwelt among us...**

> [1 Timothy 3:16] And without controversy **great is the mystery of godliness: God was manifest in the flesh...**

[Philippians 2:6-8] [Jesus] **Who, being in the form of God, thought it not robbery to be equal with God**: But made himself of no reputation, and took upon him the form of a servant, and was made in the likeness of men: And **being found in fashion as a man, he humbled himself**, and became obedient unto death, even the death of the cross.

The Lord Jesus Christ was born a King, and the wise men knew it. They arrived asking:

[Matthew 2:2] **Where is he that is born King of the Jews?** for we have seen his star in the east, and are come to worship him.

But the kingdom Jesus represented at His first coming was not a physical kingdom. It was the spiritual kingdom upon which the proper operation of the physical kingdom was contingent.

[John 18:36] Jesus answered, **My kingdom is not of this world**: if my kingdom were of this world, then would my servants fight, that I should not be delivered to the Jews: but **now** is my kingdom not from hence.

[Romans 14:17] For **the kingdom of God is** not meat and drink; but **righteousness, and peace, and joy in the Holy Ghost.**

[1 Corinthians 4:20] For **the kingdom of God is** not in word, but **in power.**

The kingdom of God is a spiritual kingdom that a person must be born into by accepting Jesus Christ as their Lord and Saviour. This brings them into an encounter with the Holy Spirit of God, Who then creates the new birth within them.

> [John 3:3] Jesus answered and said unto him, Verily, verily, I say unto thee, **Except a man be born again, he cannot see the kingdom of God.**

Christ, the child King, needed to overcome sin His entire life. It was necessary for Him to grow into a man and prove Himself both worthy and capable to rule the kingdom FOREVER. As I mentioned before, Satan offered Christ *"all the kingdoms of the earth"* if he would just bow down, but Jesus refused to bend the knee to an ungodly usurper. Instead, He pillaged Satan's kingdom for 3 ½ years as He preached the gospel. Those possessed of devils fell down before Him, and evil spirits confessed that He was Christ as they were defeated by the power of His words. Moreover, the hearts of the people were being stirred to righteousness because of His message. It was fresh and compelling. He was telling His nation that if they would seek God's spiritual kingdom first, the physical kingdom would follow.

> [Matthew 6:33] But **seek ye <u>first</u> the kingdom of God, and his righteousness; and all these things shall be added unto you.**

Luke echoed Matthews's account and added a large and welcomed measure of hope for those who would listen.

> [Luke 12:29-32] And seek not ye what ye shall eat, or what ye shall drink, neither be ye of doubtful mind. For all these things do the nations of the world seek after: and your Father knoweth that ye have need of these things. But rather **seek ye the kingdom of God; and all these things shall be added unto you. Fear not, little flock; for <u>it is your Father's good pleasure to give you the kingdom.</u>**

Satan had been strong in the earth for millennia but One stronger than he was ransacking his unholy kingdom. Obviously, the Devil saw this as a problem. Holy Jesus not only resisted sin and temptation; He also offered Israel the return of their long-awaited physical kingdom. The Devil's logic seemed perfect in its simplicity; a rightful heir to the throne of King David that could not be tempted to sin against the Creator MUST BE KILLED to prevent Him from implementing a righteous government within the long-corrupted kingdom.

The religious leaders (Sadducees, Pharisees, Lawyers and Scribes) were the best place to spread unbelief since their widespread influence could be used to turn the people against Him. It didn't take long for the accusations to begin. They accused our precious Lord of deceiving the people, operating under the power of devils, violating the Sabbath, being a glutton and a winebibber, blasphemy and whatever else they could dream up. And finally one of His own was recruited to betray Him for a paltry sum. At the trial of the Lord Jesus Christ, the King (and by extension the offer of the physical kingdom) was hanging in the balance. Even though Jesus was found innocent by both Pilate and Herod, at the insistence of the religious leaders the people of Israel were forced to make a decision and they made it. Theirs was the final word in the matter.

[Matthew 27:22-25] Pilate saith unto them, What shall I do then with Jesus which is called Christ? They all say unto him, Let him be crucified. And the governor said, Why, what evil hath he done? But they cried out the more, saying, Let him be crucified. When Pilate saw that he could prevail nothing, but that rather a tumult was made, he took water, and washed his hands before the multitude, saying, I am innocent of the blood of this just person: see ye to it. **Then answered all**

the people, and said, His blood be on us, and on our children.

Much like the people's statement above, one of the saddest replies in all of scripture is the response of Israel's chief priests to Pilate's final question regarding Israel's Messiah King.

[John 19:15] …they cried out, Away with him, away with him, crucify him. Pilate saith unto them, Shall I crucify your King? **The chief priests answered, We have no king but Caesar.**

THE CROSS

I suppose that the best-known story in the world is what happened next; and if it's not the best known story it should be. I'm speaking, of course, of the debasement, humiliation and crucifixion of the Lord Jesus Christ. But what many people do not know is that not only did the sacrifice of Christ atone for the sins of fallen man, but His crown of thorns symbolized His payment for the curse upon nature as well. Jesus, the *"last Adam"*, wore the thorns that the first Adam earned as part of his wages for sin.

[Genesis 3:17-19] And unto Adam he [God] said, Because thou hast hearkened unto the voice of thy wife, and hast eaten of the tree, of which I commanded thee, saying, Thou shalt not eat of it: **cursed is the ground for thy sake; in sorrow shalt thou eat of it all the days of thy life; Thorns also and thistles shall it bring forth to thee;** and thou shalt eat the herb of the field; In the sweat of thy face shalt thou eat bread, till thou return unto the ground; for out of it wast thou taken: for dust thou art, and unto dust shalt thou return.

The crucifixion of Christ was inevitable. It was a matter of much biblical prophecy. The redemption of sinful man and the Sabbath of the earth could not take place without it. Both man and nature required atonement. This is what Jesus accomplished on the cross. It has been well said: *"We owed a debt we could not pay. And He paid a debt that He did not owe."* In the midst of His agony on the cross, when the Lord Jesus Christ pronounced *"It is finished"*, **the atonement was complete**. Christ had effectively appeased the wrath of God against sin by becoming sin personified and taking the full blast of God's wrath upon Himself as the Lamb of God.

[2 Corinthians 5:21] **For he** [God the Father] **hath made him** [God the Son] **to be sin for us, who knew no sin;** that we might be made the righteousness of God in him.

[1 John 2:2] And **he is the propitiation for our sins**: and not for ours only, but also **for the sins of the whole world.**

PROPITIATION - The act of appeasing the wrath of an offended person *[In this case, it was God that was offended by our human rebellion.]*

But this was not the last thing He did. The sin must also be properly disposed of. Why? Because, although the Son of God became sin for us; He had no intention of remaining the personification of sin forever. The world's sin He bore in His holy body must be *taken away*

and deposited in an appropriate place so He could once again clothe Himself in the holiness of the Godhead with the Father and the Holy Spirit.

> [John 1:29] The next day John seeth Jesus coming unto him, and saith, Behold **the Lamb of God, which** <u>taketh away</u> **the sin of the world.**

But where is the appropriate place to deposit sin? Peter gives us the answer when he quotes David's sixteenth Psalm and its prophecy which pertains to the sacrifice of Christ.

> [Acts 2:27] Because **thou wilt not leave my soul in hell**, neither wilt thou suffer thine Holy One to see corruption.

Most Christians are unaware that the three-part nature of Christ, as a man, was separated and dispersed in different directions upon His death. We can see from the above verse that His **soul** was *"in hell"* (at least for a while) during the three days His body was dead. And as every believer knows, His **body** was placed in the tomb after the crucifixion. But where was His spirit? The Lord Jesus answered this question himself.

> [Luke 23:46] And when Jesus had cried with a loud voice, he said, **Father, into thy hands I commend my spirit:** and having said thus, he gave up the ghost.

It has been argued by some that the soul of Christ did not go to hell. However, all of the patterns and plain scriptural statements argue the contrary. For instance, one of the greatest types of Christ in the scriptures was the very first Passover lamb, and regarding this lamb the Jews were given very specific instructions for its preparation.

[Exodus 12:9-11] Eat not of it raw, nor sodden at all with water, but **roast with fire; his head with his legs, and with the purtenance thereof.** And ye shall let nothing of it remain until the morning; and that which remaineth of it until the morning **ye shall burn with fire.** And thus shall ye eat it; with your loins girded, your shoes on your feet, and your staff in your hand; and **ye shall eat it in haste**: it is the LORD'S passover.

The *"purtenance"* of the lamb is the internal organs. The Passover was to be done *"in haste"*. So, the lamb was roasted in the fire, along with its head, legs, body and entrails. Like the rich man who went to hell in Luke chapter 16, it was roasted in the fire whole and no water was added. Also like the rich man in hell; when Jesus was on the cross He said *"I thirst"*, but no water was given to Him.

Another example of this truth is found in Psalm 22, a crucifixion Psalm. Here, we find the Lord Jesus Christ likened to a man in hell.

[Psalm 22:6] But **I am a worm, and no man**; a reproach of men, and despised of the people.

This is the exact condition Jesus warned people about in Mark chapter 9.

[Mark 9:43-48] And if thy hand offend thee, cut it off: it is better for thee to enter into life maimed, than having two hands to go **into hell**, into the fire that never shall be quenched: **Where their worm dieth not, and the fire is not quenched.** And if thy foot offend thee, cut it off: it is better for thee to enter halt into life, than having two feet to be cast **into hell**, into the fire that never shall be quenched:

Where their worm dieth not, and the fire is not quenched. And if thine eye offend thee, pluck it out: it is better for thee to enter into the kingdom of God with one eye, than having two eyes to be cast **into hell fire: Where their worm dieth not, and the fire is not quenched.**

Moreover, when demanded by the religious leaders to produce a sign to validate His ministry, Jesus used the judgment imposed upon the prophet Jonah as a proof of His Messiahship.

[Matthew 12:40] For **as Jonas was three days and three nights in the whale's belly; so shall the Son of man be three days and three nights in the heart of the earth.**

Have you ever considered what Jonah actually said about his time in the whale's belly?

[Jonah 2:1-7] Then Jonah prayed unto the LORD his God out of the fish's belly, And said, I cried by reason of mine affliction unto the LORD, and he heard me; **out of the belly of hell cried I**, and thou heardest my voice. For thou hadst cast me into the deep, in the midst of the seas; and the floods compassed me about: all thy billows and thy waves passed over me. Then I said, I am cast out of thy sight; yet I will look again toward thy holy temple. **The waters compassed me about, even to the soul: the depth closed me round about**, the **weeds were wrapped about my head.** I went down to the bottoms of the mountains; **the earth with her bars was about me for ever**: yet hast **thou brought up my life from corruption**, O LORD my God. When **my soul fainted** within me I remembered the LORD: and my prayer came in unto thee, into thine holy temple.

We find Jonah crying out from the belly of hell, encompassed by water with weeds wrapped around his head and the bars of the earth about him forever. At this point he needed his very life brought up from corruption. When was that? It was when his soul had fainted [past tense] within him. But what does the word *"faint"* mean? In the Bible the word is used broadly. It can apparently mean anything between feeling emotionally hopeless on one end of the spectrum to physically dying on the other end. In Jonah's case it appears to mean physical death, in keeping with the first usage of the word in scripture, which is found in Genesis.

> [Genesis 25:29-32] And Jacob sod pottage: and Esau came from the field, and **he was faint**: And Esau said to Jacob, Feed me, I pray thee, with that same red pottage; for **I am faint**: therefore was his name called Edom. And Jacob said, Sell me this day thy birthright. And Esau said, Behold, **I am at the point to die:** and what profit shall this birthright do to me?

Esau said he was *"faint"*, at *"the point to die"*, but he had not yet fainted; unlike Jonah whose *"soul"* had already *fainted within him.*

In addition to this, there is the great Messianic passage in Isaiah 53 which plainly speaks of Christ's sufferings.

> [Isaiah 53:10-12] Yet it pleased the LORD to bruise him; he hath put him to grief: when **thou shalt make his soul an offering for sin**, he shall see his seed, he shall prolong his days, and the pleasure of the LORD shall prosper in his hand. He shall see of **the travail of his soul**, and shall be satisfied: by his knowledge shall my righteous servant justify many; for he shall bear their iniquities. Therefore will I divide him a portion with the great, and he shall divide the spoil with the strong; because he hath **poured out his soul unto death:**

and he was numbered with the transgressors; and he bare the sin of many, and made intercession for the transgressors.

We either believe these statements or we do not. I believe them!

ABRAHAM'S BOSOM & HIS LAND GRANT

Moreover, let us remember that every sin offering in the Bible was BURNT IN THE FIRE! So we see that the plain statements of David in Psalm 16 and Peter in Acts 2 regarding Christ's soul being in hell are confirmed in a variety of ways. But what was Jesus doing in Hell? As we've seen, He was depositing mankind's sin burden for which He had suffered. But that's not all. Peter tells us that while Christ was there He delivered two messages! The first message was preached to the disobedient spirits that were suffering on one side for their unrepentant earthly wickedness.

> [1 Peter 3:18-20] For Christ also hath once suffered for sins, the just for the unjust, that he might bring us to God, being put to death in the flesh, but quickened by the Spirit: By which also **he went and preached unto the spirits in prison; Which sometime were disobedient**, when once the longsuffering of God waited in the days of Noah, while the ark was a preparing, wherein few, that is, eight souls were saved by water.

In paradise (on the other side of Hell) Jesus delivered His second subterranean sermon. There He preached the gospel to those whom we might call *"the righteous dead"*. They weren't righteous in the same sense that God is, but they were the people who cared about what was right and wrong and had made an effort to do that which was right. God has always recognized the difference between a person who tried to do what was right and a person who didn't care. In the following verse we see that Abraham understood this and relied upon it to negotiate with God in order to save Lot and his family from the destruction that rained down on Sodom and Gomorrah.

> [Genesis 18:25] **That be far from thee to do after this manner, to slay the righteous with the wicked:** and that the righteous should be as the wicked, that be far from thee: **Shall not the Judge of all the earth do right?**

But why was it necessary for Jesus to preach to the souls of the righteous dead? The answer is simple. Since they died before the Lord Jesus Christ had made atonement for their sins, they needed an opportunity to accept Him as their Saviour. For this reason, Peter informs us that to these people the gospel was preached.

> [1 Peter 4:6] ... for this cause was **the gospel preached also to** <u>them</u> <u>that</u> <u>are</u> <u>dead,</u> that they might be judged according to men in the flesh, but **live according to God in the spirit**.

We are NOT told that the aforementioned "*spirits in prison*" heard a gospel message from Christ like these did; only that Jesus preached to them. The sermon Christ delivered to the ungodly dead was undoubtedly a message of condemnation. It was most likely delivered in the same vein as many of the messages proclaimed by the Old Testament prophets to the ungodly rebels of their day. The humanly righteous people on the desirable side were offered living water, the gospel message of eternal salvation.

All of this preaching was accomplished in the lower parts of the earth after Christ's death and before His resurrection, which was ultimately followed by His ascension into heaven.

[Ephesians 4:8-10] Wherefore he saith, When he ascended up on high, he led captivity captive, and gave gifts unto men. (Now that he ascended, what is it but that **he also descended first into the lower parts of the earth?** He that descended is the same also that ascended up far above all heavens, that he might fill all things.)

The messages the Lord Jesus Christ preached during the time He was dead were delivered to the inhabitants of hell, which was clearly divided into two parts. One part was Hell proper, a place of torment for the souls of the spiritually lost. The other side, known as *"Abraham's bosom"* or *"paradise"*, was the temporary home of those people whose sins had been remitted as they awaited the sacrifice of God's spotless Lamb to get them into heaven. Like all sinners, they deserved to be in hell. But God in His mercy was willing to make a distinction between the righteous and the wicked. And as you can see from the words of Christ in the following passage, there is no purgatory. There is only a place where ungodly people suffer for their unforgiven sin, and there is a place of comfort for those who have not rejected the knowledge of God written in their hearts.

Luke 16:19-31

There was a certain rich man, which was clothed in purple and fine linen, and fared sumptuously every day: And there was a certain beggar named Lazarus, which was laid at his gate, full of sores, And desiring to be fed with the crumbs which fell from the rich man's table: moreover the dogs came and licked his sores. And it came to pass, that **the beggar died, and was carried by the angels into Abraham's bosom: the rich man also died, and was buried; And in hell he lift up his eyes, being in torments, and seeth Abraham afar off, and Lazarus in his bosom.** And he cried and said, Father Abraham, have mercy on me, and send

Lazarus, that he may dip the tip of his finger in water, and cool my tongue; for I am tormented in this flame. But Abraham said, Son, remember that thou in thy lifetime receivedst thy good things, and likewise Lazarus evil things: but now he is comforted, and thou art tormented. And beside all this, between us and you there is a great gulf fixed: so that they which would pass from hence to you cannot; neither can they pass to us, that would come from thence. Then he said, I pray thee therefore, father, that thou wouldest send him to my father's house: For I have five brethren; that he may testify unto them, lest they also come into this place of torment. Abraham saith unto him, They have Moses and the prophets; let them hear them. And he said, Nay, father Abraham: but if one went unto them from the dead, they will repent. And he said unto him, If they hear not Moses and the prophets, neither will they be persuaded, though one rose from the dead.

From the above passage we can clearly see that Hell and Abraham's bosom were located in the same general area, which Jesus said in Matthew 12:40 is in the heart of the earth. And although there is a great gulf between them, from either side one could still see the other. In fact, though the chasm was too wide to pass over, they were still able to converse across it. The situation is somewhat like going down in a service elevator that has two doors in it. The door in front would open to Abraham's bosom which is a paradise of rest from the troubles of life while waiting for Christ's atonement to open heaven to the righteous dead. The door in the back of the elevator opens to reveal Hell fire for the wicked and Christ rejecting sinners. It's a place of torment and unrest which serves as a temporary jail cell for spiritual offenders who are waiting to go to the eternal lake of fire. Between the two sides a great canyon exists maintaining their separation. When Jesus descended into the heart of the earth after His death, He dropped sin off in Hell and preached a message of condemnation. Afterwards He went to Abraham's bosom to preach the good news of salvation to the righteous dead people who had not yet heard of Him, and they were apparently given an opportunity to accept Him as their Saviour.

But why did Jesus refer to the good side as *"Abraham's bosom"*? What is the intended significance of such a name? Webster's 1828 dictionary gives a lengthy definition for the use of the word bosom, but the 5th and 6th definitions are the most applicable to the discussion at hand.

> **BO'SOM,**
> > 5. The **breast**, or its **interior,** considered as a closed place, **the receptacle of secrets.**
> > 6. Any **inclosed place**; the interior; **as the bosom of the earth** or of the deep.

As it turns out, Jesus referring to the place as Abraham's bosom was a play on the events recorded in early Genesis when Sarai gave her gentile servant, an Egyptian named Hagar, into Abram's *"bosom"* to have a child. It was Sarai's fleshly and impatient attempt to help God fulfill His promise to give Abram a son. But her actions did not result in the fulfilling of God's promise. Quite the contrary, Sarai's lack of faith in God's ability to keep His promise resulted in seeing her gentile maid (Hagar) obtain an unintended position of favor. Hagar became the mother of Abram's first born son. This was supposed to have been Sarai's position of blessing. But Sarai's presumptuous decision to have her maid bear Abram a child failed to produce the blessing she had anticipated and she made her displeasure well known!

[Genesis 16:5] And **Sarai said unto Abram**, My wrong be upon thee: **I have given my maid into thy bosom**; and when she saw that she had conceived, I was despised in her eyes: the LORD judge between me and thee.

It's interesting to note that **Genesis 16** and **Luke 16** are the only two places in the Bible where Abraham's bosom is mentioned – another strange phenomenon! Jesus' play on words regarding Abraham's (Abram's) bosom in Luke 16 was no doubt an offense to the religious Jews who heard it. The rich man in the story was obviously a Jew who did not receive the place of favor with *"father Abraham"* that they undoubtedly expected; while Lazarus, the sore laden leprous beggar who was hanging out with "dogs" and was no doubt thought to be a lowly gentile, ended up in the favored position the Jews expected to receive. If clarification is needed regarding the Jewish perception of gentiles, see Jesus' comment in Mark 7:25-30 where a gentile syrophenecian woman is referred to as a dog.

Some people teach the story of Lazarus and the rich man as a parable, but Jesus implied no such thing. He spoke about the situation as a matter of fact, indicating the events actually took place. It must also be noted that no parable *ever* uses proper names for the people in the story. Parables always refer to people in a generic manner, like *"a certain man"*, etc., whereas here we have Lazarus, Abraham and Moses mentioned by name. Since we know Abraham and Moses were real people there is no reason to think that Lazarus, and by extension the *"rich man"*, was not real as well. It's fairly obvious the story is to be understood historically, not as a parable or allegory.

I'll ask again. Why did Jesus refer to the heart of the earth as Abraham's bosom? I would suggest Jesus called it that for the following reasons: (1) it is *secretly located* in keeping with the definition of a *bosom*, (2) like Hagar and Lazarus, the people who go there have obtained a position of *favor* even though they may not be the people you might expect, (3) and lastly because the location is directly underneath Abraham's land grant, in the *"bosom of the earth"*.

Why would the souls of dead people go to the place Jesus called Abraham's bosom? In other words, why go there as opposed to deep inside Mammoth Caves in Kentucky, or somewhere else - anywhere else? God could have sent them anywhere. He could have sent the souls of the dead to the moon or into Davy Jones' locker at the bottom of the sea. So why put them inside the earth? Why might God put them under the Temple Mount within the borders of Abraham's land grant? Perhaps the answer is as simple as this. If that's where human life actually began, if in fact Adam, the first man, was formed there wouldn't it be reasonable to send him back to his place of origin when his time was over? God actually told Adam that He was going to do exactly that, and then He apparently did it!

> [Genesis 3:19] In the sweat of thy face shalt thou eat bread, **till thou <u>return</u> unto the ground; for <u>out of it</u> wast thou taken: for dust thou art, and <u>unto dust shalt thou return.</u>**

We always picture Adam's creation as God scraping some topsoil off the surface of the ground to make a man. That's probably due to the fact that we typically see it portrayed in such a way. But the passage says Adam was taken *"out"* of the ground, which would mean that at one point he was *"inside"* it. Not just on top of it. If that's so, and it's certainly what the scripture says, then he will be returning to where he originated. I realize that Adam's body would have been buried in the ground, but a man is more than just a shell; and there's more than a strong implication that the life his flesh was given, his soul, was returned to the very place where he *"became a living soul"* in the day of his creation.

The land God promised Abraham and his descendants is a massive section of Middle East real estate that extends from the Euphrates River in the east, to the Nile River on the west.

> [Genesis 15:18] In the same day the LORD made a covenant with Abram, saying, **Unto thy seed have I given this land, from the river of Egypt unto the great river, the river Euphrates:**

In spite of the fact that the land grant is quite large from a human perspective, it's still a mere 1/450th of the earth's total surface area. This means the odds of the Promised Land containing the geographical center of earth's landmass is only 1 chance out of 450. Google search results for *"Earth's Geographical Center"* provide the following information:

- Charles Piazzi Smyth, 1864, Astronomer Royal for Scotland in *"Our Inheritance in the Great Pyramid"* cited the geographical center coordinates as 30°00′N 31°00′E, which was understood as the location of the Great Pyramid of Giza in Egypt.
- Smyth's findings (above) were corroborated by Frederick Augustus Porter Barnard, 1884, *"The Imaginary Metrological System of the Great Pyramid of Giza"* stating *"the perfect location of the Great Pyramid along the longitudinal line could only have been purposefully done by its builders."*
- Smyth's findings were again corroborated by Mason William Galliher in the September 1919 issue *of "Trestle Board Magazine"* where he acknowledged

that the Great Pyramid being the geographical center of the earth was *"determined by many years of scientific investigation"*.

Recent technological advancements have allowed the geological center to be located more accurately via the computerized satellite Global Positioning System.

- Andrew J. Woods, 1973, physicist with Gulf Energy & Environmental Systems in San Diego, using a digital global map calculated the coordinates as 39°00′N 34°00′E, in modern Turkey, 1,000 km north of Giza, Egypt
- And in 2016, Google Maps recognized Holger Isenberg's 2003 results of 40°52′N 34°34′E as the geographic center of the world by marking it as the Central Anatolian province of Çorum in Turkey.

Although there are some obvious disagreements between the older calculations which point to Giza, Egypt and the newer calculations which identify Turkey as the geological center of the earth, there is an interesting phenomenon connecting those locations. It has been pointed out that if a line is drawn both horizontally east and vertically north from Memphis, Egypt [think Exodus]; and vertically south and horizontally west from Mount Ararat [Noah's ark], when the lines intersect a rectangle will be formed. Inside the rectangle will be the greater part of what is recognized as the *"Bible lands"*; meaning almost all of the Old Testament took place within this area. That rectangle is around 440,000 square miles. It is 450 times smaller than the total area of the earth's surface. Statistically, it is noteworthy that the geographical center of the earth would be located in this area as opposed to one of the other 449 possible locations on this planet.

It is even more significant in light of the fact that the scriptures make the claim of Israel's geographical centrality. Israel is said to *...dwell in the midst of the land.* [Ezekiel 38:12] And the ancient Jewish Sages explained their understanding of the text as described below.

Midrash Tanchuma, Kedoshim, Siman 10:1

> The Land of Israel sits at the center of the world; Jerusalem is in the center of the Land of Israel; the sanctuary is in the center of Jerusalem; the Temple building is in the center of the sanctuary; the ark is in the center of the Temple building; and the foundation stone, out of which the world was founded, is before the Temple building.

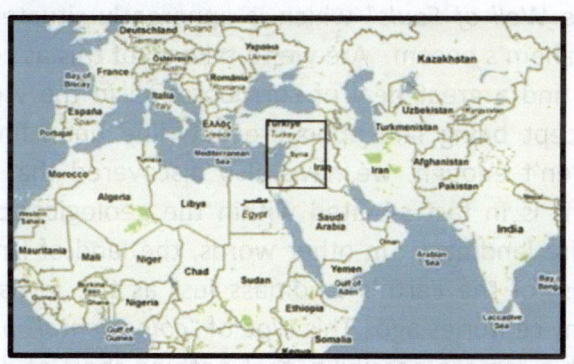

The following quote regarding the research performed by Andrew J. Woods, mentioned above, comes from an article on the Institute for Creation Research website at:

https://www.icr.org/article/the-center-of-the-earth/

"The calculations made by Woods indicate, in fact, that the average distance to all the world's land areas varies only

slightly for any central site in all this general region. For example, the average distance from the Ankara region was found to be 4,597 miles, whereas the average distance from the Jerusalem area is 4,612 miles and from the Ararat region is 4617 miles, a difference of only 15 miles and 20 miles, respectively, or about 1/3 of 1%. In terms of practical applications, the difference is negligible."

Within that rectangle is the ultimate location for the nation of Israel, of which Jerusalem is the capitol. You will recall that we have previously discussed the possibility that Israel is the area where the Garden of Eden once existed. In fact, the very Foundation Stone of the world is said to be located on Mount Zion, the Temple Mount. And the cave behind the Foundation Stone that goes down into the mount is historically referred to as *"The Well of Souls"* which is apparently situated directly above Abraham's bosom. Are we to take all of this as coincidence or do we find a great deal of corroboration in the word of God with precept being laid upon precept, line upon line? And if that weren't enough, we have also discovered that Abraham's land grant is in fact situated within the geological center of earth's entire landmass. In other words, the land of Israel is within the midst of the Earth's landmass just as the Jewish Sages insisted many centuries ago. This type of *"coincidental"* phenomenon is of such a remote possibility that nothing short of divine providence can account for it.

PART 9

GOING ONCE, GOING TWICE...

A PROPHECY FUFILLED ...IN PART

Satan's plan to destroy Israel's Messiah wasn't as perfect as he may have imagined. For whatever reason, he obviously did not expect Christ to defeat death and be resurrected. Perhaps he thought he would be able to cause Jesus to sin by having Him scourged and crucified, and thereby render Him defeated. Or maybe he thought that his victory would be complete once Jesus was dead. I don't know. But I do know that Christ's death fulfilled a great prophecy. It shows us that Jesus was not killed for Himself, but for a greater purpose.

> [Daniel 9:26] And **after threescore and two weeks shall Messiah be cut off, but not for himself**: and the people of the prince that shall come shall destroy the city and the sanctuary; and the end thereof shall be with a flood, and unto the end of the war desolations are determined.

Daniel's prophecy of the 70 Weeks, mentioned above, works out with an amazing mathematical precision. A more complete examination of this prophecy is included in the appendix at the end of this book . However, for the purposes of this section I will simply provide the text of the prophecy with a few clarifying notations bracketed in bold print.

> [Daniel 9:24-27] Seventy weeks are determined upon thy people **[the Jews]** and upon thy holy city **[Jerusalem]**, to finish the transgression, and to make an end of sins, and to make

reconciliation for iniquity, and to bring in everlasting righteousness **[Christ's Millennial Kingdom],** and to seal up the vision and prophecy, and to anoint the most Holy **[Jesus].** Know therefore and understand, that from the going forth of the commandment to restore and to build Jerusalem unto the Messiah the Prince shall be **[#1]** seven weeks, and **[#2]** threescore and two weeks: the street shall be built again, and the wall, even in troublous times. And after threescore and two weeks shall Messiah be cut off, but not for himself: and the people of the prince that shall come shall destroy the city and the sanctuary; and the end thereof shall be with a flood, and unto the end of the war desolations are determined. And he shall confirm the covenant with many for **[#3]** one week: and in the midst of the week he shall cause the sacrifice and the oblation to cease, and for the overspreading of abominations he shall make it desolate, even until the consummation, and that determined shall be poured upon the desolate.

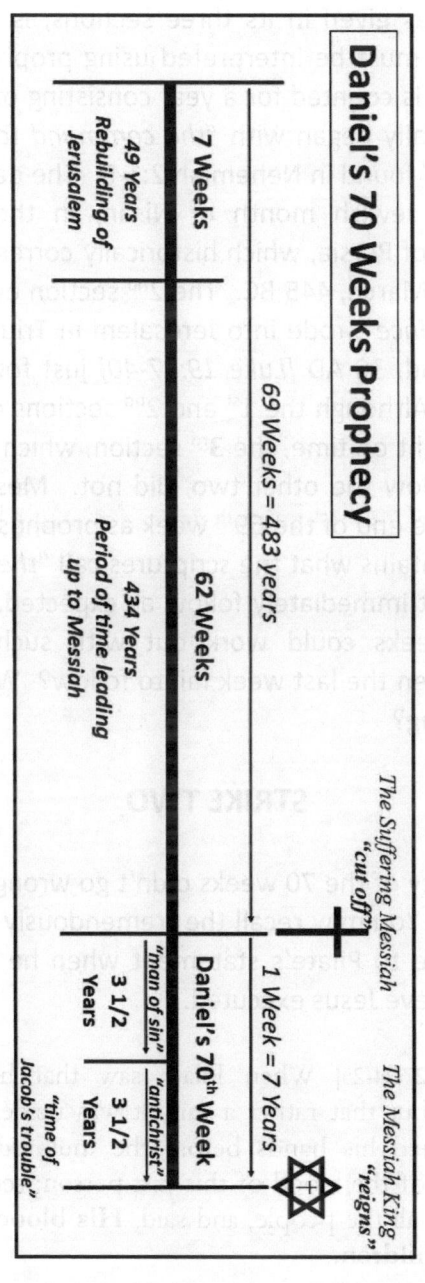

Daniel's 70 Weeks Prophecy

7 Weeks

49 Years
Rebuilding of
Jerusalem

69 Weeks = 483 years

62 Weeks

434 Years
Period of time leading
up to Messiah

The Suffering Messiah
"cut off"

The Messiah King
"reigns"

1 Week = 7 Years

Daniel's 70th Week

"man of sin"
3 1/2
Years

"antichrist"
3 1/2
Years

"time of
Jacob's trouble"

This prophecy, as given in its three sections, is depicted in the above chart. It must be interpreted using prophetic chronology where each day is counted for a year consisting of 360 days. The 1st section officially began with *"the command to restore and to build Jerusalem"* found in Nehemiah 2:1-6. The date given in that passage is the Jewish month of Nisan, in the 20th year of Artaxerxes king of Persia, which historically corresponds to about the 13th day of March, 445 BC. The 2nd section ends when Jesus, *"Messiah the Prince"*, rode into Jerusalem in Triumphal Entry on Sunday, April 2nd, 30 AD *[Luke 19:37-40]* just four days prior to His crucifixion. Although the 1st and 2nd sections of the prophecy were fulfilled right on time, the 3rd section, which was apparently supposed to follow the other two, did not. Messiah the prince was cut off at the end of the 69th week as prophesied but the 70th week, which contains what the scriptures call *"the time of Jacob's trouble"*, did not immediately follow as expected. How is it that the first 69 weeks could work out with such mathematical precision and then the last week fail to follow? What happened? What went wrong?

STRIKE TWO

Daniel's prophecy of the 70 weeks didn't go wrong, but Israel did. Let me explain. You may recall the tremendously sad reply Israel gave in response to Pilate's statement when he saw they were determined to have Jesus executed.

> [Matthew 27:24-25] When Pilate saw that he could prevail nothing, but that rather a tumult was made, he took water, and washed his hands before the multitude, saying, I am innocent of the blood of this just person: see ye to it. Then answered all the people, and said, **His blood be on us, and on our children.**

Their response was one that grieved the very heart of God and would have incurred His righteous wrath if it were not for the prevailing intercessory prayer of their rejected King as He hung on the cross, bearing their sin.

> [Luke 23:34] Then said Jesus, **Father, forgive them; for they know not what they do**.

Honoring the request of His obedient Son who was languishing near death, the Father willingly granted His chosen people, Israel, another opportunity to receive the kingdom that He so eagerly wanted to give them. Perhaps they would yet become the light to the world God intended them to be when He chose their patriarchal fathers to bring forth both His word and the messianic blood line.

After His resurrection, the Lord Jesus Christ addressed the issue of Israel's long-awaited kingdom with His disciples.

> [Acts 1:6-7] **When they therefore were come together, they asked of him, saying, Lord, wilt thou at this time restore again the kingdom to Israel?** And he said unto them, **It is not for you to know** the times or the seasons, which the Father hath put in his own power.

The apostles were interested in the restoration of the physical kingdom of Israel, and rightly so, for it had been given to old father Abraham and his descendants by an unconditional promise, and therefore it could not rightfully belong to anyone else. But Jesus had sidestepped the question, because although the kingdom was ready for them, Israel was not yet ready for the kingdom. A truly righteous King had been found, and He had proven Himself worthy of the throne, even unto death. But Israel needed to be willing to accept the King and join Him in His righteousness. So on the day of Pentecost, the disciples, having believed on their Messiah King and having been filled with the Holy Ghost, preached to the nation of Israel the news of the recently fulfilled prophetic events regarding their promised Messiah.

> [Acts 2:29-36] Men and brethren, let me freely speak unto you of the patriarch **David**, that he is both dead and buried, and his sepulchre [tomb] is with us unto this day. Therefore **being a prophet, and knowing that God had sworn with an oath to him, that of the fruit of his loins, according to the flesh, he would raise up Christ to sit on his throne;** He seeing this before **spake of the resurrection of Christ, that his soul was not left in hell, neither his flesh did see corruption. This Jesus hath God raised up,** whereof we all are witnesses. Therefore being by the right hand of God exalted, and having received of the Father the promise of the Holy Ghost, he hath shed forth this, which ye now see and hear. For David is not ascended into the heavens: but he saith himself, The LORD said unto my Lord, Sit thou on my right hand, Until I make thy foes thy footstool. **Therefore let all the house of Israel know assuredly, that God hath made that same Jesus, whom ye have crucified, both Lord and Christ.**

All the dwellers at Jerusalem were well aware of the crucifixion of Christ, for it had been a public spectacle. A great miracle worker, who many had proclaimed as the Messiah, had been crucified. Now they were being made aware of His victory over the grave, having risen in resurrection power and no longer subject to the power of death. He had risen as a righteous King that would be able to hold on to the throne of the physical kingdom, Israel's kingdom, the kingdom of heaven, FOREVER. The problem that had long plagued Israel, its inability to maintain possession of their kingdom, had finally been solved. But it seemed that a new snag had arisen in the process. Not only had they rejected and crucified their long-awaited King, but he was no longer on earth to sit on the throne of David. He had reportedly gone to heaven.

[Acts 2:34-35] For David is not ascended into the heavens: but he saith himself, The LORD said unto my Lord, **Sit thou on my right hand, Until I make thy foes thy footstool.**

Jesus had ascended into heaven and was sitting at the right hand of God. In light of this new development, the people hearing Peter's message asked the apostles a purely logical question.

[Acts 2:37] Now when they heard this, they were pricked in their heart, and said unto Peter and to the rest of the apostles, **Men and brethren, what shall we do?**

The question was a simple one. What do we do now? In other words, they're saying, *"It's pretty clear that we messed up, so how do we fix this mistake?"* And the answer comes back just as simple.

[Acts 2:38-40] Then Peter said unto them, **Repent, and be baptized every one of you in the name of Jesus Christ for the remission of sins, and ye shall receive the gift of the Holy Ghost.** For the promise is unto you, and to your children, and to all that are afar off, even as many as the Lord our God shall call. And with many other words did he testify and exhort, saying, **Save yourselves from this untoward generation.**

The answer is essentially threefold. First, they were to repent and make a public declaration acknowledging the truth that Jesus is both Lord and Christ, Israel's Messiah King. This was accomplished by being baptized in His name. Second, a promise was given to those who obey that they would receive the gift of God's Holy Ghost. And third, they were required to separate themselves from the *"un-toward"* people, that is, the people who would not go towards the Lord Jesus and accept Him regarding this new development in the advancing plan of God.

None of the New Testament had yet been written, but the Apostles preached what they knew. Jesus was going to return one day, and Israel's kingdom would be restored. There was a need for the nation to repent and get ready for His return.

> [Acts 3:17-23] And now, brethren, I wot that through ignorance ye did it [kill the Messiah], as did also your rulers. But those things, which God before had shewed by the mouth of all his prophets, that Christ should suffer, he hath so fulfilled. **Repent ye therefore, and be converted, that your sins may be blotted out, when the times of refreshing shall come from the presence of the Lord; And he shall send Jesus Christ, which before was preached unto you: Whom the heaven must receive until the times of restitution of all things**, which God hath spoken by the mouth of all his holy prophets since the world began. For Moses truly said unto the fathers, A prophet shall the Lord your God raise up unto you of your brethren, like unto me; him shall ye hear in all things whatsoever he shall say unto you. And it shall come to pass, that **every soul, which will not hear that prophet, shall be destroyed from among the people.**

The book of Acts chronicles the development of the Christian church as God's plan transitioned from Old Testament Judaism to

New Testament Christianity. A very brief outline of that history is as follows.

> **THE ACTS OF THE APOSTLES:**
> **Chapter 1** – Jesus ascended into heaven
> **Chapter 2** – the Holy Ghost was given and Christ's resurrection was preached
> **Chapter 3** – the apostles preached Christ's resurrection and that he would return
> **Chapter 4** – Israel's religious leaders commanded the apostles to stop teaching in the name of Jesus
> **Chapter 5** – the apostles were beaten for continuing to teach about Jesus anyway
> **Chapter 6** – the first deacons of the New Testament church were chosen
> **Chapter 7** – Israel's leaders rejected their Messiah and had deacon Stephen stoned to death for preaching Jesus Christ

Chapter seven is a pivotal chapter in the book of Acts. It is in this chapter that Israel's leadership officially rejected their resurrected King; consequently, the offer of the kingdom was withdrawn. The King was ready, but His subjects (Israel) were not. Up to this point Daniel's prophecy of the 70 weeks was fulfilled with meticulous precision. But here the prophetic clock stops and gets reset. The 70th week, which contains *"the Time of Jacob's Trouble"* and by all accounts should have immediately followed the 69thweek, did not proceed as expected. The 70th week, which would have lasted seven years [exactly 2,520 days] was intended to culminate in the return of the Messiah King to deliver Israel from the opposing enemy nations and institute Earth's 1,000-year Sabbath kingdom of rest.

[Jeremiah 30:7-10] **Alas! for that day is great, so that none is like it: it is even the time of Jacob's trouble; but he shall be saved out of it.** For it shall come to pass **in that day,** saith the LORD of hosts, that I will break his yoke from off thy neck, and will burst thy bonds, and strangers shall no more serve themselves of him: But they shall serve the LORD their God, and David their king, whom I will raise up unto them. Therefore fear thou not, O my servant Jacob, saith the LORD; neither be dismayed, O Israel: for, lo, I will save thee from afar, and thy seed from the land of their captivity; and **Jacob shall return, and shall be in rest,** and be quiet, and none shall make him afraid.

I have previously mentioned the implication of a 2,000-year era existing within the first and second verses of Genesis chapter one. I pointed out how such a period of time would not only be consistent with the biblical doctrine of the present earth's creation but also fit perfectly with the offer of the 1,000-year Sabbath rest of Christ's kingdom being preached during His first coming. And it would explain Adam being created to exercise dominion in what was previously Lucifer's territory. Moreover, it explains how spiritual beings were present when the foundation of the earth was laid, and it provides a more reasonable amount of time for Lucifer to become dissatisfied with his position and subsequent decision to formulate a rebellion. The following chart reflects this understanding.

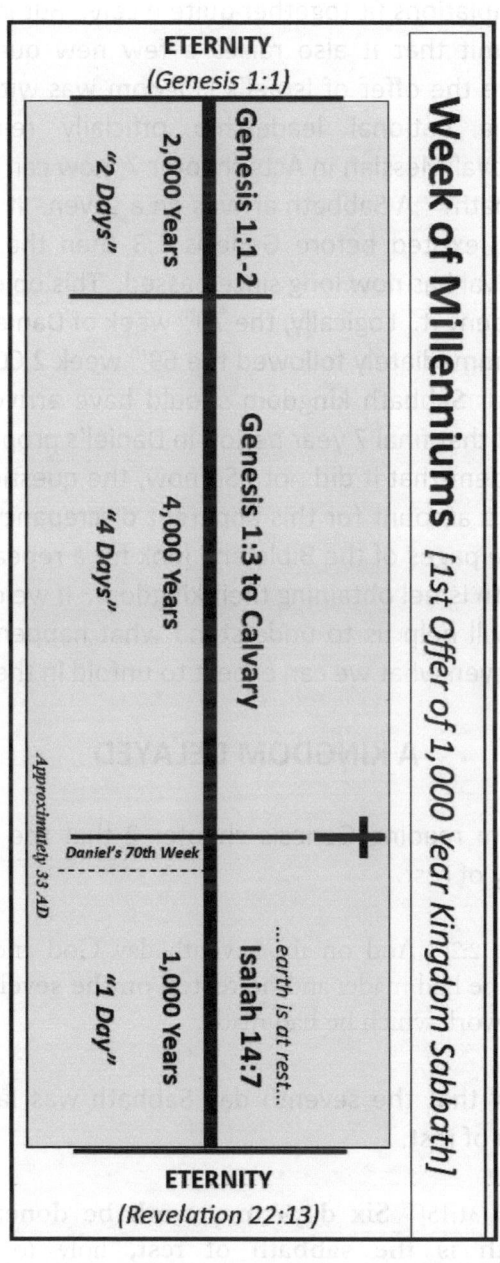

These contemplations fit together quite nicely. But in all honesty, I have to admit that it also raises a few new questions. For instance, since the offer of Israel's kingdom was withdrawn as a result of the national leadership officially rejecting their resurrected royal Messiah in Acts chapter 7, how can the kingdom still be a Sabbath? A Sabbath arrives on a seven. If a 2,000-year block of time existed before Genesis 1:3 then the time of the Sabbath's arrival has now long since passed. This objection is true and I cannot deny it. Logically, the 70th week of Daniel's prophecy should have immediately followed the 69th week 2,000 years ago. The 1,000-year Sabbath kingdom should have arrived upon the completion of that final 7 year period in Daniel's prophecy and yet it is quite evident that it did not. So now, the question becomes, how are we to account for this apparent discrepancy? I suggest we turn to the pages of the Bible and look for a repeating pattern associated with Israel obtaining their kingdom. If we can find such a pattern it will help us to understand what happened long ago and perhaps even what we can expect to unfold in the future.

A KINGDOM DELAYED

We know from reading Genesis chapter 2 that the seventh day was God's day of rest.

> [Genesis 2:2] And on the seventh day God ended his work which he had made; and **he rested on the seventh day** from all his work which he had made.

And we know that the seventh day Sabbath was later given to Israel as a day of rest.

> [Exodus 31:15] **Six days may work be done; but in the seventh is the sabbath of rest,** holy to the LORD:

whosoever doeth any work in the Sabbath day, he shall surely be put to death.

I have previously discussed the advancing pattern of Sabbaths God established through Israel's holy days as He built up to the 1,000-year kingdom of Christ in the seventh millennium. Though their entrance was to be a time of warfare before they entered into rest, let's consider what Israel's past attempt to enter the kingdom looked like. For instance, what happened under the leadership of Moses? A cursory reading of the Bible will reveal that after Israel left Egypt they were supposed to enter the *"promised land"*, but it did not work out as smoothly as Moses might have anticipated. You may recall how twelve spies were sent to search out the land and bring back a report on what they saw so a plan of conquest could be developed. The land was indeed good, just like Moses had said, but there was a problem. A race of evil giants lived there and their presence caused ten of Israel's twelve spies to give an evil report of the land. Their fearful report discouraged the hearts of the people so they did not want to enter.

[Numbers 13:32-14:4] And they [the ten spies] brought up an evil report of the land which they had searched unto the children of Israel, saying, **The land, through which we have gone to search it, is a land that eateth up the inhabitants thereof**; and all the people that we saw in it are men of a great stature. And **there we saw the giants, the sons of Anak, which come of the giants: and we were in our own sight as grasshoppers,** and so we were in their sight. And all the congregation lifted up their voice, and cried; and the people wept that night. And all the children of Israel murmured against Moses and against Aaron: and the whole congregation said unto them, Would God that we had died in the land of Egypt! or would God we had died in this wilderness! And wherefore hath the LORD brought us unto this land, to fall by the sword, that our wives and our children should be a prey? were it not better for us to return into Egypt? And **they said one to another, Let us make a captain, and let us return into Egypt.**

Two of the twelve spies, Joshua and Caleb, were of a different heart in the matter.

[Numbers 14:6-9] And Joshua the son of Nun, and Caleb the son of Jephunneh, which were of them that searched the land, rent their clothes: And they spake unto all the company of the children of Israel, saying, The land, which we passed through to search it, is an exceeding good land. **If the LORD delight in us, then he will bring us into this land, and give it us; a land which floweth with milk and honey. Only rebel not ye against the LORD,** neither fear ye the people of the land; for they are bread for us: their defence is departed from them, and the LORD is with us: fear them not.

The end result of Israel's national faithlessness was that the offer of the forthcoming kingdom was withdrawn. The opportunity to obtain the long-awaited kingdom had passed. God was their King [1 Samuel 8:7], but they had no faith in Him even though they had seen His many miracles.

[Numbers 14:22-23] Because all **those men which have seen my glory, and my miracles,** which I did in Egypt and in the wilderness, and have tempted me now these ten times, and have not hearkened to my voice; Surely **they shall not see the land which I sware unto their fathers,** neither shall any of them that provoked me see it:

GOING ONCE, GOING TWICE...

This was Israel's first attempt to enter the kingdom but it ended in failure. It would be forty long years before they would get another shot at it. But when the opportunity did finally arise Joshua was still present and ready to command their armies. Moses was Israel's undisputed leader but Joshua had apparently been Israel's captain since the time they left Egypt, or at least nearly so. Joshua led the troops in the battle against the Amalekites [Exodus 17:9]; went up Mount Sinai with Moses when he got the 10 Commandments [Exodus 24:14]; entered the Tabernacle with Moses when no one else was permitted [Exodus 33:11]; was one of the spies that searched the land [Numbers 14:38]; was anointed by Moses as the next national leader [Numbers 27:18-20]; and he ended up being the man that actually led Israel in their conquest of the promised land [Deuteronomy 1:38]. Joshua was truly a great captain but he encountered a far greater captain than he when they entered the Promised Land. Joshua met the Captain of the LORD's host, the Lord Jesus Christ.

[Joshua 5:15] And **the captain of the LORD'S host** said unto Joshua, Loose thy shoe from off thy foot; for the place whereon thou standest is holy. And Joshua did so.

We have seen that even though Joshua would have led them into the Promised Land when it was first offered, their faithlessness prevented them from entering. The book of Hebrews spells this out for us.

[Hebrews 3:17-19] But with whom was he [God] grieved forty years? was it not with them that had sinned, whose carcases fell in the wilderness? And to whom sware he that they should not enter into his rest, but to them that believed not? **So we see that they could not enter in because of unbelief.**

Now that we see the picture, let us compare it to the offer of the kingdom at Christ's first coming. As previously mentioned, forty years later Israel did eventually enter the Promised Land under Joshua but that wasn't the end of their troubles. They seemed unable to maintain possession of the kingdom. Good kings are apparently quite rare and even the best earthly rulers have some serious chinks in their breastplate of righteousness. Accordingly, God stepped up to solve the problem. He took upon himself the form of a man and lived a perfectly righteous life clear to the very end. Here was the much needed incorruptible, perfect King. He had overcome sin and death and rose again in eternal resurrection power. Moreover, during His earthly ministry Christ performed miracles of unprecedented magnitude, and His detractors admitted it.

> [John 11:47] Then gathered the chief priests and the Pharisees a council, and said, **What do we? for this man doeth many miracles.**

Yet even though the *"many miracles"* He performed validated His claims of divine authority, the people still refused to believe.

> [John 12:37] But **though he had done so many miracles before them, yet they believed not on him:**

Finally, the right King had arrived and He was offering Israel the kingdom of heaven once again, but there was one prerequisite, and it shouldn't have been too difficult. All they had to do was accept Him and His righteousness and the long-awaited Kingdom would be theirs.

> [Matthew 6:33] But **seek ye first the kingdom of God, and his righteousness;** and all these things shall be added unto you.

Alas, it seems that one prerequisite was apparently one too many. Jesus was rejected and crucified like a common criminal. And though the Son of God was shamefully mistreated, the Father still gave Israel an opportunity to obtain their kingdom. The apostles faithfully preached Christ to the nation on Pentecost and continued to do so during the weeks and months that followed. However the apostles were unable to reach the hearts of Israel's national leaders. Ultimately, the offer was rejected, and faithful Stephen became Christianity's first martyr in Acts chapter seven. Israel of old did not enter the kingdom under Moses because of their unbelief. Many centuries later, the Lord Jesus Christ, the One whom the scriptures call the *"prophet like unto Moses"*, had finally arrived, and Israel again failed to enter and for the very same reason – UNBELIEF. The pattern had repeated and the offer of the physical kingdom was once again put on hold.

Joshua [Hebrew to English] and Jesus [Greek to English] are the same name; both mean *"Jehovah is Salvation"*.

> [Matthew 1:21] And she shall bring forth a son, and **thou shalt call his name JESUS: for he shall save** his people from their sins.

And we have seen, Joshua was Israel's captain, but then, so is Jesus!

> [Hebrews 2:10] For it became him, for whom are all things, and by whom are all things, in bringing many sons unto glory, to make **the captain of their salvation** perfect through sufferings.

Israel's first offer to enter the kingdom under Joshua was a disaster and so was their first offer under the Lord Jesus Christ, their TRUE Joshua. But God is not finished with Israel. And in like manner, as it happened in the Old Testament, so again will the offer of the kingdom be extended to Israel in the future, and they will accept it.   However, this time Israel will not get by with a mere forty-year delay like they did in the past. This time the postponement will be more akin to forty Jubilees: in other words, 40 Jubilee's x 50 years per Jubilee = 2,000 years.   And if appearances are any indication, we are approaching that time at an accelerated pace. We can now observe a rapidly changing world where the stage is being set for the final drama to unfold.

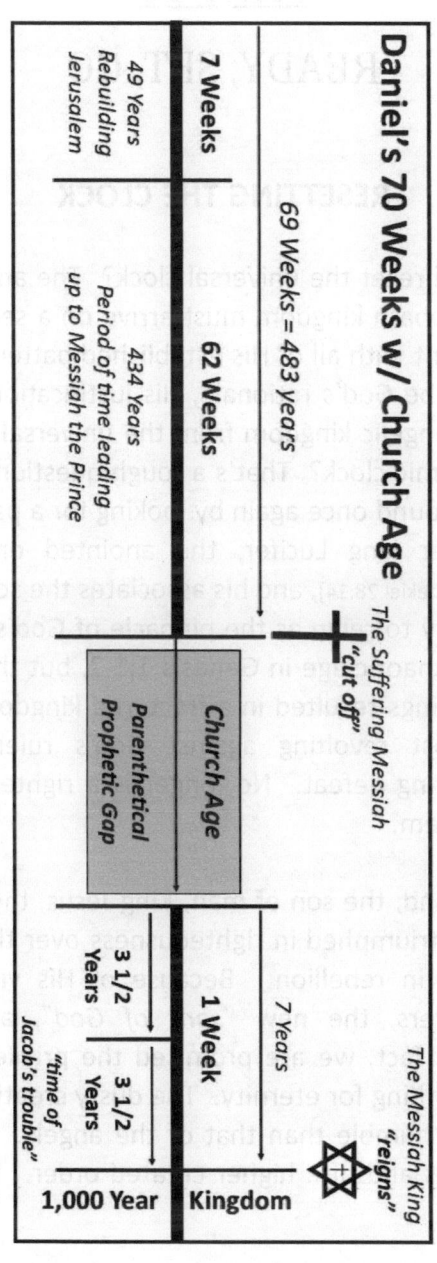

PART 10

READY, SET, GO

RESETTING THE CLOCK

Why would God reset the universal clock? The answer is simple. Because the Sabbath kingdom must arrive on a seven in order to remain consistent with all of His established patterns. That being so, what might be God's rationale, His justification, for dropping 2,000 years of angelic kingdom from the universal count in order to reset the cosmic clock? That's a tough question but maybe an answer can be found once again by looking for a pattern. We can see that former king Lucifer, the anointed one among the heavenly host [Ezekiel 28:14], and his associates the sons of God, had their opportunity to reign as the pinnacle of God's created order during the pre-chaotic age in Genesis 1:1-2, but their free will as independent beings resulted in a fractured kingdom with part of the angelic host revolting against God's rulership and the offenders suffering defeat. No longer is a righteous king to be found among them.

On the other hand, the son of man, King Jesus, the anointed one of Adam's race triumphed in righteousness over the temptations that can result in rebellion. Because of His victory the true Christian believers, the new *"sons of God"*, are more than overcomers. In fact, we are promised the privilege of reigning with our Saviour King for eternity. The dusty creation of man was no doubt more humble than that of the angels. They truly are mighty creatures and of a higher created order. But no created

being is higher than the Creator, and it is He that condescended to
our low estate in order to raise us up.

> [Hebrews 2:6-9] But one in a certain place testified, saying,
> What is man, that thou art mindful of him? Or the son of
> man, that thou visitest him? **Thou madest him a little
> lower than the angels**; thou crownedst him with glory and
> honour, and didst set him over the works of thy hands: Thou
> hast put all things in subjection under his feet. For in that he
> put all in subjection under him, he left nothing that is not put
> under him. **But now we see not yet all things put under
> him. But we see Jesus, who was made a little lower than
> the angels for the suffering of death, crowned with glory
> and honour**; that he by the grace of God should taste death
> for every man.

The first group of created beings, the angelic host of heaven,
officially lost their exalted status when Jesus Christ the son of man
triumphed over sin. It seems their segment of history has been
removed from God's reckoning. It's as if He reset the clock of
creation to the moment when the Earth was resurrected from the
formless void of Genesis 1:2, which void resulted from Lucifer's
attempted coup. He has in essence turned over the hourglass of
history and now the sands of time have begun to flow from the
re-creation we find in Genesis 1:3. Because of Christ's victory, the
kingdom of heaven now rightfully belongs to the descendants of
Adam (the new sons of God) which are those who have believed
on their sinless King. Jesus, the son of God/victorious son of man,
is both Lord and Christ. It is therefore fitting that the biblical
timeline should now be reckoned according to the dispensation of
things concerning the sons of man/sons of God as well.

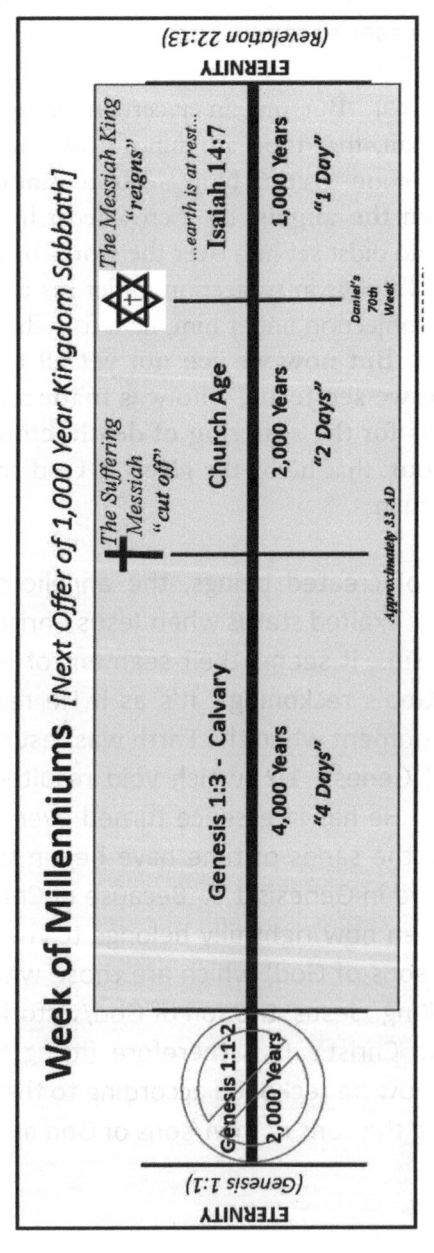

THE CHURCH AGE

For nearly 2,000 years the gospel of Jesus Christ has been preached to the lost souls of mankind's masses. Many have been saved but regrettably many more have perished while being lost and undone, in the world without hope and without God. Jesus Himself said that salvation belonged only to the few who would seek the narrow way.

> [Matthew 7:13-14] Enter ye in at the strait gate: for wide is the gate, and broad is the way, that leadeth to destruction, and many there be which go in thereat: Because **strait is the gate, and narrow is the way, which leadeth unto life, and few there be that find it.**

If the pattern of the *many* through the broad way verses the *few* who enter the narrow way holds true even among celestial beings, one would have to wonder how many of the angels took the path to perdition with Lucifer in his foolish ambition to try and usurp the throne of God. No doubt some people would say that He took a third of the angels with him when he fell, and they would cite Revelation 12 as the proof text.

> [Revelation 12:3-4] And there appeared another wonder in heaven; and behold **a great red dragon,** having seven heads and ten horns, and seven crowns upon his heads. And **his tail drew the third part of the stars of heaven,** and did cast them to the earth: and the dragon stood before the woman which was ready to be delivered, for to devour <u>her child</u> as soon as it was born.

Many people teach Revelation chapter twelve in the past tense. They suppose that the battle between Michael and Satan mentioned in the passage happened 6,000 years ago when Satan rebelled. They believe that the child mentioned in the passage is the Lord Jesus Christ Who was incarnate 2,000 years ago, and it's easy to see why they might think so. The problem is that the chapter is filled with prophecies about things that will happen in the future, just like the rest of John's Revelation. Consequently, it's impossible to view it as a reference to the birth of Christ without destroying the continuity of the chapter. Truthfully, some parts of Revelation are difficult to unravel and this may well be one of those places, for if the passage speaks of the future then not only is the identity of the child unknown, but the third part of the angels mentioned in the chapter are yet to fall. If that be the case, it seems the majority of angels may not have done any better with their free will than humanity has fared. They may have experienced just as many losses as mankind will ultimately suffer. Time will tell. In the meantime, the church age is drawing to a close and all indications are that the time of *"the end"* is rapidly approaching.

> [Daniel 12:4] But thou, O Daniel, shut up the words, and seal the book, even to <u>the time of the end</u>: **many shall run to and fro, and knowledge shall be increased.**

The past 150 years represent only 2 ½% percent of the 6,000 years of recorded human history from Genesis 1:3 to today. During the last century and a half the modernization of travel has increased not only the number of travelers in orders of magnitude, but it has also increased the pace of travel to staggering speeds. Man is no longer limited to traveling about 20 miles per day on horseback as he had been for the previous 5,850 plus years. We now routinely drive our cars 70 miles in an hour. Bullet trains are available that run 200 miles an hour. Passenger jets can zip through the sky at 500 MPH, the supersonic SR-71

Blackbird hit speeds of 2,193 MPH in 1976, and NASA's X43A Scramjet can clip off over 7,350 MPH. If that's not enough to lay claim to Daniel's end time prophecy, the US Space Shuttles managed to orbit the earth at an incredible 17,500 MPH before the fleet was retired in 2011. In other words, travel speeds have increased by a factor of 875 times.

Not only do many *"go to and fro"* like never before, but knowledge has increased exponentially as well. It has been shown that over 95% of everything man has ever invented has come into being in the past 100 years. Today, vast numbers of inventions are devised by simply marrying technologies that have not been previously joined. Artificial Intelligence has become a reality with the creation of computer programs that are capable of learning and rewriting their own code, and the reality of quantum computing is now coming into sight. In his 10/16/2019 article *"Quantum Computing Is Poised to Change Everything"*, Ray Schroeder reported on Google's new *"qubit"* computer's ability to crack the code of a sophisticated random number generator, saying:

> *"Google's 53-qubit computer reached computing supremacy, and from now on the world will never be the same."*

> *"Google's quantum computer was reportedly able to solve a calculation -- proving the randomness of numbers produced by a random number generator -- in 3 minutes and 20 seconds that would take the world's fastest traditional supercomputer, 'Summit', around 10,000 years. This effectively means that the calculation cannot be*

> *performed by a traditional computer, making Google the first to demonstrate quantum supremacy."*
>
> *"That's astounding -- 200 seconds compared to 10,000 years."*
>
> *"The IBM Summit computer at Oak Ridge Labs is no slacker; it boasts specs of "a peak performance of 200 petaflops, or 200,000 trillion calculations per second."*

If this doesn't qualify as the prophetic fulfillment of knowledge being increased then it's doubtful that man will ever attain such a lofty status. Surely the 70th week of Daniel's prophecy is just over the horizon, and the *"time of Jacob's trouble"* is quickly approaching. Could the great tribulation really be more than just a tick or two away on the world clock?

WHOSE TEMPLE IS THIS ANYWAY?

Biblical prophecy has an unequalled and flawless track record. Prophecy is one of the many infallible proofs that the Bible is the authentic word of God. How could anyone other than God truly know the end from the beginning? There are people who occasionally get a prediction or two correct, and when they do, the world marvels and fawns all over them. Yet it seems that relatively few people are willing to acknowledge the Bible's predictive superiority. Regardless, the scriptures are very clear; the Temple Mount will once again have a Jewish Temple sitting on it, and it will be there before the middle of Daniel's 70th week arrives. Nearly two thousand years have passed since the previous temple was destroyed, but the obsession with the Temple and the desire to build it yet again continues with a fevered pitch. The renowned *Temple Institute* has labored diligently to research and recreate the many implements needed for the institution of proper Jewish worship so that all will be ready once the third Temple is constructed. And there is ONLY one place it can be built, on the threshing floor of Ornan the Jebusite, with the Foundation Stone located within the Holy of Holies. I covered this previously in *The Location of the Jewish Temple*. And as you may recall, there is an obvious obstruction prohibiting the building of the third Temple; it's called the *"Dome of the Rock"*. But when God is ready for things to happen, He has a way of removing everything that stands in the way of His plan. No one knows for sure how the Lord will bring about the dome's removal. It may fall in an earthquake, or a freak storm may destroy it, or for that matter it may wind up as unintentional collateral damage in a botched Islamic missile attack. Time will tell. But the hard cold truth is that it must come down for the Jewish Temple to go up.

But when the Jews finally get to rebuild their Temple, what will it look like? That's a good question, because although the scriptures speak often about the temple, and give many details of its making, there is insufficient information to construct it. We know that King David had plans made for Solomon to use in the construction of the first Temple, and it was necessary for Solomon to precisely follow the plans as God gave them. Why? Because, as I have shown, God uses patterns to teach His eternal truths; thus, the patterns are of great importance.

> [1 Chronicles 28:19] All this, said David, **the LORD made me understand in writing by his hand upon me, even all the works of this <u>pattern</u>.**

The problem is that those blueprints or patterns no longer exist. According to the Temple Institute it will only take a year to eighteen months to build the Temple with modern building techniques, significantly shorter than the forty-six years it took to rebuild the second temple. Still, there's the nagging question: *"In what manner shall the third Temple be built? What pattern will it follow?"* There are two conceivable solutions to this dilemma, which are:

> 1) It can be built after the pattern of Messiah's Temple in Ezekiel chapters 40-46.
>
> 2) Or, it can be built after the pattern of Herod's Temple in the first century A.D.

This being the case, let's consider both options.

First is Ezekiel's description of Messiah's Temple, but there is a major problem associated with this option. The problem is the same as that of trying to rebuild Solomon's Temple. There are many details given but they are insufficient to actually accomplish a building project. However, it is conceivable that this obstacle could be overcome if a couple of God's prophets were to arise that could supply the proper specifications where needed in order to fill in the missing details that are as yet unexplained in Ezekiel's passages. There is also the possibility that a High Priest could use the Urim and Thummim to provide the missing information as was done in the past. We find an example of this in the book of Nehemiah where certain priests could not prove their genealogies and it was determined that they would not be considered for the priesthood until a priest with *"Urim and Thummim"* had been consulted.

[Nehemiah 7:65] And the Tirshatha said unto them, **that they should not eat of the most holy things, till there stood up a priest with Urim and Thummim.**

We also know that at one point King Saul attempted to use this form of information gathering but God refused to respond to him.

[1 Samuel 28:6] And when Saul enquired of the LORD, the LORD answered him not, neither by dreams, **nor by Urim,** nor by prophets.

This method of obtaining revelation is not clearly understood today, but it was without doubt ordained by God for the benefit of the people of Israel. The Lord specifically instituted the use of it under the leadership of Joshua, Moses' successor.

[Numbers 27:18-21] And the LORD said unto Moses, Take thee Joshua the son of Nun, a man in whom is the spirit, and lay thine hand upon him; And set him before Eleazar the priest, and before all the congregation; and give him a charge in their sight. And thou shalt put some of thine honour upon him, that all the congregation of the children of Israel may be obedient. And **he shall stand before Eleazar the priest, who shall ask counsel for him after the judgment of Urim before the LORD:** at his word shall they go out, and at his word they shall come in, both he, and all the children of Israel with him, even all the congregation.

Though we can see there are methods whereby the construction of the Temple described in Ezekiel could be completed, it could only occur if the needed prophets or priests were <u>available and empowered</u> to perform the vital prophetic functions. It has been a very long time since a recognized prophet or priest has stood on the Temple Mount to proclaim God's holy words to the children of

Israel. Consequently, the accessibility of such prophetic men is a prerequisite Israel cannot rely upon to be available when the opportunity to build the temple finally arises.

The second possibility for the construction of the third Temple is to follow the pattern of Herod's Temple from two thousand years ago. Oddly enough there is a great deal more information available for that pattern than there is for Ezekiel's. Consequently, it has been decided that the third Temple will be built following the pattern of Herod's; with the understanding that when Messiah comes, He will build His Messianic Temple according to the pattern found in Ezekiel. Messiah will know and provide all the details which are currently lacking in Ezekiel's description and will be able to erect at that time, what will then be, the fourth Jewish Temple.

The decision to follow Herod's pattern is a very revealing development because the scriptures plainly state that antichrist will ultimately walk into the third Temple, sit on the ONLY seat in the house, the Mercy Seat (which is essentially God's throne) and proclaim himself to be God.

> [2 Thessalonians 2:3-4] Let no man deceive you by any means: for that day shall not come, except there come a falling away first, and that man of sin be revealed, **the son of perdition**; Who opposeth and exalteth himself above all that is called God, or that is worshipped; so that **he as God sitteth in the temple of God, shewing himself that he is God.**

But is there a previously established pattern connected with this line of thinking? In fact, there is. Paradoxically the very same person who helped rebuild the second Temple, Herod the Great, was also the person who ordered the killing of all the Jewish male children less than two years of age in Bethlehem. It was an attempt to try and kill the Jewish Messiah, Jesus.

> [Matthew 2:16] Then **Herod**, when he saw that he was mocked of the wise men, was exceeding wroth, and sent forth, and **slew all the children that were in Bethlehem, and in all the coasts thereof, from two years old and under,** according to the time which he had diligently enquired of the wise men.

Since both Herod and the antichrist are persecutors of the Jews, it seems quite appropriate that the third Temple would be built by following the pattern of Herod's namesake. What better place for the antichrist to proclaim himself God than in a likeness of the Temple named after Herod, who attempted to kill Christ by murdering a large number of innocent Jewish children. I'm sure Satan will enjoy the irony. More ironic is the realization that the Jewish people will actually build it for him, and he will vigorously persecute them for their passionate efforts. But notice where we are; once again we have arrived at the Temple Mount and it is the singular focus of Satan's plan. He simply cannot stay away from the place. Apparently, his heart cries out, *"I MUST HAVE IT"*.

There is yet another, even more ancient pattern of these things which can be partially found in the Old Testament scriptures. We know that Solomon's temple, the first Temple, was built around 1,000 BC and that it was destroyed by Babylon about 400 years later. The book of Ezra contains the account of the effort to rebuild the Temple of the LORD in Jerusalem. The authorization to begin the building project was given by Cyrus.

> [Ezra 1:2-3] Thus saith Cyrus king of Persia, The LORD God of heaven hath given me all the kingdoms of the earth; and he

hath charged me to build him an house at Jerusalem, which is in Judah. Who is there among you of all his people? his God be with him, and let him **go up to Jerusalem, which is in Judah, and build the house of the LORD God of Israel,** (he is the God,) which is in Jerusalem.

Ezra lists the leaders who volunteered to go to Jerusalem and help with the building of the Temple. Moreover, he lists the number of people that the leaders bring with them. There is one leader in particular that I will bring to your attention. His name is Adonikam, which some interpret to mean *"whom the Lord sets up"* or *"my Lord has risen"*. But there is also another interpretation which says his name means *"Lord of the rebellion"* because the "rising up" is accompanied by a negative connotation making it a rebellious rising. And anyone who pays any attention to biblical numbers at all will immediately see that the context lends itself most appropriately to the translation *"Lord of the rebellion"*. In the following passage we are given the number of people who returned with Adonikam.

[Ezra 2:13] The children of **Adonikam, six hundred sixty and six.** [666]

Adonikam is shown to accompany those people who are intent on rebuilding the Jewish Temple; and this *"Lord of the rebellion"* is directly connected to the satanic number 666.

The last time Adonikam shows up in the scriptures we find him in the book of Nehemiah when the Jews are rebuilding the city walls of Jerusalem which had been destroyed by warfare. This passage is nearly identical with the aforementioned verse in Ezra; but there is one very slight difference.

> [Nehemiah 7:18] The children of **Adonikam, six hundred threescore and seven.** [667]

Why has the number increased by one man? Why has the count changed? Is this a scribal error? If not, then who and what is the significance of this additional person? Who is this mysterious *"Mr X"*? If Adonikam is in fact an ancient picture of the antichrist, then prophetically there is no doubt about the identity of the extra person. The X-man would represent the seemingly all-powerful false prophet who will arrive on the scene LATER and help solidify the political power of the antichrist.

> [Revelation 13:11-18] And **I beheld another beast** coming up out of the earth; and he had two horns like a lamb, and he spake as a dragon. And he exerciseth all the power of the first beast before him, and **causeth the earth and them which dwell therein to worship the first beast,** whose deadly wound was healed. **And he doeth great wonders, so that he maketh fire come down from heaven on the earth in the sight of men,** And **deceiveth them that dwell on the earth by the means of those miracles which he had power to do** in the sight of the beast; saying to them that dwell on the earth, that they should **make an image to the beast,** which had the wound by a sword, and did live. And **he had power to give life unto the image of the beast,** that the image of the beast should both speak, and cause that as many as would not worship the image of the beast should be killed. And **he causeth all, both small and great, rich and poor, free and bond, to receive a mark** in their right hand, or in their foreheads: And that **no man might buy or**

sell, save he that had the mark, or the name of the beast, or the number of his name. Here is wisdom. Let him that hath understanding count the number of the beast: for **it is the number of a man; and his number is Six hundred threescore and six.**

If this interpretation of Adonikam and the *X-man* is correct, we can logically expect that a desecration eventually followed the initial rebuilding of the second Temple. And in fact, history tells us that it did.

Antiochus IV (175-164 BC) gave himself the surname "*Epiphanes*" which means "*the visible god*". He insisted that he and *Jupiter* were one and the same person, and he acted as though he really was Jupiter. His people called him "*Epimanes*" or "*the madman*". He was a violent persecutor of the Jews and attempted to exterminate both them and their religion. He devastated Jerusalem in 168 BC and defiled the Temple by sacrificing a pig upon the altar. Not content with that, he also set up an altar to institute the worship of the false god, Jupiter. Jewish Temple worship was forbidden, and thousands of Jewish families were sold into slavery. Moreover, every copy of the scriptures that could be found was destroyed, and anyone found in possession of a copy was slaughtered along with it. Any form of torture imaginable was used in an effort to force the Jews to renounce their faith in Jehovah God. What's really amazing is that apart from the dates, every bit of this narrative could be read into the upcoming tribulation without doing any harm at all to the prophecies found in the book of Revelation.

JACOB'S IN TROUBLE

Jesus wrote of such a day.

[Matthew 24:14-22] And **this gospel of the kingdom** shall be preached in all the world for a witness unto all nations; and then shall the end come. **When ye therefore shall see the abomination of desolation, spoken of by Daniel the prophet, stand in the holy place,** (whoso readeth, let him understand:) **Then let <u>them which be in Judaea</u> flee** into the mountains: Let him which is on the housetop not come down to take any thing out of his house: Neither let him which is in the field return back to take his clothes. And woe unto them that are with child, and to them that give suck in those days! But pray ye that your flight be not in the winter, neither on the sabbath day: **For then shall be great tribulation,** such as was not since the beginning of the world to this time, no, nor ever shall be. **And except those days should be shortened, there should no flesh be saved:** but for the elect's sake those days shall be shortened.

Unfortunately, much of *"Christianity"* has defected from the doctrinal understanding of the physical kingdom which God promised the nation of Israel. Many now operate under the presumption that God is finished with the Jews. And some modern bibles, such as the Amplified Version help them along in this doctrinal error with their sloppy translating of where Paul speaks of the Jews, saying:

[1 Thessalonians 2:15-16, AMP] [the Jews] ...killed both the Lord Jesus and the prophets, and harassed and drove us out; and [they] continue to be highly displeasing to God and [to show themselves] hostile to all people, forbidding us from speaking to the Gentiles (non-Jews) so that they may be saved. So, as always, they fill up [to the brim] the measure of their sins [allotted to them by God]. But **[God's] wrath has come upon them at last [completely and forever].**

Contrast the Amplified reading above with the KJV below.

> [1Thessalonians 2:15-16, KJV] Who both killed the Lord Jesus, and their own prophets, and have persecuted us; and they please not God, and are contrary to all men: Forbidding us to speak to the Gentiles that they might be saved, to fill up their sins alway: **for the wrath is come upon them to the uttermost.**

In case you don't see it, the difference between these two statements is quite profound. The phrase *"completely and forever"* found in the Amplified speaks of God's wrath being both complete in its severity and forever in its duration. In other words, the Jews are permanently FINISHED, which of course, is quite obviously false since they are still walking around on Earth 2,000 years later. The KJV phrase *"to the uttermost"* speaks only of the severity of the wrath on the Jews and not of the duration. Simply put, because of the Jewish people's rebellion against their Messiah King, God exposed them to EXTREME wrath as is evidenced by their continual persecution throughout history. But the punishment of the nation will not last forever. It is only a temporary interval in His dealings with them like the forty years in the wilderness. Moreover, we are specifically told by Paul that God will, without fail, be renewing His dealings with Israel in the future.

> [Romans 11:25-26] For I would not, brethren, that ye should be ignorant of this mystery, lest ye should be wise in your own conceits; that **blindness in part is happened to Israel, until the fulness of the Gentiles be come in. And so all Israel shall be saved**: as it is written, There shall come out of Sion the Deliverer, and shall turn away ungodliness from Jacob:

As if this were not enough, the apostle John also tells us of a coming time when Israel will yet again be persecuted, this time in the tribulation. In Revelation chapter seven we can read about the sealing of the 144,000, which are 12,000 male virgins from each of the twelve tribes of Israel. And seven chapters later, in chapter fourteen, we see the 144,000 standing on heavenly Mount Sion with the Lord Jesus Christ before the throne of God, having been redeemed from the earth. These are not *"spiritual Jews"*, as some gentile Christians refer to themselves. They are not *"the circumcised in heart"* [Romans 2], or *"the Israel of God"* [Galatians 6], and they are not Mormon's or Jehovah's Witnesses. They are literally from the twelve tribes of the nation of Israel to whom God has made promises and to whom He intends to keep His word. Even so, it must be noted that the tribes of Dan and Ephraim have been replaced among the names of the tribes, and in their place we find Levi and Joseph are substituted. The reasons for this are apparent in the Old Testament. Dan dove into idolatry in Judges Chapters 17 and 18 and never recovered; and regarding Ephraim, Hosea plainly says:

[Hosea 4:17] **Ephraim is joined to idols: let him alone.**

There is simply no doubt that the 144,000 are from the twelve tribes of Israel. The antichrist will persecute them just as Herod did, but he won't be satisfied with only killing the children under two years old. His ambition will be to extinguish the entire nation. As I pointed out previously, Jesus declared in Matthew 24 that the gospel of the kingdom will be preached in all the world for a witness to all nations. The persecution against Israel will force them to flee into the wilderness and for the elect's sake the days will be shortened; otherwise none of them would survive the onslaught. Those will be dark times indeed, but another pattern will repeat when Israel's true *"Joshua"*, the Messiah King, will return to defeat their enemies and lead them into the promised kingdom.

Why did I refer to Jesus the Messiah as the true Joshua? It's because an interesting phenomenon occurs in the Bible that links Jesus and Joshua together. The Hebrew name **"Yehoshua"**, which is rendered in English as *Joshua*, means *"Jehovah is Salvation"*. And when the Hebrew name *Yehoshua* is transliterated into Greek it becomes **Iesous**. It is commonly taught that the New Testament was written in ancient koine Greek, so when the Greek name *Iesous* is brought over into English it becomes the name we know as **JESUS**, which also means *"Jehovah is Salvation"*. This truth is made apparent in the prophecy concerning Christ's birth.

> [Matthew 1:21] And she shall bring forth a son, and thou shalt call his name **JESUS:** for he shall save his people from their sins.

This realization sets the stage for the amazing Bible phenomenon which now follows. Just before Stephen, who was full of the Holy Ghost, was stoned in Acts chapter seven, he made an interesting statement, saying:

> [Acts 7:44-45] Our fathers had the tabernacle of witness in the wilderness, as he had appointed, speaking unto Moses, that he should make it according to the fashion that he had seen. **Which also our fathers that came after brought in with Jesus into the possession of the Gentiles,** whom God drave out before the face of our fathers, unto the days of David;

The question arises: *"Why does this verse say that Jesus was among those who brought the Old Testament Tabernacle into the possession of the gentiles (the Promised Land) when we know that Jesus was not even born until about 1,400 years later?"* The answer is that the Greek name *Iesous* which means *Jehovah is Salvation* can ONLY be transliterated into English as *Jesus*. That Greek word CANNOT be properly brought over into English as *Joshua*. PERIOD!

So then, another question arises: Does the appearance of the word Jesus in that passage create an historical error in the King James Bible? The truth is that some people would say it does, and for that reason the modern translations seek to correct the text by altering it to read *"Joshua"* even though it's not possible to translate a Greek text that way. But what if they're wrong? What if it doesn't create an historical mistake? What if God actually knew what He was doing when He had Stephen's message written in Greek? Is there anything relevant we can discover if we look deeper into the scripture instead of just skimming the surface of the text?

As usual, there is more treasure to be found when the Bible is approached with the open eye of faith instead of a closed mind of doubt. For instance, we know that in the Old Testament the various pre-incarnate appearances of the Lord Jesus Christ are referred to as an *"Angel of the LORD"*. An interesting example of that would be His travels with them in the wilderness after the Exodus.

> [Exodus 23:20-23] Behold, **I send an Angel before thee, to keep thee in the way, and to bring thee into the place which I have prepared.** Beware of him, and obey his voice, provoke him not; for he will not pardon your transgressions: for **my name is in him.** But if thou shalt indeed obey his voice, and do all that I speak; then I will be an enemy unto

thine enemies, and an adversary unto thine adversaries. For **mine Angel shall go before thee**, and bring thee in unto the Amorites, and the Hittites, and the Perizzites, and the Canaanites, the Hivites, and the Jebusites: and I will cut them off.

This being the case, it can be truthfully said that Jesus, the Angel of the LORD, did in fact enter with them when they brought the ark of the testimony into the Promised Land. But that isn't all. Once they were in the land Joshua encountered Jesus there in a very special way. He actually met the *"Captain"* of our salvation.

> [Joshua 5:13-15] And it came to pass, when Joshua was by Jericho, that he lifted up his eyes and looked, and, behold, there stood a man over against him with his sword drawn in his hand: and Joshua went unto him, and said unto him, Art thou for us, or for our adversaries? And he said, Nay; but **as captain of the host of the LORD am I now come.** And Joshua fell on his face to the earth, and did worship, and said unto him, What saith my lord unto his servant? And **the captain of the LORD'S host said unto Joshua, Loose thy shoe from off thy foot; for the place whereon thou standest is holy.** And Joshua did so.

It appears that the unbelieving mindset of the modern translators has caused them to overlook some pretty vital information. But this isn't the end of the matter, because we have yet to discuss how the proper rendering of the word JESUS in Acts 7:45 raises a flag that draws attention to a significant pattern that is pertinent to this study. Instead of considering the word *"Jesus"* to be a mistake in the text, we should ask: *"Why did God make this passage appear, at first glance, as though it was an error? What is He trying to accomplish by this?"* The answer is simple. Joshua is presented to us as a type of Jesus Christ. Not only do both their names mean *"Jehovah is Salvation"*, but both are also *"captains"* of the Lord's people. However, this is just the beginning of the fascinating things we can learn as a result of this connection. You may remember that Moses (the law) was able to bring Israel near the Jordan River. They could see the Promised Land, but Moses couldn't take them over into the new life on the other side. Only Joshua (*Jesus*) could do that.

And we're told that when Joshua took them across that dirty, crooked, Jordan River that flowed down from the city of Adam, it was overflowing all its banks [Joshua Chapter 3]. What are we shown by this? It's an Old Testament  illustration of how the overflowing, uncleanness of mankind, which has followed humanity all the way down from Adam, prevents them from entering into and obtaining God's promises. Man cannot get to the other side without the help of Jesus who can stop the corrupt flow long enough to get a man across. Once a man makes it to the other side he must be circumcised, and his flesh is discarded. You can read about the spiritual aspects of this in Colossians Chapter 2. And after the believer is circumcised, he must be prepared to put on the full armor of God and go to war because he has not entered *"the sweet by and by"*. That comes later. The Promised Land is the place where *"the nasty now and now"* is fought out against the enemies of God, and you can read the spiritual application of this in Ephesians Chapter 6. Bondage to the world is to be replaced by battle for God's kingdom. Pretty cool so far - but there's more, because just as in Exodus Israel fled from Pharaoh, called the dragon in Ezekiel 29:3, the dragon, which is Satan, will seek to destroy Israel in the tribulation (Revelation Chapter 12). Fortunately for them, *"Jehovah is Salvation"* [Jesus] will deliver them yet again, and so the Exodus pattern is repeated in Revelation. Notice the similarities below.

> [Exodus 19:4] Ye have seen what I did unto the Egyptians, and how **I bare you on eagles' wings**, and brought you unto myself.

> [Revelation 12:14] And **to the woman** [Israel] **were given two wings of a great eagle, that she might fly into the wilderness**, into her place, where she is nourished for a time, and times, and half a time, from the face of the serpent.

All of this great truth and more is found by simply believing the Bible. What some people see as errors because of their corrupted biblical philosophy stemming from unbelief in the preservation of scripture, other people see as flags that draw their attention to greater and deeper truths. We see this phenomenon regarding the name of Jesus repeated in a slightly different way in the book of Hebrews. Again, though the text CANNOT be properly translated into English as Joshua, modern translators change it anyway, and having done so, the flag God raised to draw our attention has been removed through their misguided efforts to help God out by correcting His supposed mistakes.

> [Hebrews 4:8] For **if Jesus had given them rest,** then would he not afterward have spoken of another day.

As was previously pointed out *"rest"* is an indication of a Sabbath, and we have seen that one of the purposes of the many Sabbaths is to point towards the millennial kingdom of Christ on earth. Remember, Israel did not enter the physical Promised Land under the leadership of Moses because of their unbelief. Unfortunately, fifteen centuries later at the first coming of Christ, who was *'the prophet like unto Moses'*, they missed out on the kingdom again, and for the very same reason.

> [Hebrews 4: 4-11] For he [God] spake in a certain place of the seventh day on this wise, And **God did rest the seventh day** from all his works. And in this place again, If they shall enter into my rest. Seeing therefore it remaineth that some must enter therein, and **they to whom it was first preached entered not in because of unbelief:** Again, he limiteth a certain day, saying in David, To day, after so long a time; as it is said, To day if ye will hear his voice, harden not your hearts. For **if Jesus had given them rest, then would he not afterward have spoken of another day. There remaineth therefore a rest to the people of God.** For he that is entered into his rest, he also hath ceased from his own works, as God did from his. Let us labour therefore to enter into that rest, lest any man fall after the same example of unbelief.

When Paul, in verse 7 above, writes *"saying in David"*, he is pointing back 1,000 years to a Psalm David wrote.

> [Psalm 95:7-11] For he is our God; and we are the people of his pasture, and the sheep of his hand. **To day if ye will hear his voice, Harden not your heart**, as in the provocation, and as in the day of temptation in the wilderness: When your fathers tempted me, proved me, and saw my work. **Forty years long was I grieved with this generation,** and said, It

is a people that do err in their heart, and they have not known my ways: Unto whom **I sware in my wrath that they should not enter into my rest.**

Clearly this Psalm is referring to the Israelite exodus from Egypt and their subsequent refusal to enter the Promised Land because of fear and unbelief. That decision cost them forty years in the wilderness. In the Hebrews 4:8 passage, we see that *"Jesus" (i.e. Old Testament Joshua)* did not deliver Israel the true kingdom. He eventually brought them into a TYPE of that kingdom, but that was all. Jesus Christ is the only One that can bring them into the REAL kingdom, and that day is swiftly approaching. But first, the gospel of the kingdom will be preached throughout the world and Israel will be forced to flee into the wilderness just as they did during the Exodus and just as Jesus said they would do again in Matthew 24.

POOR SOULS

Since it's not the purpose of this book to be a commentary on the book of Revelation, I'll cover just a few of the tribulation highlights that are pertinent to our subject. At this point we know that the antichrist helps the Jews get their temple built which is quite apparently in use in Revelation 11:1. And it has been determined that it will be fashioned after the pattern of Herod's temple, who typifies the antichrist, a persecutor of the Jews [Matthew 2:16]. *The temple will be built on the only authorized location for it, the Temple Mount, which is the one piece of real estate that encompasses the primary object of Satan's desire.*

In Revelation chapter six we see the four horsemen of the apocalypse. They are 1) the Antichrist, 2) War and 3) Famine, with 4) Death & Hell following. The antichrist will enter the holy of holies and proclaim he is God [2Thessalonians 2:4]. People will be forced to take the mark of the beast [Revelation 13:16-18]. The antichrist will betray the Jews with a vengeance in an attempt to kill them all off [Revelation 12:17], and a great many of them will be destroyed. It will seem as if the tiny nation will be extinguished, but during this time Israel will come to the realization that they are smack dab in the middle of Daniel's 70th week and that the real Messiah must have already come. Of course, the only person in all of history who could have possibly been the Messiah is the Lord Jesus Christ. Upon realizing this, Israel will accept Him as their Messiah Saviour [Isaiah 66:8]. Jesus will take many of them to a place of safety, and the days will be shortened for the sake of *"the elect"* [Revelation 12:6 & 14].

Many of the converted tribulation Jews and gentile followers of Christ will be executed as a result of their refusal to take the mark of the beast, and they will be killed in a very specific manner - decapitation [Revelation 20:4]. This brings us to a rather peculiar passage in the scriptures appearing only in the gospel of Luke.

> [Luke 13:1] There were present at that season some that told him [Jesus] of **the Galileans, whose blood Pilate had mingled with their sacrifices.**

Although it cannot be said for certain, it is assumed by some that the above scripture is related to the following passage in the book of Acts.

> [Acts 5:34-37] Then stood there up one in the council, a Pharisee, named Gamaliel, a doctor of the law, had in reputation among all the people, and commanded to put the apostles forth a little space; And said unto them, Ye men of Israel, take heed to yourselves what ye intend to do as

> touching these men. For before these days rose up Theudas, boasting himself to be somebody; to whom a number of men, about four hundred, joined themselves: who was slain; and all, as many as obeyed him, were scattered, and brought to nought. After this man rose up **Judas of Galilee in the days of the taxing**, and drew away much people after him: **he also perished**; and all, even as many as obeyed him, were dispersed.

If the previous assumption is correct, it appears that the event mentioned in Luke 13:1 took place within the recent memory of Gamaliel, the Pharisee and doctor of the law, who mentioned it, and the time it happened is said to be *"in the days of the taxing"*. Moreover, it is significant that Luke's is the only gospel account that mentions a time of taxing in connection with the birth of Christ and the happenings of *"those days"*.

> [Luke 2:1] And it came to pass **in those days, that there went out a decree from Caesar Augustus, that all the world should be taxed.**

In this manner, all three of these passages are connected, having Luke as the author and him as the only biblical writer to mention any of these events.

If these events are, in fact, directly related, which they appear to be, what do we find? We discover that about the time of Christ's birth a man named Judas of Galilee rose up and started a rebellion regarding the Roman taxation that was decreed. He successfully generated a large following, but Pilate brought the rebellion to a swift end. How so? Pilate apparently caught up with Judas of Galilee and some of his followers while they were offering sacrifices at the Temple. Having caught the rebels standing at the altar, Pilate took the opportunity to make a public example of them by slaying them on the spot. They were most likely decapitated with a sword in typical Roman fashion. It is the same

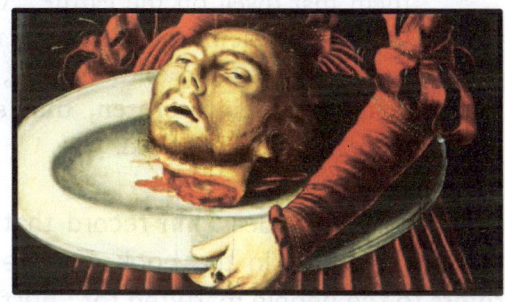

manner in which John the Baptist and James the apostle were killed. [Matthew 14:10 / Acts 12:2] And, since they were apprehended at the Temple while making an offering, their blood was "*mingled with their sacrifices*" right there at the altar.

You might ask: "*How does this tie in with the events of the tribulation that were mentioned earlier in this chapter?*" Well, as I pointed out before, people who refuse the mark of the beast in the tribulation will be executed by decapitation.

> [Revelation 20:4] And I saw thrones, and they sat upon them, and judgment was given unto them: and **I saw the souls of them that were beheaded** for the witness of Jesus, and for the word of God, and which had not worshipped the beast, neither his image, neither had received his mark upon their foreheads, or in their hands; and they lived and reigned with Christ a thousand years.

But that's not the most interesting part of the connection. What's really pertinent to this book is what John sees when the fifth seal is opened in the tribulation.

> [Revelation 6:9-11] And when he had opened the fifth seal, **I saw under the altar the souls of them that were slain** for

the word of God, and for the testimony which they held: And they cried with a loud voice, saying, How long, O Lord, holy and true, dost thou not judge and **avenge our blood** on them that dwell on the earth? And white robes were given unto every one of them; and it was said unto them, that they should rest yet for a little season, until **their fellowservants also and their brethren, that should be killed as they were**, should be fulfilled.

Only two times does John record that he saw the souls of the tribulation saints in the book of Revelation, and both times it refers to the people martyred for Christ. When he sees them the first time they are **under the altar** at the temple in Jerusalem, which is right *underneath the very spot where Judas of Galilee was killed* two thousand years previous and where, over 150 years before that, Antiochus Epiphanes persecuted the Jews, desecrated their temple and set up an image of the false god, Jupiter. You may recall from the earlier section in this book titled ABRAHAM'S BOSOM & HIS LAND GRANT that the area located underneath the Jewish Temple on the top of Mount Zion is called *"the Well of Souls"*. Dare we conclude that deep in the Well of Souls will be found the temporary abode of the tribulation's righteous dead while they await the time of their resurrection? Are we to think it's just a coincidence that the probable location of Abraham's Bosom is directly underneath Abraham's land grant on the surface? And are we to believe it is merely by chance that the place where they will be martyred is the very place where they too will have made their sacrifices? Their blood will no doubt be mingled with the sacrifices they will be offering when the antichrist apprehends them. How could it be a coincidence that over two millennia ago in the very same place, men were slain in the exact same peculiar manner in front of an identical Jewish Temple for the very same reason? It strains the imagination to consider a coincidence of that magnitude. Now add to it the fact that the men slain there two thousand years ago were not only persecuted Jews, but they were also from Galilee (like Christ's followers), and they were following a man named Judas, which is the New Testament translation of the Hebrew name "*Judah*" [Matthew 1:2] which means "*He shall be praised*" just like Christians praise our Jewish Jesus who was born of the tribe of Judah. Moreover, consider the likelihood that a madman, Antiochus Epiphanes, committed similar atrocities in the very same place a century and a half before Pilate. The odds against this convergence of details are simply staggering! It cannot be coincidence – it cannot be the product of mere chance occurrences.

But why would the antichrist slay those Jewish believers at the altar on the Temple Mount? Apparently at least some of the motive is simple revenge for the times when God's chosen people defiled Satan's altars in a similar way. Scripture indicates it was a common practice to defile an opposing altar. [See 1Kings 13:1-3 / 2Kings 23] It is a sign of contempt, a demoralizing of the people's religious beliefs and a bold slap in the face to their deity. It says, "*If you're a god, do something about it!*" It is a challenging of authority.

~ 229 ~

PART 11

THE LAMB THAT SLAYS A DRAGON

THE LAMB THAT IS A LION

As any student of the Bible knows, the tension during the tribulation will build as the antichrist tries to solidify his grip on the governments of mankind. A variety of God's plagues will be poured out on this rebellious world in a manner similar to those recorded in Exodus. However, the tribulation plagues will be orders of magnitude greater than those that destroyed the land of Egypt. Finally the day will come when Jesus will return to this earth to defeat the antichrist and take the throne as King of kings and Lord of lords. Sometimes people get the wrong idea about Christ's coming. The return of Christ will not initiate a mighty conflict between good and evil. It won't really be a battle at all. The first time Jesus came to this planet He came as God's sacrificial Lamb. When He comes back the next time, He will come like a fierce Lion.

The 1st Coming of Jesus Christ
[John 1:29] The next day John seeth Jesus coming unto him, and saith, **Behold the Lamb of God,** which taketh away the sin of the world.

The 2nd Coming of Jesus Christ
[Revelation 5:5] And one of the elders saith unto me, Weep not: behold, **the Lion of the tribe of Juda**, the Root of David, hath prevailed to open the book, and to loose the seven seals thereof.

Fear will strike through the hearts of Earth's rebels when they realize that the day of Christ's return has actually come upon them.

> [Revelation 6:12-17] And I beheld when he had opened the sixth seal, and, lo, there was a great earthquake; and the sun became black as sackcloth of hair, and the moon became as blood; And the stars of heaven fell unto the earth, even as a fig tree casteth her untimely figs, when she is shaken of a mighty wind. And the heaven departed as a scroll when it is rolled together; and every mountain and island were moved out of their places. And **the kings of the earth, and the great men, and the rich men, and the chief captains, and the mighty men, and every bondman, and every free man, hid themselves in the dens and in the rocks of the mountains;   And said to the mountains and rocks, Fall on us, and hide us from the face of him that sitteth on the throne, and from the wrath of the Lamb: For the great day of his wrath is come; and who shall be able to stand?**

The dragon, the beast and the false prophet, as well as the armies they were able to muster will be defeated by the Lord Jesus Christ as easily as a bug is squashed under foot. There will be no struggle, no contest, and no casualties on the side of the Messiah King. He will simply *"tread the winepress of the wrath of God"*. [Revelation 14:19] The beast and the false prophet will be effortlessly dispatched to the lake of fire.

> [Revelation 19:19-20] And I saw the beast, and the kings of the earth, and their armies, gathered together to make war against him that sat on the horse, and against his army. And **the beast was taken, and with him the false prophet** that wrought miracles before him, with which he deceived them that had received the mark of the beast, and them that worshipped his

image. **These both were cast alive into a lake of fire burning with brimstone.**

And Jesus won't even mess around with the devil. He'll just send a subordinate angel to take care of him.

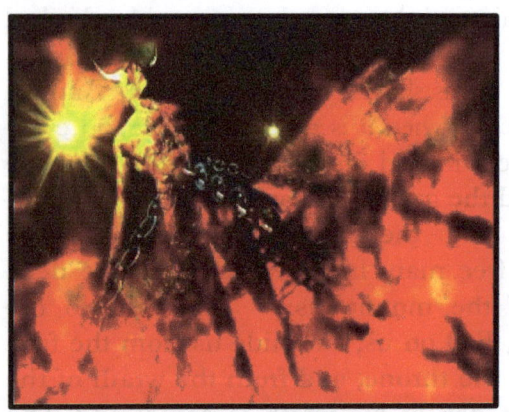

[Revelation 20:1-3] And I saw an angel come down from heaven, having the key of the bottomless pit and a great chain in his hand. And **he laid hold on the dragon, that old serpent, which is the Devil, and Satan, and bound him a thousand years, And cast him into the bottomless pit**, and shut him up, and set a seal upon him, that he should deceive the nations no more, till the thousand years should be fulfilled: and after that he must be loosed a little season.

TO THE PIT AND TO THE LAKE

We just read how the evil trinity will be dispatched at the second coming of Jesus Christ, but there are two interesting details that supply an additional link to another one of God's patterns. We are told that Satan will be bound by an angel that will *"cast him into the bottomless pit"* for a thousand years. However, the beast and the false prophet are said to end up in *"a lake of fire burning with brimstone"*. How are we to understand this? Where is this lake of fire? It's definitely not the same place where Lucifer will get thrown.

[Isaiah 14:12-15] How art thou fallen from heaven, O **Lucifer**, son of the morning! how art thou cut down to the ground, which didst weaken the nations! For thou hast said in thine heart, I will ascend into heaven, I will exalt my throne above the stars of God: I will sit also upon the mount of the congregation, in the sides of the north: I will ascend above the heights of the clouds; I will be like the most High. **Yet thou shalt be brought down to hell, to the sides of the pit.**

Lucifer's trip to the pit is spelled out quite clearly in Isaiah, and the *pit* is shown to be the same thing as *hell*, which is the area across the great gulf from Abraham's bosom in Luke 16. According to Jesus, hell, or the pit, is a place of flames created specifically for Satan and his angels, although many of Adam's descendants will be joining them there as well.

[Matthew 25:41] Then shall he say also unto them on the left hand, Depart from me, ye cursed, into everlasting fire, **prepared for the devil and his angels:**

But where are we to find this *"lake of fire"* that will hold the beast and the false prophet during the millennial reign of Christ? I'll give you two hints: one from Paul and the other from Moses.

[Romans 9:13] As it is written, **Jacob have I loved, but Esau have I hated.**

[Genesis 36:8] Thus dwelt Esau in mount Seir: **Esau is Edom.**

Historically we know that Abraham begat Isaac, and Isaac begat the fraternal *(not identical)* twin boys Jacob and Esau. The blessings and land grant of Abraham went to Isaac, and from Isaac the birthright blessing passed to Jacob, the younger of the twin boys, although both boys got a piece of the land grant. But why did Jacob end up with the birthright? He got it because:

[Genesis 25:34] ...**Esau despised his birthright.**

We are told Esau was a *...profane person ...who for one morsel of meat sold his birthright. [Hebrews 12:16]* Apparently he didn't count spiritual things as having much value and God wasn't too happy with him concerning it! But if we turn our attention at this point to Esau's land grant, we'll discover something quite fascinating. We have discussed how the land of Israel (Jacob's inheritance) is connected with the Garden of Eden, but it's not quite the same for Esau. The land of Esau ultimately becomes *"a lake of fire"* during the millennium. It seemingly rises to the surface from the bad side of the great gulf that's across from Abraham's bosom. It's apparently a precursor or type of the eternal cosmic lake of fire found in Revelation 20:15. Notice in the following passage that when the earth rejoices in the millennial kingdom, the land of Idumea (Esau, Mount Seir) will be made desolate.

[Ezekiel 35:14-15] Thus saith the Lord GOD; **When the whole earth rejoiceth, I will make thee desolate.** As thou didst rejoice at the inheritance of the house of Israel, because it was desolate, so will I do unto thee: thou shalt be desolate, **O mount Seir, and all Idumea**, even all of it: and they shall know that I am the LORD.

How desolate will it become? Let's see what Isaiah prophesied about Christ's second coming and what will happen to the land of Idumea.

[Isaiah 34:6-10] The sword of the LORD is filled with blood, it is made fat with fatness, and with the blood of lambs and goats, with the fat of the kidneys of rams: for the LORD hath a sacrifice in Bozrah, and **a great slaughter in the land of Idumea.** And the unicorns shall come down with them, and the bullocks with the bulls; and their land shall be soaked with blood, and their dust made fat with fatness. For **it is the day of the LORD'S vengeance, and the year of recompences for the controversy of Zion.** And **the streams thereof shall be turned into pitch, and the dust thereof into brimstone, and the land thereof shall become burning pitch. It shall not be quenched night nor day;** the smoke thereof shall go up for ever: from generation to generation it shall lie waste; none shall pass through it for ever and ever.

MYSTERY OF THE FUTURE PAST

> [Isaiah 66:23-24] And it shall come to pass, that from one new moon to another, and from one sabbath to another, shall all flesh come to worship before me, saith the LORD. And **they shall go forth, and look upon the carcases of the men that have transgressed against me: for their worm shall not die, neither shall their fire be quenched; and they shall be an abhorring unto all flesh.**

You may recall in the chapter called *"THE CROSS"* the matter of the *"worm"* was discussed in more detail. It is associated with suffering in Isaiah 66 just as it is in Mark chapter 9. To get a mental image of the situation, imagine throwing a living worm that couldn't die into a fire and watching it writhe in agony as it continually burned but could NEVER burn up. It's not a pretty picture, and if you're wise, you'll trust the Lord Jesus Christ as your personal Saviour and avoid that horrible fate!

Edom, the land of Esau [Idumea], is south of Israel and was part of the original land grant given to Abraham which extends from the Euphrates River to the Nile in Egypt. And we have seen how the Bible reveals that Abraham's Bosom and Hell are underneath Abraham's land grant in the innermost part of the earth. Above Abraham's Bosom is Israel, Jacob's inheritance that will be transformed as the Garden of Eden during the millennium.

> [Isaiah 51:3] For **the LORD shall comfort <u>Zion</u>: he will comfort all her waste places; and he will make her wilderness <u>like Eden</u>, and her desert <u>like the garden of the LORD</u>**; joy and gladness shall be found therein, thanksgiving, and the voice of melody.

The land of Esau will not be so fortunate. There is no paradise underneath Idumea, and when its subterranean counterpart forms on the Earth's surface in the kingdom of Christ, it will be a literal lake of fire with burning pitch and brimstone. I can't be positive, but it looks as if the ground over some massive Middle East oil wells will collapse at that time. When it does it will force the oil to the surface and create an oil lake that will be set on fire.

We started down this trail with Paul pointing out the Lord's attitude about Esau: *Jacob have I loved, but Esau have I hated.* Now look at the question Paul asks just nine verses later in light of all the information we just covered.

> [Romans 9:22-24] **What if God, willing to shew his wrath, and to make his power known,** endured with much longsuffering **the vessels of wrath fitted to destruction: And that he might make known the riches of his glory on the vessels of mercy, which he had afore prepared unto glory,** Even us, whom he hath called, not of the Jews only, but also of the Gentiles?

Clearly, Esau and the land of Idumea represents God's wrath, and conversely Jacob's inheritance, the land of Israel, is associated with His mercy, and for good reason because Abraham's bosom and Hell are not just metaphors. The heart of the earth is both: 1) the paradise where man came from; and 2) the temporary prison created for the devil and his angels. These are literal places deep in the earth, and it's as if their substance will bubble up and rise to the surface when the Lord Jesus Christ returns to reign as King of kings and Lord of lords. These abodes are part of a well-established repeating pattern of saved vs. lost, blessing vs. cursing, paradise vs. hell.

MESSIAH'S TEMPLE

Once the evil trinity is taken out of the picture, Christ's 1,000-year kingdom of peace will be established on the earth with its headquarters in Jerusalem. If you recall, in our chapter titled "WHOSE TEMPLE IS THIS ANYWAY?" we discussed the two possible options for building the tribulation Temple. The pattern must either follow that of Messiah's Temple found in Ezekiel or it must be made after the pattern of what has come to be known as Herod's Temple. Jewish leadership has already determined they have no choice but to use Herod's pattern for the next Temple *[in the tribulation]* since it's the only one they have specifications for which are sufficient enough to build. Moreover, it was determined that Messiah would build His own Temple when He arrives since He alone will be able to fill in the many details which are missing in Ezekiel's description. It is necessary then that the tribulation temple be destroyed at some point so the new one can be built. And where will Messiah's Temple be erected? On the only authorized location where the Temple can stand - the Temple Mount.

Although it's true that many details of Messiah's Temple are missing in Ezekiel's description, it's also true that there are some pretty significant details given which are pertinent to this book. For instance, Ezekiel tells us about the waters that come down from under the right side of the house of the LORD.

[Ezekiel 47:1-12] Afterward he brought me again unto the door of the house; and, behold, **waters issued out from under the threshold of the** house eastward: for the forefront of the house stood toward the east, **and the waters came down from under from the right side of the house, at the south side of the altar.** Then brought he me out of the way of the gate northward, and led me about the way without unto the utter gate by the way that looketh eastward; and, behold, there ran out waters on the right side. And when the man that had the line in his hand went forth eastward, he measured a thousand cubits, and he brought me through the waters; the waters were to the ankles. Again he measured a thousand, and brought me through the waters; the waters were to the knees. Again he measured a thousand, and brought me through; the waters were to the loins. Afterward he measured a thousand; and it was a river that I could not pass over: for the waters were risen, waters to swim in, a river that could not be passed over. And he said unto me, Son of man, hast thou seen this? Then he brought me, and caused me to return to the brink of the river. Now when I had returned, behold, at the bank of the river were very many trees on the one side and on the other. Then said he unto me, **These waters issue out toward the east country, and go down into the desert, and go into the sea: which being brought forth into the sea, the waters shall be healed. And it shall come to pass, that every thing that liveth, which moveth, whithersoever the rivers shall come, shall live: and there shall be a very great multitude of fish,** because these waters shall come thither: for they shall be healed; and every thing shall live whither the river cometh. And it shall come to pass, that the fishers shall stand upon it from Engedi even unto Eneglaim; they shall be a place to spread forth nets; their fish shall be according to their kinds, as the fish of the great sea, exceeding many. But the miry places thereof and the marishes thereof shall not be healed; they shall be given to salt. **And by the river upon the bank thereof, on this side and on that side, shall grow all trees for meat, whose leaf shall not fade, neither shall the fruit thereof be consumed: it shall bring forth new fruit according to his months, because their waters they issued out of the sanctuary: and the fruit thereof shall be for meat, and the leaf thereof for medicine.**

Providence would have it that Messiah's Temple will be the location of an underground river that will flow out from the house of the LORD. That river will get deeper and wider as it flows down into the desert and travels about seventy miles to the Dead Sea. Once the river enters the Dead Sea, it will heal the barren sea of its salinity. The Dead Sea will be dead no longer. It will literally be teeming with aquatic life, allowing fishermen to earn a living there. Moreover, this amazing river that brings life to the previously sterile Dead Sea will have the most exotic trees growing along its banks. The fruit of the trees will not rot and the leaves will be medicine for all who need it. It sounds pretty awesome doesn't it! Actually, it reminds one of a place called Eden. But then, you may remember in the chapter called "SOLOMON, THE SON OF DAVID" we discussed how the Bible reveals that the Gihon River, one of the four rivers of Eden, apparently surfaces very close to Jerusalem where the Temple Mount is located. In fact, the very headwaters of the Gihon appear to be under the Temple Mount, right where Messiah's Temple will be erected. So we see that the pattern of a river associated with Zion repeats: from Eden, to Solomon, to the pool of Siloam in the time of Christ, and even into the Millennial Kingdom.

FROM PEACE TO PIECES

Revelation chapter 20 makes it evident that the millennial reign of Christ will last a thousand years. In fact, that one chapter mentions it six different times. It will be a kingdom of peace ruled by an incorruptible King who will never die. Seemingly, Christ's earthly kingdom would be the answer the world has been longing for; a world where lion and lamb can rest together. It will be a world that is not ruled by corrupt politicians and greedy businessmen. Christ will *"destroy those who destroyed the earth"* [Revelation 11:18].

There will be no war on the planet for a thousand years [Isaiah 2:4] . The planet will be regenerated and global warming will no longer be a threat, if ever it was one. The earth will bear its produce so bountifully that  before the crops are fully gathered from the fields, it will be time to plant again [Amos 9:13]. Hunger will finally be a thing of the past and lifespans will be greatly increased along with the good health to enjoy the extra years. It will be Utopia! Or at least it could be if mankind truly desired Utopia. But it seems that a utopian society isn't all that appealing to a great many people no matter how much they appear to promote it. The truth is, after a thousand years of peace in a virtual paradise, many of our planets' inhabitants will be ready to burn the world down rather than suffer another day in a global Garden of Eden. They will despise the King and His paradise with such intensity that when Satan is loosed at the end of the millennium they will actually try to crown him king of Earth in an attempted coup against the Messiah's kingdom. It's nearly unimaginable! But the Bible is very clear on the matter.

[Revelation 20:7-9] And **when the thousand years are expired, Satan shall be loosed out of his prison, And shall go out to deceive the nations** which are in the four quarters of the earth, Gog and Magog, **to gather them together to battle**: the number of whom is as the sand of the sea. And they went up on the breadth of the earth, and **compassed the camp of the saints** about, and the beloved city [Jerusalem]: and **fire came down from God out of heaven, and devoured them.**

Again, the battle is over in an instant. But what do we learn here? The lesson is obvious to anyone who will give it a moment's consideration. The rebellious heart of fallen man causes him to love darkness rather than light because his deeds are evil, just like Jesus said [John 3:19]. Even so, the rebels will not prevail and neither will their evil master. Satan's fate is sealed and has been plainly spelled out in the scriptures. He is destined to join the other two members of the satanic trinity in the lake of fire.

[Revelation 20:10] And **the devil that deceived them was cast into the lake of fire and brimstone**, where the beast and the false prophet are, and shall be tormented day and night for ever and ever.

BACK TO CHAOS

The previous chapter ended with Satan finally meeting his well-deserved and ultimate fate, to which hundreds of millions will no doubt shout *"Halleluiah"* and give a wave of *"good riddance"*. When the devil finally gets what he deserves the universe will also meet its end. Not only will the corrupter be dealt with but all he has corrupted must be eliminated too, as shown in the very next verse.

[Revelation 20:11] And I saw a great white throne, and him that sat on it, from whose face **the earth and the heaven fled away**; and there was found no place for them.

Other biblical passages shed greater light on this event. But none do it any better than Peter.

[2 Peter 3:10-11] But the day of the Lord will come as a thief in the night; in the which **the heavens shall pass away with a great noise, and the elements shall melt with fervent heat, the earth also and the works that are therein shall be burned up.** Seeing then that **all these things shall be dissolved,** what manner of persons ought ye to be in all holy conversation and godliness,

What do we find here? The situation is very reminiscent of what we read in Genesis 1:2 which is often referred to as *"the chaotic earth"*.

And **the earth was without form, and void; and darkness was upon the face of the deep.** And the Spirit of God moved upon the face of the waters.

I can hear someone saying, *"But the chaos in Genesis involved water, and Peter describes the end of the world as fire. How do you explain that?"* It's pretty simple really. Having drowned out the earth twice [Genesis 1:2 / 7:18], God promised that He would never again destroy it with the waters of a flood.

[Genesis 9:11] And I will establish my covenant with you; neither shall all flesh be cut off any more by the waters of a flood; **neither shall there any more be a flood to destroy the earth.**

Obviously God meant what He said. He will not drown out the world again by water. However He WILL set all the water in the universe on fire, and there is a LOT of it! One day, the water of *"the deep"* [discussed under the section by the same name] will separate into hydrogen *(the most combustible element in the universe)* and oxygen *(which vigorously accelerates combustion),* and it will be ignited resulting in an explosion of universal magnitude. Like Peter said, ...**the heavens shall pass away with a great noise, and the elements shall melt with fervent heat, the earth also and the works that are therein shall be burned up... all these things shall be dissolved.**

In the same way that a defiled and unclean brasen cooking pot in the Old Testament would be purified by fire so must all the matter in the universe be purified from its corruption in a similar manner. This will purify *"the elements"* in a way that the waters of a flood, be it global [Genesis 7] or universal [Genesis 1:2], never could. The cataclysmic explosion and subsequent universal fire of the deep will be the final event before the Great White Throne Judgment in Revelation chapter 20 where all accounts will be squared with God. Those beings, whether earthly or celestial, that stubbornly refused to submit themselves to the rulership of the Creator, will be judged and sent to the lake of fire to suffer punishment for their unpardoned offenses against the King of kings.

THE FIX IS IN

The most important thing about the universal cataclysm in Revelation chapter 20 isn't the explosion – it's WHAT will explode. When the watery deep is ignited, the barrier between God and His creation will forever be destroyed, and God will finally be able to fully and openly dwell with His people as was intended when the first man was raised from earthly dust. Obtaining a *"no holds barred"* full personal intimacy with humanity has been God's intention from the first moment of man's creation. Look at the flow of the biblical context which follows the universal destruction.

> [Revelation 20:15] And whosoever was not found written in the book of life was cast into the lake of fire.

The very next thing we're told is:

> [Revelation 21:1-5] And I saw a new heaven and a new earth: for the first heaven and **the first earth were passed away; and there was no more sea.** And I John saw the holy city, new Jerusalem, coming down from God out of heaven, prepared as a bride adorned for her husband. **And I heard a great voice out of heaven saying, Behold, the tabernacle of God is with men, and he will dwell with them, and they shall be his people, and** <u>God himself shall be with them,</u> **and be their God.** And God shall wipe away all tears from their eyes; and there shall be no more death, neither sorrow, nor crying, neither shall there be any more pain: for the former things are passed away. And he that sat upon the throne said, **Behold, I make all things new.** And he said unto me, Write: for **these words are true and faithful.**

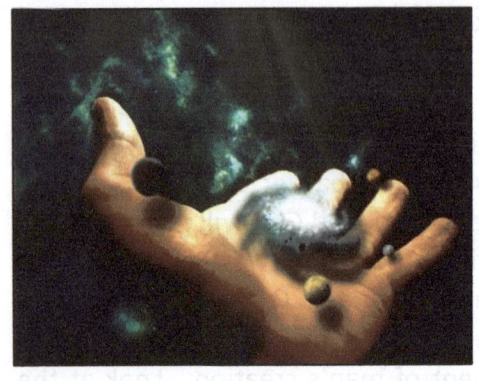

When the heavenly new Jerusalem, which is above, descends will it actually land on the new Earth? I don't know for sure, but if it does we can be certain of where it will touch down. It will no doubt land in the place of its namesake, which is Mount Zion. It will be on *the Foundation Stone* of the new world; situated just like Jerusalem is today and Messiah will continue to be the point of reference for all things.

The appearance of the deep in Genesis 1:2 and the disappearance of it in Revelation 20:11 serve as a pair of cosmic bookends for the history of the Kingdom of Heaven. Those events encapsulate the plan of God, not just for this world, but for the entire universe and its inhabitants as well. [Isaiah 9:7] . When Revelation 21:1 says *"and there was no more sea"* it isn't referring to the Mediterranean. Neither is it speaking of the Atlantic Ocean. It is speaking of the sea that must stand between the totality of God's presence and the people He desires to have fellowship with, until the sin problem is forever resolved. The story between the *"bookends"* is a revelation of God's method for fixing what the devil messed up. It reveals the process by which He will reclaim what was lost [Luke 19:10]. The bookends stand as an interruption between eternity past and eternity future. They create the bubble in which mortal history is contained. The bookends surround the story of the Kingdom of Heaven and show us how God has worked to restore it to its proper relationship with the Kingdom of God. This is what He has been working on since

Genesis 1:2. And from this point in time right now [2024], there is at least another 1,007 years to go before His plan is brought to its full fruition. Why? Because there must yet be a seven-year period [Daniel's 70th week] and the 1,000 year reign of Christ the Messiah King on Earth to follow it. The rest of the Bible, after Revelation 21:1, tells us what's in store after the fix is in! But we have now come to see the seventh and final phase of the plan of God. It is the Eternal Sabbath. This understanding.is condensed in the following points and can be seen illustrated in the chart on page 254.

1) Eternity Past

In the Beginning God... [Genesis 1:1]
This is before time, space and matter were created. There was no kingdom of heaven because there was no location called heaven. It had not yet been created. Eternal God was in fellowship with His triune self.

2) First Heaven & Earth

...God created the heaven and the earth.
[Genesis 1:1]
Here is the original creation. During this age Lucifer was made king of planet Earth, ruling over the angelic hosts known as the sons of God. It was from here that he launched his rebellion. [Isaiah 14] But it was entirely unsuccessful. Moreover, there's no evidence that an actual battle even took place. I realize that many people would point to Revelation 12:7-8 as the ancient battle of Lucifer's rebellion, but it cannot be so. The context of Revelation chapter 12, like the rest of the book of Revelation, is PROPHECY. In fact, we are specifically told that very thing four times in Revelation 22. Of course, this supposition begs the question: *"If there was no war in heaven when Lucifer rebelled, then what stopped the rebellion?"* Perhaps there is another scenario that matches up

better with the existing scriptural evidence. Since I can find no ancient heavenly battle in the Bible, it seems more likely to me that when Lucifer and his rebellious followers approached heavens shore, they effectively ran into a *"brick wall"*. In fact, they may have run into it at full speed. You might ask: *"What wall is that?"* It's the barrier; it's the frozen body of water called *"the deep"* that we discussed in the section by the same name.

Sin had entered the kingdom of heaven, which is the universe and its contents. Lucifer's rebellion failed, but it left its marks on the physical creation. From this point forward, the universe was subject to the downward spiral of entropy, where things naturally tend towards decay and disorder.

Whether Lucifer saw an impenetrable wall upon his arrival or slammed into it at light speed and bounced off falling from heaven back to earth I don't know. But I do know two things: 1) the rebellion was probably over before it ever really got started, and 2) that sin had tarnished everything contained within the second heaven - everything within the universe, including Earth.

Though God finds it undesirable, the *"deep"* satisfies the part of God's holiness that must be kept separate from all that is defiled.
- [Job 15:15] Behold, he putteth no trust in his saints; **yea, the heavens are not clean in his sight.**
- [Habakkuk 1:13] **Thou art of purer eyes than to behold evil, and canst not look on iniquity:**

It seems this is the reason the Father turned His back on Christ when He *"was made to be sin for us"* [2 Corinthians 5:21].
- ⟹ [Matthew 27:46] And about the ninth hour Jesus cried with a loud voice, saying... **My God, my God, why hast thou forsaken me?**

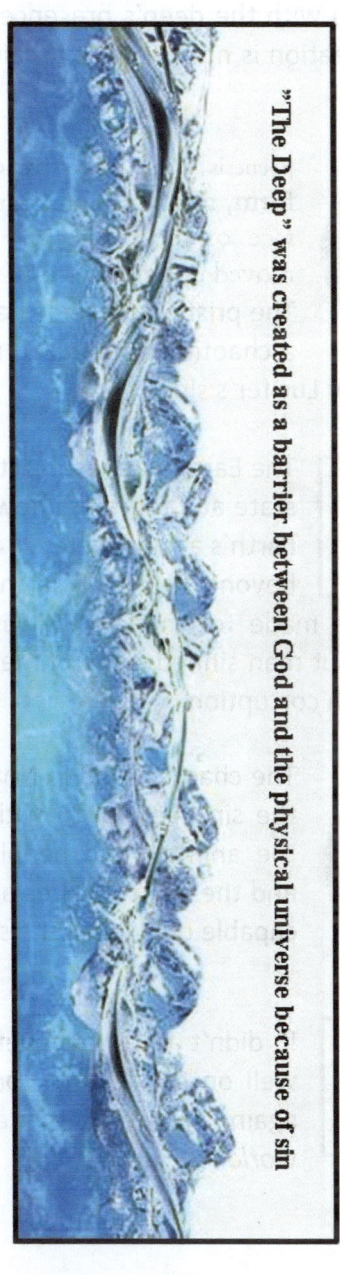

"The Deep" was created as a barrier between God and the physical universe because of sin

God's dissatisfaction with the deep's presence is the reason why the 2nd day of re-creation is not specifically said to be *"good"* like the other days.

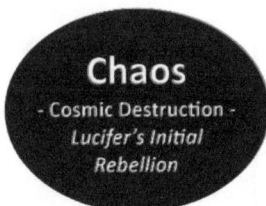

[Genesis 1:2] **And the earth was without form, and void;** and darkness was upon the face of the deep. And the Spirit of God moved upon the face of the waters.

The pristine universe had been reduced to a chaotic disorganized mess as a result of the defiling effects of Lucifer's sin.

> 3) **Re-Created Earth**

The Earth was resurrected from its chaotic state and there are now three heavens: 1) Earth's atmosphere, 2) outer space, and 3) beyond the deep is the domain of God. The new Earth was made for man, who was created to have dominion over it. But man sinned and in time the earth became filled once again with corruption.

> **Chaos**
> - Global Destruction -
> Lucifer's Son's of God
> Rebellion

The chaotic flood in Noah's day destroyed the sin filled earth with the exception of the animals and people aboard the ark, and the sea creatures and other creatures capable of living in the sea.

> 4) **Present Earth**

It didn't take long before mankind was well on the way to corrupting the world again. Paul refers to it as *"this present evil world"* [Galatians 1:14].

In the ever-nearing future the world will be plunged into *"great tribulation"*. Pestilence, plagues, war and famine will sweep the planet creating global chaos. Demonic activity will skyrocket with satanic creatures arising from the pit of hell vexing all mankind under the totalitarian rule of Satan's antichrist as the world is being destroyed.

When Christ returns to defeat Satan and his followers, the earth will experience a *"regeneration"* [Matthew 19:28] and will be more fruitful than it has been in the past 6,000 years. We are told that the *"plowman shall overtake the reaper"* [Amos 9:13], indicating that because of the abundance of crops they will not be all harvested before it's time to plant again.

At the end of Christ's 1,000-year earthly kingdom, the heavens and earth will be destroyed by a cosmic fiery explosion. Scripture says *"the heavens shall pass away with a great noise, and the elements shall melt with fervent heat, the earth also and the works that are therein shall be burned up."* [2 Peter 3:10] In this universal explosion *"the deep"*, the barrier between the 2nd and 3rd heaven, will be ignited plunging the universe into the flames of a cosmic chaotic destruction. The Great White Throne Judgment will then take place. Sin, death, hell, Satan and his followers will never plague creation again.

After the "Deep" is destroyed God will once again fully join His creation

6) New Heaven & Earth

After the last judgment is over God will create a new heaven and earth *"wherein dwelleth righteousness"*. [2Peter 3:13] John records *"I saw a new heaven and a new earth: for the first heaven and the first earth were passed away; and there was no more sea."* [Revelation 21:1] Which sea is John talking about? It's the first one he mentioned in his book of Revelation. He said when he got called up to heaven *"before the throne there was a sea of glass like unto crystal"*. [Revelation 4:6] How do we know this is the sea that Revelation 21:1 is discussing? We know by what follows in the next verse.

7) Eternal Sabbath

[Revelation 21:2-4] **And I John saw the holy city, new Jerusalem, coming down from God out of heaven, prepared as a bride adorned for her husband. And I heard a great voice out of heaven saying, Behold, the tabernacle of God is with men, and he will dwell with them, and they shall be his people, and God himself shall be with them, and be their God.** And God shall wipe away all tears from their eyes; and there shall be no more death, neither sorrow, nor crying, neither shall there be any more pain: for the former things are passed away.

⇨ *This is the 7th and final Sabbath. It is the Sabbath of the universe, the Sabbath of all creation.*

A Completed Sabbath Pattern Emerges

1) **A *"Week"* of Days**, six days of work and the 7th day is a Sabbath of rest.

2) **A *"Week"* of Weeks**, a period of 7 weeks between the holy days of Passover and Pentecost.

3) **A *"Week"* of Months**, with the exception of the weekly Sabbath, all of Israel's God ordained original holy days fall in the first 7 months of the year.

4) **A *"Week"* of Years**, they would plant their fields for 6 years and in the 7th year the land would rest.

5) **A *"Week"* of Weeks of Years**, 7 groups of 7 years were to be between Israel's Jubilee celebrations.

6) **A *"Week"* of 1,000 YEARS**, six groups of 1,000 years, and the 7th group is the Sabbath of the earth.

7) **A *"WEEK"* of AGES** completes God's recurring pattern of Sabbaths, for when the Lord gets to seven He is finished. From here, humanity goes out into an eternal Sabbath of rest with the Creator; and all is as it should be.

Week Of Ages

1) Eternity Past

2) First Heaven & Earth

Chaos
- Cosmic Destruction -
Lucifer's Initial Rebellion

3) Re-Created Earth

Chaos
- Global Destruction -
Lucifer's Son's of God Rebellion

4) Present Earth

Chaos
- Tribulation Destruction -
Lucifer's Antichrist Rebellion

5) Millennial Earth

Chaos
- Universal Destruction -
Lucifer's Final Rebellion

6) New Heaven & Earth

7) Eternal Sabbath

A DIVINE INVITATION

Having completed this examination of the "Mystery of the Future Past", it seems appropriate to end this book with the same words that my Lord and Saviour Jesus Christ chose for the ending of His book, the Bible. His words are simple and heartfelt. He says:

> [Revelation 22:16-20] I Jesus have sent mine angel to testify unto you these things in the churches. I am the root and the offspring of David, and the bright and morning star. And **the Spirit and the bride say, Come. And let him that heareth say, Come. And let him that is athirst come. And whosoever will, let him take the water of life freely.** For I testify unto every man that heareth the words of the prophecy of this book, If any man shall add unto these things, God shall add unto him the plagues that are written in this book: And if any man shall take away from the words of the book of this prophecy, God shall take away his part out of the book of life, and out of the holy city, and from the things which are written in this book. **He which testifieth these things saith, Surely I come quickly.**

God has graciously extended an invitation to the billions of sinners on this planet. He wants each and every one of them to join Him on the other side of the flood, beyond the last bookend for the Eternal Sabbath. He wants YOU to join Him in that universe to come where there is no more sickness, sorrow, pain or death. We can dwell with Him where the fellowship is sweet and pure, where the glory and holiness of the Creator can be enjoyed by all of His creation – as it should be. You have nothing to lose and literally everything to gain. He wants you to have the endless enjoyment of a perfect universe so desperately that He PERSONALLY paid the price of your admission. It's such a desire of His heart that He can't even finish His book without giving you one more invitation to join Him. Truly, *"the Spirit and the bride say, Come. And let him that heareth say, Come. And let him that is athirst come. And whosoever will, let him take the water of life freely."* [Revelation 22:17] Come and drink deeply of the things of God. Drink in all the goodness of God. Don't wait another minute. Accept the Lord Jesus Christ as your very own Saviour now, while your heart is crying out and while there is still time to do it. Let Him give you a new heart for loving and new eyes for seeing. I hope to see you beyond the final bookend!

Eternal Life IS A Free Gift!

Dear Friends,

While reading this book you may have realized that you haven't yet trusted the Lord Jesus Christ as your own personal Saviour but would like to do it now. Fortunately, God wants you to have eternal life. And because He wants you to have it, He has made it very easy to obtain. In fact, it's free! That's right, the Bible says,

> **"For the wages of sin is death; but the gift of God is eternal life through Jesus Christ our Lord."** [Romans 6:23]

So how do you get this gift?

1) **ADMIT** that you are a sinner and that you deserve to find yourself condemned under the righteous judgment of a Holy God. *"For all have sinned, and come short of the glory of God;"* [Romans 3:23]

2) **BELIEVE** in your heart that the Lord Jesus Christ died for YOU! And, that His sacrifice has been accepted by God the Father as a complete payment for YOUR sins. The Bible tells us *"...the blood of Jesus Christ his [God's] Son cleanseth us from all sin."* [1 John 1:7]

3) <u>CONFESS</u> the Lord Jesus Christ as your personal Saviour. Tell someone that you have accepted God's gift of salvation by receiving His Son, the Lord Jesus Christ! *"For the scripture saith, Whosoever believeth on him shall not be ashamed."* [Romans 10:11]

If you have trusted the Lord Jesus Christ as your personal Saviour today, why don't you write and let me know. I would love to hear about it and rejoice with you! You will find my e-mail address below.

May you be abundantly blessed!
Mark A Weller

MysteryPast@yahoo.com

PART 12

APPENDIX

The Pre-existing Earth is not a New Teaching

The Confessions of Saint Augustine
Book XII, by Saint Augustine: [400A.D.]

For very wonderful is this corporeal heaven; of which firmament between water and water, the second day, after the creation of light, Thou saidst, Let it be made, and it was made. Which firmament Thou calledst heaven; the heaven, that is, to this earth and sea, which Thou madest the third day, by giving a visible figure to **the formless matter, <u>which Thou madest before all days</u>. For already hadst Thou made both an heaven, <u>before all days</u>; but that was the heaven of this heaven; because In the beginning Thou hadst made heaven and earth.**

Of course, this does not mean that Augustine's teaching was accepted by all ancient Christians, nor does it mean that it was taught the same way as I have presented it in this book. It only demonstrates that some students of scripture believed the heaven and earth in Genesis 1:1-2 existed prior to the seven days of creation that follow in the same chapter. Some modern creationists assert that the pre-existing earth belief didn't arise until the 1800's. As you can see, that assertion is verifiably false.

SOME REPEATING BIBLICAL PATTERNS

In some ways, studying the Bible is like looking inside a diamond through its several facets. Through each facet you will be able to see inside the diamond, but each view of the inside will be a little different. And each view will provide a little more information. In this way, the more facets you examine, the more you will discover about its contents. The preponderance of the evidence will reveal the truth. Our job is to simply follow the evidence. We must always ask: Do the pieces fit properly? Do they create a pattern of evidence? What do they point to? What do they tell us?

I have included a small list of repeating biblical patterns for your convenience. It is by no means extensive, but it is both fascinating and informative. No doubt, many of you will be able to add much more to it. I hope you'll consider sharing your discoveries with me as you find them. My email address is on page 257.

Creation
Original Earth, Genesis 1:1 - Current Earth, 2 Peter 3:7 - New Heaven & New Earth, Revelation 21:1

The Deep and its Types
The Deep, Genesis 1:2 - Vail of the Tabernacle & Temple, Exodus 30:6 - Crossing the Jordan River, Joshua 1:2 - Sea of Glass like Crystal, Revelation 4:6

States of Major Chaos
Satan's Initial Rebellion, Genesis 1:1-2 - Satan's Sons of God Rebellion, Genesis 6 - Satan's Antichrist Rebellion, Revelation 13 - Satan's Final Rebellion, Revelation 20

Foundations
Original Earth, Genesis 1:1 - Current Earth, Job 38:4-7 - Jewish Temple, 1 Kings 6:37 - Jesus Christ *the Chief Cornerstone*, 1 Peter 2:6 - New Testament Church, Ephesians 2:28 - New Jerusalem, Revelation 21:14

Gardens
Lucifer in Garden of God, Ezekiel 28:13 - Adam in Garden of Eden, Genesis 3 - Jesus *"the last Adam"* in the Garden of Gethsemane, John 18:1-2 - Jesus Buried in a Garden Tomb, John 19:41-42 - Zion Made Like a Garden, Isaiah 51:3 - The Garden Paradise of God, Revelation 2:7

Gihon River Appearances
Garden of Eden, Genesis 2:13 - Solomon's Coronation, I Kings 1:45 - Pool of Siloam, 2 Chronicles 32:30 - Millennial Temple, Ezekiel 47:8 - New Jerusalem, Revelation 22:1

Tree of Life
Garden of Eden, Genesis 2:9 - Millennial Kingdom Leaves of Tree for Medicine, Ezekiel 47:12 - Paradise of God, Revelation 2:7 - New Jerusalem Leaves for Healing of the Nations, Revelation 22:2

Well of Souls
Adam's Creation in the Heart of the Earth, Psalm 139:15 - Abraham's Bosom, Lazarus and the Rich Man, Luke 16:19-31 - Jesus Descending after Death, 1 Peter 3:18-20 / 1 Peter 4:6 - Martyred Tribulation Saints, Revelation 6:9

Kings of Earth
Lucifer, Isaiah 14:12 - Adam, Genesis 1:26 - Satan, Job 41:1&34
- Noah, Genesis 9:1-3 - Satan, Luke 4:5-7 - Jesus, Revelation
19:16

Sabbath Patterns
Week of Days, Exodus 20:11 - Week of Weeks, Deuteronomy
16:9 - Week of Month's, Leviticus 23:34 - Week of Years,
Deuteronomy 15:1-2 - Week of Weeks of Years, Leviticus 25:8-10
- Week of Millenniums, 2 Peter 3:8-10 - Week of Ages, Ephesians
3:5 / 2:2

Sons of God
Angels, Job 1:6 / 2:1 - Adam, Luke 3:38 - Israel, Exodus 4:22-23
- Jesus Christ, Mark 1:1 - Christians, 1 John 3:1-2

Focal Points of History
Israel, Deuteronomy 11:10-12 - Jerusalem, Zechariah 2:2 -
Temple Mount, Psalm 78:67-68 - Holy of Holies, 1 Chronicles
13:6 - Foundation Stone, Isaiah 28:16

Ornan's Threshing Floor
*1Chronicles 21:1 Connections to antichrist: See chapter "ORNAN
OR ARAUNAH? [REVISITED]"* - Satan provoked David to number
Israel - Ornan = *"Light Perpetuated"* - 6660 grams/number of
the beast - Gold indicates "deity" even in idols - location of
Satan's tribulation Temple

Araunah's Threshing Floor
2Samuel 24:1 Connections to Jesus Christ and/or antichrist's deception - See chapter "ORNAN OR ARAUNAH? [REVISITED]" - God moved David to number Israel - Araunah = "*Joyful Rising of Jehovah*" - 555 grams number of death/grace - Silver indicates redemption - location of Messiah's Millennial Temple

Various Arks
Noah's giant ark, Genesis 6:14 - Baby Moses' ark of bulrushes' Exodus 2:1-4 - Moses wooden ark of covenant, Deuteronomy 10:1-3 - Bezaleel's golden ark of covenant, Exodus 37:1-9 - Ark of the testament in heaven, Revelation 11:19

Temples
Solomon's Temple, 1 Kings 6:1-38 - Herod's Temple, Mark 13:1-2 - Antichrist Temple, 2 Thessalonians 2:3-12 - Messiah's Temple, Ezekiel chapters 40-46

Arks of the Covenant Compared
One ark made of wood by Moses; One ark covered with gold by Bezaleel - One ark with stone tables God made; One ark with stone tables Moses made - One ark with 10 commandments whole; One ark with 10 commandments broken - One ark where Satan sits in tribulation; One ark where Christ sits in millennium

Fishing
The "Deep" is water, Genesis 1:2 - Ark's are a Boat: Genesis 6:14, Exodus 2:3, Psalm 29:10 - Apostles were Fishers of men, Matthew 4:19 - Jesus is the bait, a worm, Psalm 22:6 - The apostles were to get people above the water (the deep) and into heaven where God's ark is located, Psalm 29:10

Antichrists
Pharaoh kills male babies, Exodus 1:16-22 - Herod kills male children, Matthew 2:16 - Nebuchadnezzar kills young men in temple, 2 Chronicles 36:17 - Antiochus Epiphanes, see: "WHOSE TEMPLE IS THIS ANYWAY?" - Pilate mingles their blood with sacrifices, Luke 13:1 - Antichrist beheads saints in the tribulation, Revelation 20:4

Image's Set Up
Israel's golden calf, Exodus 32:4 - Absalom's pillar, 2 Samuel 18:18 - Solomon's Molech, Chemosh, etc., 1 Kings 11:6-7 - Nebuchadnezzar's golden image, Daniel 3:1 - Antichrist's image of the beast, Revelation 13:14-15

Persecutions
Nebuchadnezzar "slew their young men with the sword in the house of their sanctuary", 2 Chronicles 36:17 - Pilate mingled their blood with sacrifices, Luke 13:1 - John the Baptist killed by Herod, Luke 6:22-28 - Apostle James Zebedee killed by Herod, Acts 12:1-2 - The Two Witnesses, Revelation 11:3-9 - Tribulation Saints, Revelation 20:4

Offers to Enter the Kingdom
Failed to enter under Moses but entered with Joshua - Failed to enter under the prophet like Moses (Jesus 1st coming, Acts 3:22) but will enter when Jesus returns at the end of the tribulation (Joshua = Jesus)

Gentile Brides

Joseph married Asenath an Egyptian, Genesis 41:45 - Moses married Zipporah an Ethiopian, Numbers 12:1 - Solomon married the Shulamite, Song of Solomon 1:5 - Jesus will marry a predominately gentile Church, John 3:29 / Romans 11:13 / Ephesians 5:25

Human Condition: Saved/Lost

Jerusalem: Mount Zion/Calvary - Middle East: Israel/Edom - Global: Abraham's Bosom/Hell - Galactic: North Star/Southern Cross - Cosmic: New Jerusalem/Lake of Fire.

Daniel's Prophecy of the Seventy Weeks
Amended from: Clarence Larkin, Dispensational Truth

Daniel, an Old Testament prophet, received information of a future event from the angel Gabriel. This prophecy was given so the Jews would be aware when the time of the Messiah drew near. Daniel 9:24-27 reads:

> Seventy weeks are determined upon thy people [the Jews] and upon thy holy city [Jerusalem], to finish the transgression, and to make an end of sins, and to make reconciliation for iniquity, and to bring in everlasting righteousness [Christ's Millennial Kingdom], and to seal up the vision and prophecy, and to anoint the most Holy [Jesus]. Know therefore and understand, that from the going forth of the commandment to restore and to build Jerusalem unto the Messiah the Prince shall be **(#1)** seven weeks, and **(#2)** threescore and two weeks: the street shall be built again, and the wall, even in troublous times. And after threescore and two weeks [62 weeks] shall Messiah be cut off, but not for himself [for us]: and the people of the prince that shall come shall destroy the city and the sanctuary; and the end thereof shall be with a flood, and unto the end of the war desolations are determined. And he [the prince that shall come] shall confirm the covenant with many for **(#3)** one week: and in the midst of the week he shall cause the sacrifice and the oblation [offerings] to cease, and for the overspreading of abominations [evil deeds] he shall make it desolate, even until the consummation [the end], and that determined shall be poured upon the desolate.

Let's review a few things about this prophecy. First, it is said to cover a period of seventy weeks which it divides into three distinct periods of time. These are **(#1)** 7 weeks, **(#2)** 62 weeks, and **(#3)** 1 week. Also, notice that the prophecy begins with the order to rebuild Jerusalem and then combines the 7 week period with the 62 weeks, thereby totaling 69 weeks. It then concludes with Messiah the Prince *(Jesus)* being cut off but not for himself. The final 1 week period follows these events. By ***allowing scripture to interpret scripture*** we can arrive at the information God wants His people to have.

This prophecy officially began with the order to rebuild Jerusalem which can be found in Nehemiah 2:1-6. The date given is the Jewish month of Nisan, in the 20th year of Artaxerxes king of Persia. This corresponds to about the 13th day of March, 445 BC according to our modern calendar. Jesus, Messiah the Prince, rode into Jerusalem in Triumphal Entry on Sunday, April 2nd, 30 AD *[Luke 19:37-40]*. The problem is that there are more than 69 literal weeks between the 13th of March, 445 BC and April 2nd, 30 AD. In fact, 445 BC+30 AD = 475 years. How are we to resolve this obvious discrepancy? First we must make sure we are using a scriptural approach in our attempt to decode the prophecy. 2 Peter 1:20-21 says:

> ... **no prophecy of the scripture is of any private interpretation.** For the prophecy came not in old time by the will of man: but holy men of God spake as they were moved by the Holy Ghost.

This being the case, we will turn to the pages of the Bible and allow it to unfold itself before us. When we examine the account of the Israelite exodus from Egypt under the leadership of Moses, specifically, the account of their first attempt to enter *the Promised Land,* we find something very interesting. *[See Numbers chapters 13 & 14].* *In a nutshell,* here's what happened. As the Israelites were preparing to enter the land, Moses sent out twelve spies to search it and bring back a report of what they found there. When the spies returned from searching the land for 40 days, they gave their report. Of the twelve spies that went, ten reported it was not possible to conquer the inhabitants who were living there. The remaining two spies gave the following report, knowing that God was on their side.

> And Caleb stilled the people before Moses, and said, Let us go up at once, and possess it; **for we are well able to overcome it.** [Numbers 13:30]

However, the multitude believed the report of the ten and because of their fear and unbelief the Israelite people refused to enter the land that God had promised them. Consequently, God decided to punish them. Now, it is the *scale* God used for the method of punishment that is of interest. The Lord said:

> After the number of the days in which ye searched the land, even forty days, **each day for a year**, shall ye bear your iniquities, even forty years, and ye shall know my breach of promise. [Numbers 14:34]

The *scale* God used was *"each day for a year"*. You can find this same scale used in Ezekiel 4:6. In both cases God is dealing with Israel during a disciplinary period. For each day they messed up the price is one year. The prophetic time scale for such a situation is a day equals one year.

Daniel's prophecy consists of a period of seventy weeks and of course there are seven days in each week.
70 weeks x 7 days = 490 days

However, our focus is on the first 69 weeks of the prophecy. So, what we are actually contemplating is this.

69 weeks x 7 days = 483 days

By advancing to the next step and applying the scale of *one day stands for one year,* we find that we are dealing with a period of 483 years. This is a problem because 445 B.C. + 30 A.D. = 475 years, not 483. What should we do? Well, there are a several ways to measure a year. For instance, a *Lunar* year has 354 days in it, a *Solar* year consists of 360 days and an *Astronomical* year has 365 1/4 days. Obviously, the question becomes: *How does the word of God measure a year?* By turning to Genesis we can find the answer. In Genesis 7:24 we find that during Noah's flood:

> ...the waters prevailed upon the earth **an hundred and fifty days**.

Looking again in Genesis, this time at 7:11 and 8:4 we are told that the flood began,

> ...in **the second month, the seventeenth day** of the month.

And ended:

> ...in **the seventh month, on the seventeenth day** of the month.

Therefore, the Bible reckons that from the 17th day of the 2nd month to the 17th day of the 7th month, or 5 complete months, is equal to 150 days. This works out as 30 days to the month when counting *Biblical Chronology.* This same measure is used consistently throughout the Bible.

Now let's do some calculating. From 445 BC to 30 AD equals 475 Astronomical years or 476 years *inclusively*.

476 years x 365 1/4 days per astronomical year = 173,859 days.

To this figure we must add the 21 days inclusive which are found between the earlier March 13th date and the later April 2nd date.

173,859 days + 21 days equals 173,880 days total

Since there are 30 days in a biblical month, we can easily see that 30 days x 12 months = 360 days in a biblical year. The next step is to divide our Astronomical calculation of 173,880 days by 360 days in a biblical year. Therefore:

173,880 days divided by 360 days equals 483 biblical years

Finally, we divide the 483 biblical years by 7 days in a week.

483 biblical years / 7 days in a week = 69 Prophetic Weeks

This is precisely where we started when we began to study Daniels prophecy. It is an amazingly accurate testimony for the Lordship of Jesus Christ. It works out to the very day of His Triumphal Entry into Jerusalem. If you reject this evidence, you do so at your own peril, for:

...the testimony of Jesus is the spirit of prophecy.
[Revelation 19:10]

~END~